CAMPING
BRITISH COLUMBIA,
the ROCKIES, and the YUKON

JAYNE SEAGRAVE

CAMPING

BRITISH COLUMBIA,
the ROCKIES, and the YUKON

9th EDITION

The COMPLETE GUIDE *to*
GOVERNMENT PARK CAMPGROUNDS

Heritage House Publishing Company Ltd.
heritagehouse.ca

Cataloguing information available from Library and Archives Canada

978-1-77203-399-1 (paperback)
978-1-77203-400-4 (e-book)

Ninth edition edited by Nandini Thaker
Interior design and typesetting by Jacqui Thomas
Cover photograph: Banff National Park, driving to Moraine Lake, by Trevor Julier

Interior photos are by Jayne Seagrave, unless otherwise indicated. See page 310 for
additional image credits.

The interior of this book was produced on 100% post-consumer recycled paper, processed
chlorine free, and printed with vegetable-based inks.

Heritage House gratefully acknowledges that the land on which we live and work is within
the traditional territories of the Lkwungen (Esquimalt and Songhees), Malahat, Pacheedaht,
Scia'new, T'Sou-ke, and WSÁNEĆ (Pauquachin, Tsartlip, Tsawout, Tseycum) Peoples.

We acknowledge the financial support of the Government of Canada through the Canada
Book Fund (CBF) and the Canada Council for the Arts, and the Province of British Columbia
through the British Columbia Arts Council and the Book Publishing Tax Credit.

27 26 25 24 23   1 2 3 4 5

Printed in Canada

CONTENTS

> **PUBLISHER'S NOTE** 1

> **INTRODUCTION** 3

> **THE CAMPING EXPERIENCE** 6

Reservations 6

Arriving at a Provincial, Territorial,
or National Park Campground 9

Selecting Your Spot and Setting Up Camp 9

Fees 11

Facilities 13

Campfires 13

Security Issues 14

Potential Hazards 14

What to Take Camping 16

Green Camping 18

Camping with Kids 19

Camping for Seniors 23

> **THE REGIONS AND THEIR PARKS** 25

The Islands 27

Vancouver Coast and Mountains 67

Thompson Okanagan 95

BC Rockies—Provincial 147

Rockies—National 180

Cariboo–Chilcotin Coast 200

Northern BC 217

The Yukon 262

> **MULTI-DAY CAMPING TOURS** 286

> **SPECIAL INTEREST CAMPING RECOMMENDATIONS** 298

> **USEFUL INFORMATION** 303

> **INDEX OF PARKS** 306

> **IMAGE CREDITS** 310

PUBLISHER'S NOTE

THE ORIGINAL EDITION of Jayne Seagrave's BC camping guide was published more than two decades ago and enjoyed great success over the subsequent eight editions. Over the years, the text has grown to include both national parks in the Rockies and thirty-nine parks spread throughout the Yukon.

In recent years, the uncertainties and restrictions of the pandemic, coupled with the unpredictable forces of climate change, have challenged government parks boards throughout western Canada to provide safe and efficient service to the public. For that reason, and recognizing both the volatility of the situation and the need for adaptability, we are modifying the approach how to best use this book. We encourage campers to visit the the national, provincial, and territorial parks websites (see pages 303–4), as well as the webpages for individual parks, for regular notifications of changing conditions. Also, we will update any important issues that affect camping on our own website (heritagehouse.ca) semi-annually. Circumstances may change rapidly, and the websites will help to accurately reflect information about emergency measures such as medical and evacuation orders, park closures, or travel restrictions.

We have come to recognize that destination and special interest campers are often anxious to explore natural sites; recreational activities; and food, beverage, and entertainment amenities that surround them. Because our primary book distributor throughout BC, the Rockies, and the Yukon is the lead distributor for several BC publishers and a multitude of recreational guidebooks for all regions included in this book, our editors have introduced suggestions for key regional books available from many local bookstores and giftshops (see pages 298–301). For reference, you can access descriptive details of these titles at hgdistribution.com and review content related to outdoor activities such as hiking, foraging, and simply exploring the historic landscape that Western Canada has become. Our editors have inserted titles of key best-selling guidebooks that may aid your enjoyment of assorted activities such as gold panning, birdwatching, or visiting "secret beaches." We encourage all tourists and campers to shop local, support craft fairs, and have an "eat fresh" mentality that helps sustain local farms, fishers, vineyards, and ranchers.

DISCLAIMER

While this guide has been fact-checked against the most current information available about camping in BC, the Rockies, and the Yukon, both online and through communications with park administrators, conditions can and often do change rapidly. Heritage House strongly recommends that visitors to provincial, territorial, and national parks educate themselves about how to stay safe while responsibly and respectfully exploring the outdoors, including wildfire safety, plant safety, and encounters with wild animals. The websites for BC Parks, the Yukon Government, and Parks Canada provide excellent guidelines for safe and responsible camping, and this book provides an additional list of helpful resources and recommendations (see pages 303–4). Before heading out for your adventure, please pay attention to the news as well as the official websites and social media of parks authorities for notices on trail closures, road conditions, and notices of potential hazards and evacuation orders resulting from climate events such as wildfires, floods, landslides, and earthquakes.

INTRODUCTION

CAMPING BRITISH COLUMBIA, *the Rockies, and the Yukon* was written out of a love of camping and a deep respect for Canada's westernmost provinces and territory. As Canada's third largest province, BC covers around 944,735 square kilometres, including about 18,000 square kilometres of inland water. BC has more land designated to provincial parks than any state in the US except Alaska and Hawaii, and it boasts over 400 different locations for day use and camping. In addition, seven national parks are found in the province, including Gulf Islands National Park Reserve, and five of these have developed camping facilities. With all this space for exploration and over 13,000 camping spots, it is little wonder that the "camping experience" has become an integral part of recreational life for BC residents and visitors alike.

The Yukon is, for the most part, a vastly unexplored region; 80 percent of it is pristine wilderness. Comprising 483,450 square kilometres and including over 8,000 square kilometres of water, it makes up almost 5 percent of Canada's total land and offers over 1,000 wonderful camping spots set among this splendour.

Written both for those who camp in tents and those who use recreational vehicles (RVs), this book describes the location, facilities offered, and recreational activities available for all provincial, territorial, and national parks with campsites in BC and the Yukon that are accessible by vehicle (with the exception of Sidney Spit and Sayshutsun/Newcastle Island), and that provide at least the basic amenities of drinking water, picnic tables, fire pits, and pit toilets. No user-maintained campgrounds nor privately owned campgrounds are included, although many of these offer wonderful camping facilities. For convenience, these campgrounds are grouped into eight chapters (The

Camping is a popular and enjoyable activity for families.

Islands, Vancouver Coast and Mountains, Thompson Okanagan, BC Rockies—
Provincial, Rockies—National, Cariboo–Chilcotin Coast, Northern BC, and
The Yukon).

The introductory chapter of this guide details important background information on camping in these areas. To offer guidance to the novice and provide
reminders to the seasoned camper, I describe selecting a camping spot, packing for a camping trip, the reservation process, potential hazards, camping
with kids, and camping for seniors. For those wanting to visit multiple campgrounds, I have suggested 7-, 14-, and 21-day camping itineraries, which are
found in the "Multi-Day Camping Tours" chapter. The selections are based on
my personal experiences and amenity evaluations, and cover reasonable daily
travel distances.

THIS NINTH EDITION of *Camping British Columbia, the Rockies, and the Yukon* builds upon and updates the information contained in my previous books. From 2020 through 2022, following the COVID-19 pandemic and the restrictions on travel this created, there was an unprecedented demand for campsites and camping experiences in BC. From 2014 to 2019, BC experienced a 23 percent increase in the number of visits to parks. BC parks now receive more than 23 million visits per year. In 2020, 270,000 camping reservations were made. Many who had never camped before went camping for the first time and discovered what many of us have known for years: that camping in BC and the Yukon's parks is fantastic. It is enjoyable, affordable, and (when the weather is good) a truly wonderful experience. During the pandemic the demand for campground sites far out-stripped supply, and while BC Parks tried to initiate policies to cope with this—for example, by reassigning group camping sites to family camping spots, restricting reservations to residents of BC, and increasing the number of reservable sites—demand continued to increase. In March 2021, when the reservation website opened, it immediately crashed as the number of those wanting access to it was so great. I predict this demand will continue in the future. Gone are the days of selecting a campground and driving to it, finding a space, and pitching a tent. Planning is now required, especially if you want to camp in the peak summer months. In April 2020, BC Parks announced an additional $83 million for the next three years for the creation of new campsites, investment in trails, and a strengthening of the park system.

Camping is a personal experience; what appeals to one person may not appeal to another. However, British Columbia, Alberta, and the Yukon are blessed with some of the most breathtaking scenery in the world. Many of the provincial, national, and territorial parks are nestled in the heart of this beauty and are yours to experience at relatively little cost. Over the last thirty years, I have travelled and camped in every region of BC and have been amazed at the stunning beauty the province offers. More recently, I have extended my camping experience to include the Yukon and those magnificent national parks that straddle the BC–Alberta border, and after exploring these areas I wanted to convey their beauty. I hope this book encourages more individuals to take the plunge and use the excellent facilities provided in their country's parks. A wealth of adventures and experiences can be enjoyed by those of every age. So, what are you waiting for?

THE CAMPING EXPERIENCE

....

THE AIM OF this chapter is to provide some of the basic ground rules for camping in BC and the Yukon's national, provincial, and territorial parks. While the contents of this chapter are intended primarily for the uninitiated to show them what to expect, those who camp regularly will find information on making reservations, what to take, and how to deal with bears and other hazards. It also includes sections on websites, internet access, camping with children and teenagers, and camping for seniors.

RESERVATIONS

Most of the provincial and national park campgrounds in BC can be reserved ahead of time. In 1996, BC Parks created the Discover Camping reservation service that enabled advance reservations to be made in forty-two of the more popular provincial parks. The Discover Camping reservation service saw a 91 percent increase in demand in the last six years, and in 2022, BC Parks overhauled the whole system and relaunched a new site with upgraded capacity. Today, reservations can be made for over a hundred provincial parks (online or by phone; see sidebar on opposite page) and some campgrounds are 100 percent reservable. It is now also possible to make site-specific reservations in a number of campgrounds. For those who have found a full house at a popular campground on the times they have tried to visit, making a reservation well in advance is a way to avoid uncertainty. However, while the process has come a long way, each year there are always would-be campers who cannot find a space during the peak summer months. During the COVID-19 health crisis, this problem became acute as the demand for camping spots in 2020 and 2021 far outstripped supply, especially for the months of July and August. While

RESERVATION INFORMATION

Many campsites in provincial and national parks in BC can be reserved. Consult the online systems for a drop-down list of all parks that accept reservations.

BC Provincial Parks
Discover Camping Reservation Service
camping.bcparks.ca
1-800-689-9025 / 1-519-858-6161 overseas
Call centre availability: 7:00 AM–7:00 PM PT daily, except December 25 and January 1
NOTE: There is a $5.00 surcharge per transaction.

National Parks
Parks Canada Reservation Service
reservation.pc.gc.ca
1-877-737-3783 / 1-519-826-5391 overseas
Call centre availability: 8:00 AM–6:00 PM local park time

Yukon Parks
Yukon Camping Permit
yukon.ca/en/camping-permit
Yukon Parks Backcountry Reservation System
yukon.goingtocamp.com
1-867-667-5648 / 1-800-661-0408, ext. 5648 toll-free in the Yukon

reservations offer the advantage of assuring accommodation for the night, unless you have the option of choosing your spot, you may end up next to a particularly well-used thunderbox or at the busy entrance to the campground.

In 2022, the fee to reserve a site in a BC provincial park was $6.00 per night to a maximum of $18.00 for three to fourteen nights, in addition to the camping fee. An additional $5.00 surcharge is charged for phone reservations. A few of the most popular campgrounds restrict reservations to seven nights. Campers pay the reservation and campsite fees when making their reservation. Payment is taken by MasterCard or Visa and includes GST. Reservations are taken seven days a week from 7:00 AM to 7:00 PM Pacific Time (weekdays), and 9:00 AM to 5:00 PM (weekends). As of January 1, 2023, sites can be reserved up to four months prior to the campground's first reservable date, and as late as two days prior to arrival. Reservations for statutory holiday weekends must be for a minimum of three nights (exceptions for specific holidays are posted on the BC Parks reservation website). In 2022, free day-use passes were required for day visitors at Garibaldi, Golden Ears, and Joffre Lakes provincial parks during peak season.

For national parks, reservations can be made through the Parks Canada Reservation Service (online or by phone; see sidebar on previous page). The service includes the Gulf Islands parks of Prior Centennial and SMONEĆTEN (McDonald). For many of the most popular campgrounds in BC, especially those on Vancouver Island and in the Lower Mainland and Okanagan, you must make a reservation if you want to camp during July and August. Beginning in January for the forthcoming year, you can reserve a campsite in a national park up to midnight on the day prior to your arrival. In 2022, the cost to make a reservation was $11.50 per stay if made online and $13.50 if made through the call centre, and you pay the campsite fee for the number of nights included in your stay at the same time. However, you will still be required to pay the park's daily entry fee upon arrival at the park ($3.90 to $9.80 per person per day). You will also be charged to change or cancel a previously confirmed reservation. Many payment options are available, and they vary according to whether you reserve online or by phone. Check out the reservation website for more information.

The parks managed by the Yukon government (yukon.ca/en/outdoor-recreation-and-wildlife/camping) can be reserved for the first time in 2022. The Government of Yukon website provides a guide about the typical availability of its campgrounds according to the season. A daily camping permit is required and can be purchased at any road-accessible Government of Yukon campground. Pre-paid daily and Yukon resident annual permits can be purchased at many local establishments outside of Whitehorse or at Department of Environment offices (a complete list of vendors can be found at yukon.ca/en/where-buy-yukon-angling-hunting-and-camping-permits-or-licences). Yukon residents can also purchase annual permits online at env.eservices.gov.yk.ca.

ARRIVING AT A PROVINCIAL, TERRITORIAL, OR NATIONAL PARK CAMPGROUND

All national, provincial, and territorial park campgrounds are well signposted from major highways. A sign (blue for provincial and territorial parks, brown for national parks) 2 kilometres before the campground turnoff is the first warning you will receive, followed by another one 400 metres from the campground, which will direct you to the access road. The park operator will post notices on these roadside signs to state when a campground is full or closed. You will come to appreciate what a real advantage this is if the campground is located 60 kilometres from the highway on a rough gravel road.

SELECTING YOUR SPOT AND SETTING UP CAMP

Presuming you do not have a reservation (see "Reservations"), the excitement upon arrival is selecting your spot. Depending on the season, time of day, and location of the park, this decision may already be out of your hands. The park may be full or there may be only one place left. Some parks have areas specifically designated for tents, but most have spots suitable for both RVs and tents. A number of parks offer "double spots," ideal for two families camping together, and pull-through spots for larger RVs. A map of the campground at the park entrance shows where these spots are found, but it is easy to just "cruise" around to select the most desirable spot. If the park offers a reservation service, the reserved sites will be listed at the park's entrance and on the sites themselves. However, if the site has not been reserved there will frequently be a notice at the site that reads "Available for one night." Campsites by any beach, lake, river, or creek are the most desirable locations, so head for them first, making a mental note of where the water tap is located. Try to avoid areas of stagnant water (mosquito breeding grounds) or spots close to the "thunderboxes" (pit toilets), which, during the park's warm summer months, may exude unpleasant odours or attract flies, and whose banging doors can cause a disturbance. At first glance, spots near the flush toilets and showers may seem convenient, but remember that between 5:00 AM and 11:00 AM, and between 7:00 PM and 11:00 PM, most people at the campground will be visiting these facilities at least twice and walking past your site in order to do so. On the other hand, if you have children in your party or want to meet people, you may deem these spots ideal.

Once you have driven around and made a mental note of your preferences, return to the gatehouse and claim your first choice. Should you not want to pitch camp immediately, leave a plastic tablecloth or water jug on the picnic table to state to the world that this is your spot, then head back to the gatehouse to register and pay the associated fee. If there's a staffed gatehouse or welcome centre at the campground, that's generally where you'll register and pay for your campsite (unless you have a reservation). You will be asked to provide your name, the number of people in your party, vehicle licence-plate number, and where you are from. You can request a particular spot to camp if you've picked one out, or you'll be given a choice of available sites. You can pay for as many nights as you want, up to a maximum of fourteen nights in

Notice boards near park entrances provide useful information for campers.

provincial, territorial, and national parks (some parks, such as sẁiẁs (Haynes Point) and Pacific Rim, may limit your stay to seven nights, while early on in the season it is possible to secure a long-term spot for a month in a few provincial park campgrounds).

In most parks, if you don't register and pay upon arrival, you can drive around and select your own spot and an attendant will come and collect payment during the early-evening hours. (Park attendants are good sources of information on weather conditions, local activities, the best fishing locations, and so on.) Some parks operate a self-registration honour system whereby you deposit the campground fee in an envelope, place it in a box at the entrance to the park, and secure a receipt. All campgrounds in the Yukon operate under this system. For such instances, it is good to ensure that you have small bills and change, although fellow campers are usually willing to help you out. Instructions on self-registering will be printed on a sign at the park's entrance and on the deposit envelope. Once you've completed the self-registration form, you post the receipt at your spot.

If you delay pitching your tent or going to collect water, just don't forget what time it gets dark. This is particularly relevant if you are camping in the shoulder seasons of early spring and late summer, when darkness falls as early as 7:00 PM. Arriving at a campground late, pitching your tent in the dark, and cooking dinner by flashlight is challenging to say the least. In contrast, relaxing by the fire while the sun goes down and the stars come out is a highly pleasurable experience when you know your bed is made, dinner is over, and the dishes done. Once established in your new home, you are ready to explore the campground. The first port of call should be a return visit to the information board at the park's entrance, where you will find a map of the campground and details about any hazards in the area.

FEES

For the most up-to-date fees for particular provincial parks, visit the BC Parks website at bcparks.ca; for national parks, visit pc.gc.ca; and for Yukon territorial parks, visit yukon.ca/camping. During the early-evening hours in most parks, an attendant will come and collect payment and will offer to sell you firewood. Cash is preferred, but credit cards are increasingly accepted, as long as the wireless connections are available. Be advised that many campgrounds, because of their location away from reliable cell phone and internet networks, are unable to accept credit cards. Camping fees vary depending on the facilities provided; campgrounds with showers tend to be the most expensive, whereas less developed campgrounds cost less. Fees include GST and in 2021 ranged from $13.00 to $35.00 (excluding hook-up costs) for provincial parks and up to $38.80 for national parks. In addition, a daily entrance fee is charged at national parks, even if you are staying overnight ($10.50 for adults, $9.00 for seniors, $21.00 for families and groups, while youths aged 17 and under can enter for free), but there are also annual passes available for single locations (in BC, only Pacific Rim) or all national parks (the Discovery Pass). Before June 15 and after Labour Day, residents of BC who are 65 or older may camp for half price in provincial parks. From June 15 to Labour Day, full rates apply. With the correct documentation, persons with disabilities who are residents of BC may be exempt from campsite fees.

Camping in the Yukon was $20.00 in 2022 if paid with cash on site, and $18.00 if pre-paid at a vendor or online. In 2022, the Yukon started a new reservation system to cope with the increasing demand. The cost of camping is reduced by 50 percent for those over 65 throughout the season.

If you intend to fish in national parks, you will have to purchase a permit ($10.25 per day or $35.75 per year). In BC, any angler over the age of 16 needs a Freshwater Fishing Licence to fish in provincial parks ($10.00 per day, $36.00 per year for BC residents; $20.00 per day, $55.00 per year for non-residents) and a tidal waters sport fishing licence from Fisheries and Oceans Canada if fishing in salt waters ($5.47 per day, $21.85 per year for Canadian residents). In the Yukon, a fishing licence is required for anglers over the age of 16 and under 65 ($10.40 per day, $26.01 for the season for non-residents); youths under 16 and seniors can fish for free. Parks request payment for firewood. Prices range from $8.00 to $15.00 per bundle—and the bundles do vary considerably in size. The farther north you travel in BC, the cheaper and larger the bundle becomes. National parks also charge $9.25 to campers intending to have a fire. If a sani-station is provided, there is usually a fee to use it ($5.00 in provincial parks, $9.25 in national parks). Firewood is free in the Yukon and there are no sani-stations in territorial parks.

FACILITIES

All campgrounds included in this book provide at least the basic amenities of drinking water, wood for sale, picnic tables, fire pits, and pit toilets; some larger campgrounds may also have sani-stations, flush toilets, showers, wheelchair access, interpretive programs, visitor centres, and/or group camping. A few campgrounds have power hook-ups. Since the COVID-19 pandemic, many campgrounds now supply hand sanitizer. Washroom facilities are generally well maintained, clean, and, unlike many campgrounds I have stayed in abroad, never run out of toilet paper. (I was preconditioned in Europe, so it took me years to stop carrying a spare roll with me.) Gravel camping spots are tidied and raked after each visitor departs, garbage is regularly collected, and recycling is encouraged. Overall, the facilities provided in BC's national and provincial parks and the territorial parks of the Yukon are excellent. No "user-maintained" campgrounds are included as these tend to be in remote areas and are often not easily accessible.

Staying connected to the internet while camping is very much dependent on where the campground is located. Some have Wi-Fi access, especially if adjacent to urban areas, but many do not, or may be located in the shadow of a mountain or in a valley, which prevents reception. Do not go camping expecting to get a reliable Wi-Fi connection.

CAMPFIRES

For many people, myself included, building and enjoying a campfire is an essential part of camping. In 2004, BC Parks started to charge for bundled firewood, and national parks now require that you purchase a campfire permit for each fire. A few campgrounds (e.g., Porpoise Bay and Stawamus Chief) have even gone so far as to ban individual campfires at all times while others actively discourage fires for environmental reasons. When conditions are excessively hot and dry, as they were in the summer of 2021, campgrounds in arid areas ban fires altogether. With global warming, fire bans in certain areas have become the norm rather than the exception. If you need a campfire to make your camping experience complete, contact the campground you want to stay in to determine if fires are allowed, or check the campground noticeboard when you arrive. If there is a fire ban, numerous signs and notices are posted along highways and at the campgrounds, and fines levied for those ignoring the law can be heavy. For general information about BC wildfires and current campfire restrictions, see bcwildfire.ca.

SECURITY ISSUES

Over the last thirty years, and since the publication of the first edition of *Camping British Columbia*, I have taken part in a number of radio phone-in interviews and given advice and guidance on camping issues. A sad development in these yearly events is the increase in the number of people calling the radio station to relay stories of being victims of crime at a campground, usually the theft of unsecured possessions. I still maintain that camping is very safe, but it cannot be denied that crimes do take place. Generally, they tend to occur in the larger campgrounds nearer to centres of population (e.g., Golden Ears, Cultus Lake, Sx̱ótsaqel/Chilliwack Lake). Many of these parks now have security patrols to deter theft. Crime can occur anywhere, and it is the responsibility of the camper to minimize the opportunity for it to take place, especially in parks that have been targets for deviants in the past. BC Parks frequently displays signs informing campers that the campground has been a target for crime in the past and suggesting extra vigilance.

POTENTIAL HAZARDS

Any hazards to be found in a particular park are posted at the campground entrance, but here are the more common problems and how to avoid them.

- **Swimmer's itch** Parasites living in freshwater snails and waterfowl can cause swimmer's itch (a.k.a. cercarial dermatitis), a temporary skin irritation caused by the parasites' larvae entering the skin. The larvae thrive close to the shore in the warm waters of lakes and ponds where Canada geese and other waterfowl are found. Because children go in and out of the water frequently and have tender skin, they are particularly vulnerable. Swimmer's itch can be avoided by applying an oil, such as baby oil, to the skin before swimming, towelling off briskly, and showering after swimming. The presence of swimmer's itch is indicated by small red spots that can develop into small blisters. Although unpleasant, the condition can be treated with calamine lotion and usually clears up by itself within a week. The information board at the campground entrance will indicate whether swimmer's itch is a problem at the lake you plan to visit.

- **Poison ivy** This low, glossy plant with three green leaves and white berries can produce severe skin rashes. It is prevalent in sunny areas on Vancouver Island and in the Okanagan. Calamine lotion is an effective treatment.
- **Sunburn** You are living largely outdoors when camping, and it is easy to forget how long you have been exposed to the sun. Apply and reapply sunscreen, wear a hat, and be especially careful when you're around water or snow, which reflect the sun and can increase your chance of sunburn.
- **Water** Lifeguards are not employed in BC parks, so a watchful eye must be kept on those who cannot swim. Some parks have designated swimming areas; others do not. Weather conditions may change rapidly in some locations, with winds suddenly developing and causing a hazard for boating enthusiasts. Again, information on the park's notice board will state whether this is a problem.
- **Bears** The area covered by this book is home to almost a quarter of all the black bears in Canada and about half of all grizzlies. Although encounters between people and bears are rare, campers should remember they are always in bear country. Respect bears as strong, fast, wild animals, and act responsibly at all times.

Generally, bears go out of their way to avoid people, but all bears are dangerous. They can rip apart tents and vehicles in their search for food, run as fast as a racehorse, and have excellent sight, hearing, and sense of smell. They are strong swimmers, and black bears and young grizzlies are agile tree-climbers. Upon leaving the city, you are in bear country and should use caution.

Anyone planning to camp or spend time in the outdoors should learn how to recognize a black or grizzly bear and how to respond accordingly. Black bears can be black, brown, cinnamon, or blond with a straight-face profile, short curved claws, and a small shoulder hump. Grizzly bears can also be black, brown, or blond, but they are bigger than black bears and have long curved claws and a prominent shoulder hump.

When walking in bear country, watch for warning signs, such as tracks, overturned rocks, clawed trees, chewed roots, and droppings. Talk loudly, wear bear bells, or sing to make your presence known. If you see a bear in the distance, leave the area immediately. If you encounter one at close range, avoid eye contact, move away slowly, and stay calm. If the bear stands up as it approaches you, it is trying to identify what you are. Talk quietly so it knows you are human. If it is lowering its head, flattening its ears, snapping its jaws, and snorting, the bear is displaying aggression. This is serious. Do not run, but continue to back away. If a grizzly shows aggression, consider climbing a tree. Generally, the key is to do nothing to threaten or arouse the animal. If a grizzly attacks, play dead and adopt a tight, curled-up position with your head on your knees and your hands behind your neck. Do not move until the bear leaves the area. If a black bear attacks, try to retreat to a safe place and use weapons, such as rocks and branches, to deter the animal.

Never approach or feed bears. Food-conditioned bears—those that scavenge food from garbage cans and picnic tables—begin to associate food with people, lose their natural fear of humans, and become a threat to campers and to themselves. With caution and sensible behaviour, you can safely camp in and enjoy bear country. Some campgrounds in the Yukon are closed to tent camping at certain times of the year if the bear activity in the area has been deemed considerable. Information on BC wildlife and safety can be found at wildsafebc.com.

WHAT TO TAKE CAMPING

To the uninitiated, it would appear that some people take everything camping. On one occasion, I camped next to a couple who had a large RV with two mountain bikes tied to the front, a boat on the roof, and a small four-wheel-drive vehicle towed behind. Their picnic table displayed several coolers of assorted sizes, wine glasses, a breadbasket, and a red-checked tablecloth; overhead was an ornate striped awning. Artificial grass, potted plants, lanterns, and numerous plastic lounge chairs with cushions were strategically positioned around a huge barbecue. This campsite had more accoutrements than my home (and was certainly worth more). It is impossible to provide the definitive list of necessities, but there are a number of items that will make your camping experience more enjoyable, whether you are a tenter or an RVer.

I started my BC camping career in 1992 with a two-person tent (designed for two very small people) and toured the province in a 1974 Ford Pinto. On

CAMPING ESSENTIALS

- Aluminum foil
- Axe
- Barbecue, hibachi, or camping stove (plus briquettes or fuel)
- Biodegradable dish soap and scrubbing pads
- Bungee cords
- Candles or camping lantern
- COVID-19 kit: hand sanitizer, disinfectant wipes, soap, face masks
- First-aid kit, including calamine lotion
- Flashlight
- Flip-flops for the shower
- Food
- Garbage bags
- Insect repellent
- Matches and newspaper if you intend to have a campfire
- Paper towels
- Pocket knife
- Pots, dishes, and cutlery
- Rainy-day activities (books, portable radio, travel games)
- Rope
- Sleeping bag, pillow, and camping mattress
- Sunglasses, hat, and sunscreen
- Tarp
- Tent and fly, tent trailer, camper, or RV
- Toilet paper
- Towels
- Water container and funnel

this first excursion I was totally unprepared. My partner and I had no axe, so to make a fire we had to arrive at a campground early enough to collect the unused wood that had been cut by our predecessors. On one occasion, this option was not available, so we approached a neighbouring site and asked a camper if we could borrow his axe. He came over from his well-equipped RV to supply the tool and chat. After surveying our meagre tent and picnic table (displaying two plastic plates, two plastic mugs, and one plastic grocery bag of food), he started to explain how he started as we were doing, with barely the basics, but assured us that as each year progressed our commitment to camping would grow and more "comforts" would be acquired. He was right. We now arrive at our campsite in a 2019 seven-seater van, sleep on self-inflating Therm-a-Rests in two large tents we can stand up in, have tarps, a red-checked tablecloth, clotheslines, coolers, a gas barbecue, and, yes, even an axe. On three separate occasions we have been lucky enough to camp in a 28-foot RV—real luxury. Occasionally we see novice campers starting out as we and many others have done, and we look knowingly at each other, content in the thought that it will not be long before they, too, start to collect the camping necessities. One of the tremendous joys of camping is learning how to do it. That said, there are a few essentials you'll want to pack right from the beginning. See adventuresmart.ca for more information on essential gear and other tips for safe camping.

GREEN CAMPING

Some would argue that true tent camping is, by its very nature, green, but like the rest of our society this has changed over the last fifty years with the introduction of recreational vehicles. In most campgrounds now, tents are the exception rather than the rule. But while huge RVs, with their own generators and heavy gas consumption, remain a regular sight in many BC parks, there are ways that camping is reverting back to its more traditional roots as our concern for preserving the environment increases. Some evidence of this shift includes:

- **Recycling** Most parks have recycling facilities. When camping, we now take along a separate bag for collecting bottles and cans, so even if the campground does not recycle, we still can.
- **Fires** Twenty years ago, firewood was provided free of charge and fires burned all day. With the concern for air quality and the environment, provincial parks now charge for wood, and national parks now require you to pay for campfires. Some campgrounds also prohibit individual fires entirely. Fees for firewood vary from campground to campground, as does the ability to have a fire. To an increasing extent, fires are prohibited during the summer season because of the real risks of devastating forest fires. BC Parks is discouraging the use of campfires and promoting the use of stoves instead, in an effort to conserve the environment.
- **Boating** An increasing number of lakes are being closed to powerboats, water-skiers, and those dreaded Jet Skis. Other parks have instituted restrictions on the types of motors allowed.

- **Fuel costs** In 2021, the cost of fuel soared to $300 to $400 to fill the gas tank of a 24-foot RV. Transportation costs for all vehicles may discourage long road trips, and more campers may choose to camp nearer to home. Consequently, campgrounds near population centres may become more crowded, and those in the remoter areas of the province, and on islands only accessible by increasingly expensive ferry rides may suffer a decline in attendance. Yet all signs point to heavy demand for campground sites on Vancouver Island and it is unlikely that parks will suffer any decline in attendance.

- **Generators** BC Parks permits the use of generators only from 9:00 AM to 11:00 AM and from 6:00 PM to 8:00 PM in an attempt to limit noise pollution and disturbance to other campers, especially those in tents.

CAMPING WITH KIDS

Twenty-five years ago, I did not have children and camping was a wonderful, tranquil experience. Now, my two sons are young adults and camping with the parents is no longer on their agenda. I lament (but totally understand) the fact they do not want to spend time with me and their father. In years past, we camped every summer as a family, and as the boys grew older, their love of camping increased until they reached the teenage years. Now I am delighted to report they go camping with their friends. In 2020, my younger son drove to the Yukon with four friends, two of whom had never camped before. He was surprised his contemporaries had not been exposed to what he saw as an integral part of growing up.

Although it saddens me that our family camping days are over, I (and my children) have so many priceless memories of these trips that when anyone asks if the challenges of taking children camping are worth it, I advise them to not think twice and do it (and to consult my other camping book, *Camping with Kids in the West*). It is a cliché to say children grow up too quickly and our time with them as young individuals is short, but it is true. The opportunities for family camping trips and the unique bonding that occurs when a family interacts in the elements are very rare, so when this chance does occur it should be seized. When he was 10, I asked my oldest son what his best summertime experience had been. I expected him to say the three-week trip we'd had to visit relatives in England, but instead it was the four-day trip we'd taken to Alice Lake Provincial Park. Often, when you reflect on your childhood, it is the outdoor summer activities that are the most memorable. Camping and all it entails is a wonderful thing to do with kids, who are totally oblivious to the weather and seem to be able to play in a lake whatever the water's temperature.

While camping is a popular affordable family vacation, what you can and cannot do when camping with kids depends on the age of your offspring, as each age brings unique experiences, joys, and challenges.

- **Camping with babies or toddlers** If your baby is not yet a crawler, camping is easy. Okay, you do have to take more stuff, but you can leave the baby happily goo-gooing in the car seat on the picnic table while you erect the tent. Playpens are great and can be used for a baby to sleep in as a crib, and a mosquito net can be easily laid over the top, should insects be a problem. Camping with toddlers, however, is another matter. This age can be the most challenging because of all the equipment they require, their need for diapers, and their propensity to put everything in their mouths. The great outdoors, replete with animals, rocks, stones, water, dirt, vegetation, and insects, can't be childproofed as easily as your home. I believe the secret to camping with toddlers is being relaxed about it. So they don't have a wash before going to bed, or they sleep in the clothes they've been in all day, or they delight in treading on the ants and poking the banana slugs with pinecones; let them do it.

  The biggest problem I found while tent camping with toddlers was in their early-morning waking. The dawn arrives and their excitement over seeing you sleeping next to them stimulates their delight and curiosity; so you get up at 5:30 AM and experience the campground at a time few others will. Afternoon naps may also be a challenge if you try to get them to sleep in the unfamiliar tent. A better option is a gentle push in the stroller around the campground's roads, especially if these are gravel—an almost surefire way to send them to sleep.

  Most of the difficulties of this tent-based experience are, of course, avoided by camping in a recreational vehicle, camper, tent trailer, or towing trailer. If there is ever a time when you get rid of the tent and choose an RV, it is at this age. On the plus side, kids of this age are still quite portable, so you can hike with them in a backpack—something that is not an option with the preschooler.

- **Camping with preschoolers** While you can't send these young ones off to explore the campground on their own, children at this age are a real delight to take camping. The under-fives can actively get involved with camping and what it means to set up home outdoors away from the urban centre. They can help select flat ground to put up the tent, get sticks for toasting marshmallows, explore adjacent undergrowth without eating it, take a ride on the tricycle, and run around and make noise. Expect them to stay up late, get dirty, make friends with the kids from the next campsite, play the best imaginary games, and have a ball.

  Camping with this age group also means you can vacation in May, June, or September and avoid the crowds and the added expense. Make the most of it and remember to teach them your campsite number upon arrival, as well as basic safety information. Also remember to pack fishing nets, water shoes, sidewalk chalk, and toys.

- **Camping with schoolchildren** By setting boundaries and following a few simple rules, children this age will learn to love the camping experience. Provincial, national, and territorial parks provide wonderful safe environments for children to explore by themselves. Parents do not have to worry about unsafe roads and fast drivers, video arcades or TV. Children can gain some independence by exploring safely on their own. Parks are fantastic for cycling, rollerblading, swimming, and exploring with new-found friends or with friends brought from home. Remember their board games, art supplies, sidewalk chalk, balls, bikes, rollerblades, and books, and they will be sure to entertain themselves. If you have to agree to screen time, which you will, try to limit this to a couple of hours at the end of the day, and remember, the decision may be out of your hands as many campgrounds do not have Wi-Fi access. The big disadvantage with this age group is the restriction of having to camp during school holidays and weekends when parks are most crowded. A little planning ahead helps a lot, though; these are the times when you really appreciate the reservation system (see "Reservations" on page 6). BC Parks have produced three "Activity Guides" for children aged 3–5, 6–8, and 9–11. These are available for free at many of the larger campgrounds and are informative for both children and adults.

Camping with teenagers A few years ago, when I asked my two teenage sons what advice I should give in this section of the book, they both said that you should not even consider camping with teenage girls, as they would be far too interested in their clothes, make-up, and Facebook friendships to tolerate camping. While teenagers can be challenging in any environment, a campground may indeed be one step too far for some. But for those of us who are willing to ride over the initial objections, there are a number of benefits, and if you are prepared to host one of their friends on the trip, many issues can be curtailed.

When my kids were 12 and 14, I took our family on a three-week trip to the Yukon, despite numerous protests. We listened as a family to numerous books on the CD player during the long car journeys, each one of us deciding in turn what we should listen to. The boys took complete responsibility for erecting their own tent and getting their beds made. They chose the location of the camping spot, collected wood and water, made fires, cooked dinner each night (as they had no desire to wash up, and the deal was whoever cooked did not have to wash up), decided what food to buy, explored

Lakeside sites at the Lost Ledge Campground, Kootenay Lake Provincial Park. Camping is an excellent way to explore the different regions of the province.

the campgrounds independently, and advised on the activities for each day. Our long camping excursion was broken up every third or fourth day by a night in a motel and dinner in a restaurant of their choice. The trip was a wonderful bonding experience, punctuated with activities they wanted to do (whitewater rafting, eating at Boston Pizza, locating the only internet cafe with Wi-Fi and remaining there for two hours so they could reconnect with friends).

Camping with teenagers involves not only including them as equal partners but also becoming involved in activities you may not want to do to keep them happy, forgetting the rules that are enforced at home (like regular washing, changing clothes, and meeting curfews), and introducing them to environments they rarely see. It is brave to embark on any family holiday with teenagers, but if you do take the plunge, the memories will be priceless.

CAMPING FOR SENIORS

I started camping in BC at the age of 30, sleeping on the ground in a very small tent. Thirty years later, I have no desire whatsoever to return to that tent. Enjoying BC's provincial and national parks is not age dependent but, as we age, does evolve. For the committed older camper, this may be the time to invest in renting or purchasing that recreational vehicle. During the shoulder seasons many RV rental companies offer discounts, adding to the incentive to continue a love of the outdoors with a little bit of luxury.

One of the benefits of camping when older is that you are not tied to school holidays or fixed two-week periods. Discounts are offered for camping during the shoulder season in BC parks and camping is reduced by 50 percent in the Yukon for anyone over the age of 65. Throughout this book I have identified campgrounds that are suitable for an older cohort (see Special Interest Camping). These tend to be smaller, with less structured activities, while still offering a tranquil experience, and because of this they are patronized by an older crowd. One of the delightful observations I have found is that in aging, everyone seems to be more open to initiating conversations, has time to stop and talk, and embraces life outdoors at a slower pace. In my experience, camping is anything but a lonely activity. That being said, as an older camper, certain activities, which were undertaken with ease when younger, may need to be adapted. For example, many campgrounds have walks or trails that are easily completed but may require walking at a slower pace and stepping aside to let others pass. An additional understanding of the length of these excursions and the necessity of taking a cell phone is also a good idea. You may want to find out if there are toilets en route (getting up after squatting in the undergrowth gets increasingly difficult with age). Remember all parks listed in this book make fantastic picnic and rest stops, even if you do not intend to camp. There really is no excuse for not getting out there.

THE REGIONS
AND THEIR PARKS

C AMPGROUNDS IN THIS book are divided into eight chapters that reflect the main geographical regions of BC, the Alberta Rockies, and the Yukon: the Islands; Vancouver coast and mountains; Thompson Okanagan; BC Rockies; national parks of the Rockies; Cariboo–Chilcotin coast; northern British Columbia; and the Yukon. Maps at the beginning of each section show the location of each campground and the main highways and centres of population. However, these maps should serve only as a general guide; more accurate information should be obtained by referencing a good map of the province, such as those found in the *British Columbia Road & Recreational Atlas* or the *British Columbia Road Map and Parks Guide*. BC Parks provides excellent maps of each of these regions at no cost. These are available from tourism information offices across the province and at some of the larger campgrounds, and an authoritative digital road atlas can be downloaded for free from the BC

Bamberton Provincial Park borders on Saanich Inlet on Vancouver Island and has a great beach that is connected to the camping area by several trails.

Government website. Additional information on parks in the various regions can be found online; a list of useful websites is included at the back of this book.

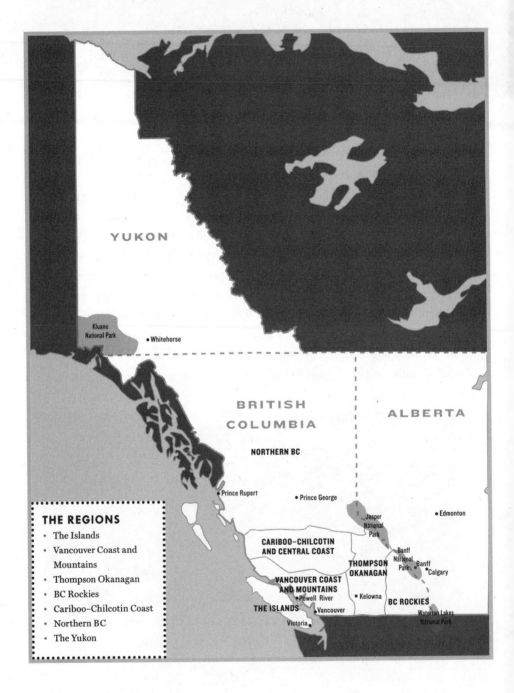

YUKON

Kluane
National Park

● Whitehorse

BRITISH
COLUMBIA

ALBERTA

NORTHERN BC

● Prince Rupert

● Prince George

● Edmonton

Jasper
National
Park

THE REGIONS

- The Islands
- Vancouver Coast and
  Mountains
- Thompson Okanagan
- BC Rockies
- Cariboo–Chilcotin Coast
- Northern BC
- The Yukon

**CARIBOO–CHILCOTIN
AND CENTRAL COAST**

**THOMPSON
OKANAGAN**

Banff
National
Park

Banff
● Calgary

**VANCOUVER COAST
AND MOUNTAINS**
● Powell River

● Kelowna

THE ISLANDS
↘Vancouver

Victoria ●

BC ROCKIES

Waterton Lakes
National Park

THE ISLANDS

THIS CHAPTER INCLUDES campgrounds located on Vancouver Island and the Gulf Islands. Vancouver Island is the largest North American island in the Pacific Ocean and stretches 450 kilometres. Named after Captain George Vancouver, one of the first European visitors in 1778, this varied region includes mountains, farmlands, kilometres of breathtaking coastline (lots of it inaccessible by road), and unique wildlife. The Gulf Islands are situated between Vancouver Island and the Mainland and for many residents offer a serene and alternative lifestyle away from the populations of the Lower Mainland and southern Vancouver Island. Tourists, too, find the islands a delight. Despite the number of campgrounds available, the popularity of the region and the convenience of its location close to large centres of population mean that many idyllic spots are very busy, especially during July and August. As the campgrounds on Vancouver Island are very popular, if travelling from the Mainland, it is advisable to make a reservation on the ferry. This is especially true if travelling on a weekend and imperative if travelling on the weekend of a statutory holiday.

FERRY SCHEDULES
Current BC Ferries schedules are always available at Tourism BC centres, in some newspapers, and on the BC Ferries website at bcferries. com, or by calling 1-888-223-3779 from anywhere in North America. For up-to-the-minute updates on service changes, see the BC Ferries Twitter account, @BCFerries.

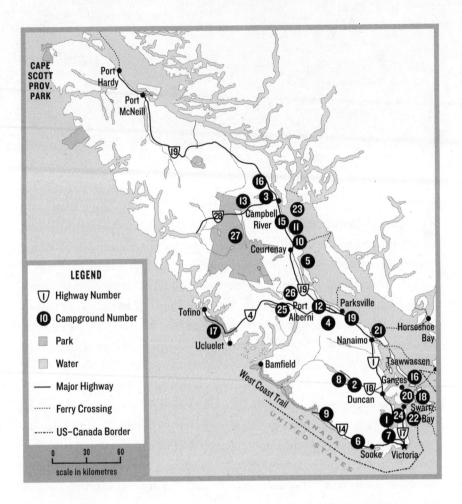

THE ISLANDS

1. Bamberton
2. Cowichan River
3. Elk Falls
4. Englishman River Falls
5. Fillongley
6. French Beach
7. Goldstream
8. Gordon Bay
9. Juan de Fuca
10. Kin Beach
11. Kitty Coleman
12. Little Qualicum Falls
13. Loveland Bay
14. Miracle Beach
15. Montague Harbour Marine
16. Morton Lake
17. Pacific Rim (NP)
18. Prior Centennial (NP)
19. Rathtrevor Beach
20. Ruckle
21. Saysutshun (Newcastle Island Marine)
22. Sidney Spit Marine (NP)
23. Smelt Bay
24. SMONEĆTEN (McDonald) (NP)
25. Sproat Lake
26. Stamp River
27. Strathcona

To reach campgrounds on Vancouver Island or the Gulf Islands, you will have to take one of the BC Ferries vessels, such as this one that runs between Swartz Bay and Salt Spring Island.

BAMBERTON

> Location

A true family-friendly campground and a really picturesque location, Bamberton looks onto the Finlayson Arm of the Saanich Inlet, across the Gulf Islands to Mount Baker and beyond. Bamberton is situated about half an hour's drive from Victoria, 1 kilometre east of Highway 1 on Bamberton Road. Services are available on the highway, in Victoria to the south, and in Duncan to the north.

> Facilities

Nestled in a lightly forested area, which includes arbutus trees unique to the west coast, are 53 well-appointed, private camping spots, 41 reservable. There are flush and pit toilets but no sani-station or showers. The park is wheelchair-accessible and reservations are accepted. This is one of the few campgrounds open year round.

> Recreational activities

This is a popular family recreational area, as the warm waters of the Saanich Inlet together with over 225 metres of beach make it a pleasant place for families to congregate, swim, play, and rest. Creeks that run through the park have little fishing potential, but it is possible to catch salmon in the inlet. Small trails lead from the campground to the beach area, and interpretive programs are offered in the summer months. Canoeing and windsurfing are also possible. As this provincial park is so close to Victoria (30 minutes to the south) and Duncan (20 minutes north), there are many additional things to see and do outside the immediate area. For example, Duncan has a forest museum displaying logging artifacts and giving the history of an industry that is very much a part of Vancouver Island's heritage.

> Additional information

Bamberton was given to the people of BC by the British Columbia Cement Company, and the name was chosen to commemorate H.K.G. Bamber, a former managing director of the Portland Cement Construction Company of London, England. Its proximity to Victoria and the population of southern Vancouver Island means Bamberton is a popular place for locals and schoolchildren, and therefore it can be very busy. The park contains a high number of arbutus trees—Canada's only broadleaf evergreen—which in Canada grow only on Vancouver Island and the Lower Mainland. It is a far more desirable camping area than nearby competitor SMONEĆTEN (McDonald).

COWICHAN RIVER

> Location

This is one of BC's newer provincial parks, established in 1995. The Cowichan River was designated a Canadian Heritage River and a BC Heritage River because it is internationally renowned for its wild salmon and steelhead. This park is very popular, especially among the angling community. Located between Lake Cowichan and Duncan, the 1,414-hectare park can be reached from Highway 18 on a good gravel road or from Highway 1 south of Duncan by a 17-kilometre paved and gravel road. Services are available in both Lake Cowichan and Duncan.

> Facilities

Thirty-nine vehicle camping spots are located at Stolz Pool on the Cowichan River with four walk-in sites. Most of these campsites are open and quite close together, offering little privacy. Water, pit toilets, picnic tables, and fire pits are all provided. Reservations are available for 27 sites. Open all year.

> Recreational activities

The Cowichan River is one of Vancouver Island's most popular fishing environments. It flows 47 kilometres from its headwaters at Cowichan Lake (the name of the body of water is the reverse of the town's name) to the sea and is known as an angler's paradise with rainbow and steelhead trout and excellent salmon runs. A section of the Cowichan River Footpath, a 20-kilometre trail leading to some of the best fishing holes, passes within the park boundaries. As well as the excellent fishing potential, the park has swimming, canoeing, kayaking, hiking, and tubing possibilities and is therefore attractive to all ages. More recently, snorkeling and scuba diving have become pastimes here. A section of the Trans Canada Trail runs through the park where the Holt Creek Trestles provide spectacular views of the river (see tctrail.ca).

> Additional information

In addition to being the delight of many fishers, this location is ideal for exploring the communities of Lake Cowichan and Duncan. Duncan calls itself the "City of Totems" and is home to over eighty totem poles, which have been erected primarily in the downtown area. Some employ traditional design while others are less traditional. Duncan is also the site of the Quw'utsun' Cultural and Conference Centre, on the banks of the Cowichan River, which has a longhouse, a theatre, and an arts and crafts centre. When we stayed at the Stolz Pool Campground, there seemed to be hundreds of teenagers sunbathing on the large slab rocks, with huge tubes lying by their sides. Every vehicle in the parking lot had an inner tube tied to it. In this respect, at the height of summer it is a place that attracts a younger crowd. However, these youths were not loud and seemed aware of the "rules of camping." I imagine that during the shoulder season this campground is a wonderful (and quieter) place for people of every age to visit.

ELK FALLS

> Location

This is a beautiful 1,087-hectare provincial park that features a cascading 25-metre waterfall created by the Campbell River falling into a walled canyon.

In spring, the waters tumble (or, in late summer, trickle) over a deep gorge and provide a beautiful vista which can be viewed from a new suspension bridge and upgraded stairs. Elk Falls is located on Highway 28 just 2 kilometres north of Campbell River, where all services are available. Elk Falls is one of the most popular campgrounds on Vancouver Island.

> Facilities

Elk Falls boasts 122 large, private camping spots surrounded by trees. Approximately 25 of the more desirable spots are situated along the banks of the Quinsam River; the rest are among an area of second-growth forest. There are a couple of flush toilets and a sani-station; however, only some park areas are wheelchair-accessible. Reservations are accepted for over half the sites. The day-use area is separate from the campground, making for quite a peaceful provincial park.

> Recreational activities

The primary attraction of the area is fishing, which is excellent in both Campbell River and Quinsam River. Depending on the time of year, steelhead, rainbow, and cutthroat trout and Dolly Varden can be caught. Another feature of this provincial park is the extensive 12-kilometre trail system. The Quinsam River Trail leads to the Quinsam Salmon Hatchery, and the Canyon View Trail, with recently completed stairs and bridge sections, takes explorers to the John Hart power-generating facility and an impressive bridge over the river. Other trails lead through woodland to wonderful waterfalls and wildlife-viewing opportunities. For children there is an adventure playground and sports field, and swimming and paddling are possible in the river at the day-use area.

The nearby community of Campbell River is a pleasant town to explore and provides a number of attractions, including a pier where you can rent fishing rods and buy ice cream. Keep an eye out for the logger up the pole by the shopping centre, and watch for seals in the Strait of Georgia.

> Additional information

In 1997, a magazine produced by BC Parks stated: "The undisputedly cheapest overnight rate in the salmon capital of the world is located in Elk Falls Provincial Park. Just $9.50/night buys a quiet river setting, a campsite, a convenient location and a fishing extravaganza." The prices have since increased to $22.00, but it is still a real bargain for those who love fishing, are in search of a base from which to explore Campbell River, or just want an idyllic place to camp.

ENGLISHMAN RIVER FALLS

> Location

Established in 1940 to protect an area of old-growth forest around stunning waterfalls, this 97-hectare provincial park is a delight to visit at any time of the year. English-man River Falls is found 13 kilometres southwest of Parksville off Highway 4 on a  paved road. Qualicum Beach, Parksville, and Nanaimo are nearby.

> Facilities

The campground has 103 spacious campsites set in a forest of Douglas fir interspersed with Rocky Mountain maple trees and ferns. There are no showers, only one flush toilet block near the day use area and no sani-station, and only the basic camping facilities (pit toilets, drinking water, picnic tables, fire pits). This park is wheelchair-accessible. Reservations are accepted for over two-thirds of the sites.

> Recreational activities

In this park you can walk to the beautiful waterfalls amidst a mixed forest of cedar, Douglas fir, and hemlock. Three kilometres of trails offer views of the river, but at the time of writing swimming was prohibited. A deep pool at the bottom of the canyon is a good place to seasonally view spawning salmon, steelhead, and trout (fishing in this park is prohibited). The park's proximity to Nanaimo (48 kilometres away), Port Alberni (50 kilometres), and Courtenay (88 kilometres) means the activities and facilities of these communities are easily accessible, as is the beach at Parksville (14 kilometres), where at low tide the sea recedes nearly 100 metres and leaves a vast expanse of sand and pools to explore and beachcomb.

> Additional information

Once named Rio De Grullas—"River of Cranes"—by the Spanish explorers of the eighteenth century, this river was renamed a century later in memory of an English immigrant who died here. The campground is frequently used when the one at Rathtrevor Beach is full. It is well worth visiting in the fall when the trees are turning beautiful shades of gold and red, or in the spring when the wildflowers are at their best.

FILLONGLEY

> Location

There is something for everyone in this 26-hectare provincial park that includes a beach, a marshy estuary, a forest rich in old-growth firs, and the remnants of what was once a large estate. Found on Denman Island and featuring views of Lambert Channel, Fillongley is reached by taking a ferry from Buckley Bay, south of Courtenay, to Denman and then driving the 4-kilometre paved road to the east side of the island where the campground is situated. Denman Island has food, gas, and basic supplies.

> Facilities

The biggest drawback of Denman Island's only provincial park is that there are only 10 camping spots available here, and they are lined up side by side at the parking area. For more privacy, it is possible to pitch tents under nearby trees. All the basic amenities are provided (drinking water, pit toilets, picnic tables, fire pits), and the park is wheelchair-accessible. In 2021, reservations were accepted for all spaces.

> Recreational activities

The campground is situated near a lovely rocky beach from which it is possible to swim, kayak, beachcomb, and look for oysters and clams. Hiking trails through old-growth forest have also been developed and offer an alternative to the shoreline recreational pursuits. A salmon spawning stream runs through the park. The island is ideal for cycling enthusiasts as there is little traffic (except near the ferry terminals) and it is relatively flat. Denman Island is a delightful place to explore, for it has a beautifully relaxed atmosphere and many arts and crafts shops. In addition, nearby Hornby Island, which is also easy to reach, has hiking trails and lovely beaches.

> Additional information

The park was created from a bequest by George Beadnell, one of the first pioneers to settle in the area. He named his estate Fillongley after his home in England and built a tennis court, bowling green, clubhouse, and greenhouse, as well as a large impressive home. Following Beadnell's death in 1958, these facilities fell into disrepair and were eventually destroyed. Beadnell is buried in the park; his grave can be seen from the Homestead Trail. This is a fantastic, tranquil camping spot with a rocky beach and shallow waters. I spent a wonderful night here watching the sun set after having dinner on the beach. It's one of the best-kept secrets of BC Parks but is often full, so be sure to make a reservation.

FRENCH BEACH

> Location

French Beach Provincial Park, which boasts 1,600 metres of beach and exceptional views across the Strait of Juan de Fuca toward the Olympic Mountains in Washington State, is a marvellous place to visit. The 59-hectare park is located just 20 kilometres west of Sooke on Highway 14 (Sooke is

38 kilometres from Victoria). Services are provided at stores in Sooke and Jordan River (11 kilometres away).

> Facilities

Set in a forest of Douglas fir, Sitka spruce, western hemlock, and western redcedar are 69 shaded camping spots. There is a sani-station and recent upgrades were undertaken to allow access to larger RVs. Flush toilets were installed but the campground does not have showers. The park is wheelchair-accessible and reservations are accepted for all the camping spots. The campground is open year round.

> Recreational activities

One of the biggest attractions here is whale watching. Magnificent grey whales migrate to their feeding grounds in the spring and return in the fall. If you're lucky, you can view them from the beach or, if you are an experienced paddler, at closer range in a kayak. Roaming pods of killer whales are also sometimes observed. Looking offshore, it is not unusual to see river otters, seals, and sea lions playing, while ospreys and bald eagles frequent the skies overhead. The extensive sand-and-gravel beach, rimmed by the forest, is a beautiful place to swim from—although it is considerably wilder than the beaches on the east side of the island. Small nature trails wind through the second-growth forest, and there is a playground for children. Once you have had enough of the natural beauty, go and explore Victoria's many attractions.

> Additional information

Many years ago, a friend of mine tried to persuade me not to include French Beach in this book; she wanted to keep it all to herself and hated the thought of it becoming too well known. The biggest draw for her and for me to this provincial park is the huge beach—a beautiful place to sit and watch the sun go down or to stargaze. This is a rugged beach that is great to explore at any time of the year. In 2021, I returned to this park after an absence of about five years; it was just as wonderful as when I had first visited over twenty-five years ago.

GOLDSTREAM

> Location

The BC Parks webpage for Goldstream reads: "Massive trees, majestic water-falls, a meandering river that meets the sea, flowers, birds and fascinating fish are but a few attractions that draw people to Goldstream Provincial Park." This description, coupled with the fact that the park is only 16 kilometres northwest of Victoria off Highway 1, makes it a very popular location for both locals and tourists. A small store and pub are located at the park entrance.

> Facilities

This 477-hectare park has 173 well-appointed camping spots available for every type of recreational vehicle. There are showers, a sani-station, flush and pit toilets, and wheelchair accessibility. Reservations are accepted for 152 spaces, and strongly advised. The campground is open year-round, but certain services (water, firewood, sani-station) are only available between March and October.

> Recreational activities

Goldstream is blessed with a number of hiking and walking routes, some accessible to mountain bikers. In 2015, bike skill trails were constructed. Trails take hikers through Goldstream's two distinctive vegetation zones to views of 600-year-old Douglas fir trees and many other deciduous and evergreen trees and plants. The Gold Mine and Lower Falls trails lead to Niagara Falls, which is higher than its namesake (and fortunately much less commercialized—no honeymoon suites here). Swimming and fishing are possible within the park, and in the summer months, naturalists conduct interpretive programs in the outdoor theatre. An excellent visitor centre is also located here, which has exhibits and snacks, and offers programs throughout the year.

> Additional information

Goldstream River was first named Gold Creek in 1858 by Lieutenant Peter Leech, an engineer with the Vancouver Island Exploration Committee, who discovered gold in the waters. Subsequent exploration revealed only small deposits, but there is nothing stopping the fortune seeker from further exploration. The Goldstream River is now the spawning site of chum salmon, and from mid-October to November it draws many thousands of visitors and millions of salmon. BC Parks produces a leaflet detailing the salmon spawning process. Long ago, this area, like many others on Vancouver Island, was used as a fishing ground by the Coast Salish people. Whether you are a fortune seeker, an angler, or just a holidaymaker, Goldstream is a lovely place to visit.

GORDON BAY

> Location

Be sure you have sunscreen if you plan to holiday at Gordon Bay Provincial Park, which is one of Canada's hottest spots. This 104-hectare park is found at the southern end of Cowichan Lake, 35 kilometres northwest of Duncan and accessed by taking Highway 18 just north of Duncan. The nearby community of Lake Cowichan has most services, and there is a small store at Honeymoon Bay, 2 kilometres from the campground.

> Facilities

Positioned in an area of second-growth Douglas fir, this campground has 126 large, well-structured camping spots (those numbered 1 to 14 are closest to the bay). There are flush and pit toilets, a sani-station, showers, and full access for wheelchairs. Reservations are accepted for all sites and highly recommended, as this is one of the Island's most popular locations. The campground is open year round.

> Recreational activities

Gordon Bay is located in one of the warmest valleys on Vancouver Island. The mountains pressing close to Cowichan Lake produce a heat trap that ensures the highest average daily temperature in Canada. The waters of

Cowichan Lake are warm and supply relief from this heat (as do the shady camping spots). For the angler, the lake has reserves of Dolly Varden, rainbow and cutthroat trout, and chum, coho, and spring salmon. Windsurfing and paddleboarding are also popular. There is a boat launch in the park and water-skiing is permitted. An adventure playground has been constructed for children within the camping area. Two of the biggest attractions are the excellent pebble beach—fantastic for children of every age—and the clear, weed-free waters, ideal for swimming. Trails lead from the park over a forest floor covered with thimbleberry, salal, and salmonberry, and, in the spring, wonderful wildflowers. (Remember, picking the vegetation in BC parks is prohibited.) Interpretive programs are available in the summer; in 2022, there was a "learn to fish" program for children under the age of 16.

> Additional information

In addition to the beauty of the park itself, the immediate surrounding area provides many alternative activities. A small museum at Saywell Park offers local interest, and you can tour the Lake Cowichan Earth Satellite station. Lake Cowichan is also the hometown of Dawn Coe-Jones, a repeat winner on the LPGA tour, who learned to golf at March Meadows, the attractive nine-hole public golf course in Honeymoon Bay. Because Gordon Bay is a delightful family-oriented camping location equipped with all amenities, it's not surprising that it's one of the most popular campgrounds on southern Vancouver Island—and frequently full.

JUAN DE FUCA

> Location

This is one of the province's newest campgrounds. Its quick addition to the list of reservable sites illustrates BC Parks's recognition that it would be immediately popular. Juan de Fuca Provincial Park consists of three main areas. In addition to the campground and day-use area (known as China Beach) there is the Juan de Fuca Marine Trail, a 47-kilometre stretch of wilderness that was used at the turn of the century as a life-saving trail. It is adjacent to the shoreline, known as the "graveyard of the Pacific" because of the number of boats that have run aground here. The third area of the park is Botanical Beach, a unique shoreline and one of the richest tidal areas on the west coast. The campground is situated on the west coast of southern Vancouver Island, 35 kilometres west of Sooke and 36 kilometres east of Port Renfrew.

> Facilities
China Beach features 78 vehicle-accessible campsites in a lightly forested area. Although fire pits are available, the parks administration stresses the use of stoves to conserve the environment. There are only picnic tables, pit toilets, and drinking water. Some campground facilities are wheelchair-accessible. Reservations are accepted at 64 of the China Beach Sites.

> Recreational activities
The main feature of this park is the Juan de Fuca Marine Trail, which was developed as an alternative to the increasingly popular West Coast Trail. Although 47 kilometres may be pretty tough going for some, it is easy to select a small section of beach to wander along. From the day-use area there is a 1-kilometre trail through the forest to the beach, while Second Beach is a 2-kilometre return trip from China Beach. Nearer to Port Renfrew is Botanical Beach, where low tide reveals a wonderful array of shoreline and marine life. Red, purple, and orange starfish can be seen, as well as sea anemones and blue mussels. Sea fishing is possible, as is canoeing, kayaking, and windsurfing if the seas are not too rough. Personally, I think it is just wonderful to sit and watch the ever-changing sea.

> Additional information
The Juan de Fuca Marine Trail was the result of the Commonwealth Nature Legacy—a reminder of the 1994 Commonwealth Games that were held in Victoria—but the area was recognized as biologically significant as early as 1901, when the University of Minnesota established a marine research station here. This is a stunning park, but take caution when enjoying it: the shoreline is prone to "rogue" waves, which hit the beach occasionally and can drag you into the sea. The BC Parks website warns that thieves operate in this area and target the personal property of park users.

KIN BEACH

> Location

Kin Beach is a Class C park, which means it's co-administered by a local community board and its facilities and services vary slightly from those solely under the auspices of BC Parks. This park is located on central Vancouver Island in the Comox Valley, overlooking the Strait of Georgia, and is very close to the Comox–Powell River ferry terminal. Unlike most provincial parks in BC, which are easily found, the signposting to Kin Beach leaves a lot to be desired. My advice is to use Google Maps if you have it. Access is from Ryan Road in Comox: turn left on Little River Road, then right on Kilmorley Road. Services are available in Comox or Courtenay. A small store selling some items is positioned in the park's day-use area and appears to be operational during the summer season.

> Facilities

The 6-hectare park has 18 vehicle-accessible open, somewhat exposed, camping spots set in a large grassy field. Firewood is available for purchase, tap water is provided, and there are flush and pit toilets (with the pit toilets being a little more "rudimentary" than in other provincial parks). Reservations are recommended during the summer and can be made by calling the park directly at 1-250-339-6365.

> Recreational activities

The nearest boat launch is at Kitty Coleman Provincial Park down the road, but it is possible to canoe and kayak from this park. The beach is somewhat rocky, which makes for good rock-pool analysis (remember the bucket and tell the kids to put everything back after they've finished prodding and poking). Fishing for salmon, rockfish, and shellfish takes place here. There is a large day-use area with a grassy area, picnic tables, a woodstove, and picnic shelter. There is also a kids' playground, which seems to have been constructed in the 1950s, with metal slides and roundabouts similar to the ones I used as a child in the 1960s. I think it should have a preservation order on it.

> Additional information

I visited this park in 2017 for the first time, out of season, as it was one of the few campgrounds in this book I had not explored. The views across the Strait of Georgia are stunning and there seemed to be a number of "nooks and crannies" I imagine my kids would have loved to explore when they were younger. It is definitely a Class C park, though. It does not possess the same level of facilities other BC parks have (toilet paper hung on a huge nail in the washroom, and there was little designation between camping spaces and that antique playpark). If you require a certain level of service, travel on to Miracle Beach, but otherwise try Kin Beach (or Kitty Coleman).

KITTY COLEMAN

> Location

Like Kin Beach, just a stone's throw away, Kitty Coleman has been designated a Class C provincial park and is managed by a local community board, which means it provides a different camping experience than other provincial parks. The 10-hectare park is found on the southern side of the Strait of Georgia, 6 kilometres north of Courtenay, off Highway 19A. The signposting is not great so use the GPS if you have it. Take Coleman Road off Highway 19A, turn on Left Road then right on Whitaker Road. Alternatively, follow the signs to Kitty Coleman Woodland Gardens and you will find the campground. All services are available in Courtenay or Comox, or at a couple of gas stations on Highway 19A.

> Facilities

The campground here has 65 sites, some quite close to each other, some which overlook the park's 900 metres of shoreline. There are flush and pit toilets but no showers and pump water that can only be used to extinguish fires. Firewood is available for purchase from the park administrator. Reservations are not taken for individual sites but can be made for group camping by calling 1-250-338-1332.

> Recreational activities

The park is characterized by a mature forest of western hemlock and western redcedar and the estuary of Kitty Coleman Creek. The forest runs almost to the ocean, so the campground is quite dark and cool. A series of trails meanders through the park, and canoeing, kayaking, and swimming are popular pastimes. There are two pay-to-use boat launches, and you can fish for salmon or harvest shellfish, which at times are abundant in the area. The park is also good for spotting wildlife, including seals, sea lions, porpoises, and bald eagles. A number of picnic tables overlook the pebbly beach, awarding great views. The woodland gardens, just a short walk away, boasts 24 acres of gardens and one of the largest rhododendron collections in western Canada (woodlandgardens.ca).

> ## Additional information

BC Parks says there is a single majestic old-growth Douglas fir in the park and wild onions growing in the area. The facilities in Class C parks are very much dependent on the local community boards charged with their administration, and regular BC Parks patrons will be immediately aware that the services here are not as good as in other BC parks. Since Kin Beach and Kitty Coleman are close to each other, campers have the luxury of checking them both out (and, if neither is appealing, Miracle Beach is just a short drive away).

LITTLE QUALICUM FALLS

> ## Location

Impressive waterfalls cascading into a rocky gorge characterize this 440-hectare provincial park, claimed by some people to be the most magnificent park on Vancouver Island. Little Qualicum River drops several hundred feet down the slopes of Mount Arrowsmith in a series of waterfalls. This remarkable vista is located on Highway 4, 19 kilometres west of Parksville on Little Qualicum River. Services are available at Port Alberni and Parksville.

> Facilities

Ninety-six camping spots are here for the taking in the upper and lower camp-grounds, set among a pleasant fir and pine forest. The park is accessible to wheelchairs, and there are flush and pit toilets but no showers or sani-station. The campground is quite close to the road and railway line. Reservations are accepted at 73 spaces.

> Recreational activities

Swimming in this provincial park is wonderful and can be undertaken in lovely little green pools at the Cameron Lake picnic site just a short drive away. (Be advised that at certain times of the year swimming is prohibited—check the park noticeboard or the BC Parks website.) There are over 6 kilometres of graded walking trails, and fishing in the river is rewarding. Just outside the park is MacMillan (Cathedral Grove) Provincial Park, where magnificent west-ern hemlocks, Douglas firs, and western redcedars stand over 60 metres tall, like the columns of a cathedral. Some of these trees are more than 800 years old. Cathedral Grove has trails that lead into the depths of this spectacular old-growth forest.

> Additional information

The area around Beaufort and Cameron lakes contains salamanders and newts, which like the cool, damp cedar and fir forest area. This provincial park is conveniently located for exploring the eastern Parksville/Qualicum area and the western town of Port Alberni. From Port Alberni, it is possible to take the famous MV Lady Rose (ladyrosemarine.com) through the fjord scenery of the Alberni Inlet to Bamfield on the west coast, an unusual and rewarding boat trip that starts at 8:00 AM and returns around 5:00 PM (no vehicles). If it is not rain-ing, you are guaranteed to see some spectacular scenery and unusual wildlife.

LOVELAND BAY

> Location

I first visited Loveland Bay in May 2002, well before the crowds arrived and when wonderful birds were singing their hearts out. More recent visits suggest this is an adult-oriented campground with a low-key, relaxed feel. It is situated

18 kilometres west of Campbell River on Lower Campbell Lake and is reached by taking the gravel road from Highway 28 across the John Hart Dam, then Camp Road 5 (also gravel). Both roads are good and suitable for every type of vehicle. It is a relatively small 30-hectare site but was immediately popular once opened (likely because it is so close to some of the best fishing in the province).

> Facilities

There are currently 31 vehicle/tent campsites, but in 2023 an additional 22 will be added, according to BC Parks. All but 5 have direct access to the lake via a small pebbly beach and boast fantastic views of Lower Campbell Lake. There are 10 pit toilets and pump water is provided, but these facilities are due to be upgraded soon to include flush toilets. The park is wheelchair-accessible and, surprisingly, reservations are accepted for 28 sites.

> Recreational activities

There are few organized activities here—indeed, this campground is not geared for children. But it is an ideal place for reading and relaxing, and there is a small wharf to sunbathe on. In 2021, the beach area was upgraded. Recreational activities include boating, swimming, trout fishing, and canoeing on picturesque Campbell Lake. There is a boat launch, but be careful of the many submerged stumps and also of the wind, which can be quite strong on the lake. In the town of Campbell River, only 20 kilometres away, it is possible to rent or buy all the fishing equipment you could ever require. With the recent decline of the fishing industry, Campbell River has promoted itself as a tourist destination and is now a lovely place to wander around and people-watch. The 180-metre-long, 6.6-metre-wide pier regularly draws crowds; you can watch seals swimming below while you eat ice cream sold on the pier. Other attractions outside the park include mountain-bike trails, hiking, and the Snowden Demonstration Forest.

> Additional information

As mentioned previously, a number of provincial park campgrounds on Vancouver Island fill up during the peak summer season. For those who cannot find accommodation at Elk Falls, Miracle Beach, or Strathcona, Loveland Bay provides an ideal alternative. Only 3 percent of the population of Vancouver Island lives north of Campbell River, so for those who want to explore the less commercialized, quieter side of Vancouver Island, Loveland Bay is an ideal choice.

MIRACLE BEACH

> **Location**

Blessed with a wide sand-and-pebble beach and excellent views across  the Strait of Georgia to the Coast Mountains, this campground is attractive to both adults and children and is an ideal spot for a family vacation. Miracle Beach Provincial Park is located on the protected shores of Vancouver Island's east coast, midway between Courtenay (22 kilometres south) and Campbell River (22 kilometres north), 1.5 kilometres from Highway 19 on a paved access road. The campground has all required services conveniently located on the highway and in nearby communities. A small store is located in the nature house.

> **Facilities**

Miracle Beach is 137 hectares and boasts 202 large private camping spots in a second-growth forest of Douglas fir, hemlock, and western redcedar. All amenities are here, including showers, flush and pit toilets, a sani-station, and wheelchair accessibility. Reservations are accepted and strongly advised for 192 spaces. The campground is open year round, but full services are only provided from April to September.

> **Recreational activities**

One of the main attractions is the lovely, long sand-and-pebble beach, perfect for swimming, sunbathing, and exploring tide pools when they are accessible. Miracle Beach also has one of the best visitor centres I've visited. To supplement personal investigations, the visitor centre has saltwater aquariums and nature displays, as well as interpretive programs here, including the Jerry's Rangers program for kids. Black Creek, which runs through the park, has a coho salmon run, and there are two small walking trails. For those who choose to travel farther afield, the salmon fishing in the area is good, and short boat trips can be taken to the nearby islands of Denman, Hornby, Quadra, and Cortes. At night, clear skies make for excellent stargazing from the beach or your camping spot.

> ## Additional information

Miracle Beach is said to have received its name because it was miraculously missed by two severe forest fires that devastated much of the surrounding area in the recent past. Whenever I stay here, children seem to outnumber adults 10 to 1. This provincial park is an extremely popular camping location, especially during the summer months. If you have young children, it is the perfect place to spend a vacation, but you will probably need a reservation unless you want to camp during the last weekend of October.

MONTAGUE HARBOUR MARINE

> ## Location

When Montague Harbour Marine Provincial Park on Galiano Island opened in 1959, it was the first provincial park to serve both visitors who arrived in their own boats and those who came by car or on foot. The park encompasses an 89-hectare area that starts 5 metres below sea level and rises to 180 metres above. Galiano Island can be reached via BC Ferries, either from Swartz Bay on Vancouver Island or Tsawwassen on the Mainland (and from some other Gulf Islands). From the ferry dock at Sturdies Bay, you drive 10 kilometres north-west to the park. Full services are at Sturdies Bay, and the nearby marina has a small store and coffee bar with basic supplies.

> ## Facilities

There are 42 beautifully positioned camping spots in this 97-hectare park, 16 of them suitable for vehicles and set in a forested area. Many of the 28 walk-in sites overlook the harbour and therefore have better views than the drive-in spots. Facilities are restricted to the basic ones found in provincial parks (pit toilets, drinking water, picnic tables, fire pits); there is no sani-station, but some facilities are wheelchair-accessible. Reservations are accepted and strongly advised. The campground is open year round, but full services are only offered from March to October.

> **Recreational activities**

This gorgeous park has scenic hiking trails that lead through a forested area of arbutus, Douglas fir, hemlock, and Garry oak to beautiful beaches of white sand and shell, ideal for sunbathing or swimming. The abundant salmon and shellfish in the area attract a wide array of birds, including bald eagles, which can be easily seen fishing for their dinner. Canoes and kayaks can be hired from the adjacent marina, and there is a boat launch within the park. Interpretive programs are offered in a glass-bottomed hut, which provide an entertaining and educational introduction to the marine life of the area. Galiano Island has quite a unique feel about it. Many artists and craftspeople have chosen to live here, and the area around Sturdies Bay has a small number of restaurants, craft shops, and an excellent bakery.

> **Additional information**

The marina next to the park serves excellent cinnamon buns and coffee in the morning. The island is named after the Spanish navy commander Dionisio Alcalá-Galiano, the first European to visit the Gulf Islands in 1792. Smaller and less commercialized than Salt Spring Island, but with more amenities than Pender, Galiano is a fantastic place to spend some time. It's also a wonderful place to cycle around, and bikes can be rented at Sturdies Bay. The sunsets from the Montague Harbour Campground are astoundingly beautiful. It's one of my favourite camping spots, with the only negative being the racoons, but I understand this population is being reduced.

MORTON LAKE

> **Location**

A really serene camping experience can be had at this exquisite little park nestled in the Sayward Forest northwest of Campbell River on Mohun and Morton lakes. The park is reached by travelling north on Highway 19 past the pulp mill and then taking the Menzies Main logging road (gravel) for

12 kilometres and Morton Lake Road for 7 kilometres. Services are at Campbell River, 27 kilometres to the south.

> Facilities

There are only 24 camping spots in this 74-hectare park, but many of them have access directly onto Morton Lake and are quite charming. Only the basic amenities are available (pit toilets, drinking water, fire pits, picnic tables). Reservations are accepted for 12 sites.

> Recreational activities

Visitors to this area can enjoy fishing for Dolly Varden, rainbow, and cutthroat trout, boating, swimming, and canoeing in Mohun or Morton lakes. Mohun Lake provides access to the Sayward canoe circuit, a 47-kilometre roundtrip. Alternately, a trail leads to Andrew Lake, which provides a different venue for water-based recreational pursuits just 30 minutes away. There is a good sandy beach by the campground, and since this location is away from the nearest population centre, sunbathing and swimming can be a tranquil experience— you may even consider skinny-dipping.

> Additional information

The forest around the lake was destroyed in the Great Campbell River Fire of 1938, which burned for over a month, and has subsequently been replanted with Douglas fir and pine; cedar and hemlock have all grown back naturally. The scars of the fire are still clearly evident in the area. Morton Lake is the northernmost provincial park on Vancouver Island with basic camping amenities. Marble River and Schoen Lake provincial parks do not have potable water. In contrast to the roads south of Campbell River, Highway 19 north is a very quiet and beautiful drive; it is a great pity that there are not provincial parks located along this stretch of highway. In all my years of camping, it is only in the northern part of Vancouver Island that I have, out of necessity, stayed in a private campground. Although BC may have a large number of provincial parks in comparison to other provinces, states, and countries, there is still a need for more campgrounds, especially on northern Vancouver Island.

PACIFIC RIM (NP)

> ## Location

Pacific Rim National Park Reserve is located on the west coast of Vancouver Island on Highway 4. Three distinctly different locations make up this 51,300-hectare (including 22,300 hectares of ocean) national park, and to see all aspects of it you need at least two weeks. The park's features include the famous West Coast Trail, a 77-kilometre rugged excursion into west coast rainforest scenery (reservations are required if you intend to take this hike); the Broken Group Islands, a group of over one hundred islands in Barkley Sound; and Long Beach, with its fantastic sands. Services are available at Ucluelet and Tofino, as well as along Highway 4, which runs between these two centres.

> ## Facilities

Developed vehicle-accessible camping facilities are only available in the Long Beach area of the park (backcountry camping is possible in other areas). Located between Ucluelet and Tofino, the Green Point Campground has 94 blissful spots located high above the beach where campers are lulled to sleep by the sound of the ocean. There are also 20 non-reservable walk-in forest sites available.

Facilities include a sani-station, flush and pit toilets, a visitor centre, and wheelchair accessibility (in addition, the park has two wheelchair-accessible trails and the Kʷisitis Visitor Centre has an all-terrain wheelchair for visitor use). During the summer months, this campground is almost always full, so reservations are essential (via the Parks Canada website; see page 7). The maximum stay here is 7 nights and 2022 fees for camping ranged from $29.25 to $34.50. Five equipped campsites are also available consisting of a tent for four to six people, sleeping pads, tarp shelter, stove, lantern, picnic table, and fire pit.

> **Recreational activities**

Long Beach boasts 22 kilometres of pristine beach, providing a superb expanse of shoreline for surfers, windsurfers, swimmers, and kayakers to demonstrate their skills. The ocean temperature varies from 6 to 12°C. With the wild waves of the Pacific Ocean pounding along the sands, beachcombing and hiking are invigorating activities here in any season—as long as you have the correct attire. There are nine short (1- to 2-kilometre) walking trails covering 12 kilometres in total, which can be used to explore the rainforest or coastal flora and fauna (bald eagles frequent the area). Hikers should be very cautious on rocky points and headlands as people have been swept to their deaths here by large waves. Remember, the next wave can be higher than the one before!

There are nightly indoor interpretive programs offered from late June to early September. The Kʷisitis Visitor Centre (formerly the Wickaninnish Interpretive Centre), at the end of Wick Road and overlooking Wickaninnish Beach, has interpretive displays and a gift shop. The community of Tofino is rapidly developing into a tourism hub and offers many commercial services, including guided excursions in the area. Over the recent past, it has become very popular with Canadian and international visitors.

> Additional information

National parks charge a daily entrance fee, even if you are staying overnight (in 2022, the fees were $10.50 per adult and $21.00 per family; or you can purchase an annual pass good for all national parks). Parks Canada has produced a number of leaflets about Pacific Rim, including one listing all the hiking trails, which can be obtained from the Pacific Rim Visitor Centre, at the T-junction of the highway where you can turn to Tofino or Ucluelet. Long Beach is extremely popular in the peak summer months but offers just as many delights for those who choose to avoid the crowds and visit during cooler, wetter times of year. The region receives 300 centimetres of rain a year, so if you are visiting out of season, dress accordingly. If you do manage to camp in the campground, you may well wake to find the previous evening's ocean view obscured by a heavy morning mist. During the course of the day the mist usually disappears, allowing you to again enjoy the sight, as well as the sound, of the ocean. Check out the Parks Canada page devoted to Pacific Rim (pc.gc.ca/en/pn-np/bc/pacificrim) and the tourism sites for Ucluelet and Tofino (discoverucluelet.com and tourismtofino.com).

PRIOR CENTENNIAL (NP)

> Location

For a get-away-from-it-all camping experience, you cannot go far wrong in selecting North Pender Island's Prior Centennial, a former provincial park that has been part of the Gulf Islands National Park Reserve since 2003. Ferries to the island can be taken from Tsawwassen on the Mainland or from Swartz

Bay on Vancouver Island, and from some of the other Gulf Islands. The campground is located 6 kilometres from the ferry terminal on Canal Road. There are stores in Port Washington, Hope Bay, and Port Browning.

> Facilities

This is a relatively small 16-hectare park nestled in a pleasant forested area of ferns, cedar, fir, maple, and alder trees. Seventeen well-spaced vehicle/tent sites are available; unfortunately, they are close to the road. All basic services can be found here (drinking water, fire pits, pit toilets, picnic tables). Reservations are accepted (via phone or the Parks Canada website; see page 7).

> Recreational activities

The campground's location a few hundred metres from Medicine Beach at Bedwell Harbour makes it ideal for beachcombing and shoreline explorations. Hiking trails exist, and Pender Island is great to explore by bike. Watch for the historical markers that give details of the island's past. The small settlement of Hope Bay is a pleasant place to relax and watch the world go by, and a trail leads from the campground to the Golf Island Disc Park.

> Additional information

This park was donated to BC Parks in 1958 by Mr. and Mrs. F.L. Prior, hence its name. Pender Island is only a short ferry ride from Galiano Island and Salt Spring Island, which both have provincial parks. Many tourists vacation in the Gulf Islands by "island hopping," and residents of the Lower Mainland and Vancouver Island visit to enjoy the altogether different ambience created by the island lifestyle. Access to South Pender Island is via a wooden bridge a kilometre from the campground, and while there is more to explore on North Pender Island, it is also interesting to travel south, as the feel of the island changes. It is worth visiting the Gulf Island National Park Reserve website to look at the various maps and guides available on this and SMONEĆTEN (McDonald) and Sidney Spit parks.

RATHTREVOR BEACH

> Location

Cool ocean water lapping a long, white beach is just one of the many attractions of Rathtrevor Beach Provincial Park. Situated on Highway 19A, just 3 kilometres south of Parksville, with views over the Strait of Georgia to the Coast Mountains beyond, Rathtrevor Beach is the most popular park on Vancouver Island for camping. Services are available in Parksville, while the park's visitor centre contains a small concession selling pop, coffee, candy, and other sundries.

> Facilities

There are 250 drive-in and 25 drive/walk-in camping spots located in the Douglas fir-forested area of the 347-hectare park that can accommodate every type of recreational vehicle. This year-round campground is fully equipped with a sani-station, three shower buildings, and flush and pit toilets. It is wheelchair-accessible. Reservations are accepted, and you won't get a space without one in June, July, or August (in fact, they are required between the last week of June and Labour Day). All sites are reservable.

> Recreational activities

Famed for its beautiful sandy shingle on 2,000 metres of beach leading to warm, clear waters, Rathtrevor Beach is described by BC Parks as "unbeatable for swimming." Windsurfing and canoeing are possible (though there is no boat launch), and there are a number of walks with over 5 kilometres of trails, including some self-guided nature trails. Birdwatching is reputed to be good in the springtime and during the annual herring spawn. There are three children's play areas, and in the summer months the amphitheatre is used to deliver visitor programs, which are a daily occurrence throughout the summer. The old farmhouse is now the park visitor centre where you can rent bikes.

> Additional information

Rathtrevor takes its name from pioneer William Rath, who established a farm here in 1886. After he died in 1903, his wife was left with five children but kept the farm running and eventually developed the land into a campground, adding the suffix "trevor" for effect. BC Parks acquired Rathtrevor Campground in 1967. Today this campground is extremely popular, but visitors who arrive to find it full only have to travel 13 kilometres to find alternative camping at Englishman River Falls Provincial Park. It is the perfect place for children: huge sites, daily interpretive programs, safe cycling, great beaches, and only a 30-minute drive from the ferry in Nanaimo. Although it is one of BC's most commercial campgrounds, it is a real crowd-pleaser. It's a place that can be enjoyed for a picnic or rest stop, as well as to camp in.

RUCKLE

> **Location**

In 1974, when the Ruckle family sold a 486-hectare parcel of land to the provincial government for a nominal fee, they gave British Columbians and visitors to the province a superb camping location. The largest provincial park in the Gulf Islands, Ruckle is situated 10 kilometres from Fulford Harbour on Beaver Point Road, at the southeastern corner of Salt Spring Island. The nearest services can be found at Fulford Harbour.

> **Facilities**

This superb park contains 78 walk-in camping spots in a grassy area beside Swanson Channel, as well as 8 drive-in spaces. There is parking for RVs, but no campsites are immediately adjacent. The walk from the parking area to the campground is flat, and in less than five minutes you can pitch your tent on a site directly overlooking the ocean. All the basic amenities are found here (pit toilets, drinking water stations, picnic tables, fire pits). There is no sani-station or wheelchair access. Reservations are accepted for 10 vehicle and tent-pad sites.

> ## Recreational activities

Campers can observe otters, harbour seals, porpoises, sea lions, and—if they're very fortunate—killer whales as they swim in the adjacent waters. Ruckle Park has more than 7 kilometres of shoreline, characterized by pocket beaches, rocky coves, and headlands waiting to be explored. There are over 15 kilometres of walking trails, leading around the headlands and through the forested areas. While there is no designated swimming area, beachcombing, fishing, windsurfing, ocean kayaking, and scuba diving are all possible here, while a maze of paved roads makes cycling a delight. Interpretive programs are offered during the summer.

> ## Additional information

The park area was originally settled in 1872 by the Ruckle family, which still resides and works in the area. The continuous use of the land for farming purposes from the late 1800s until today makes it one of BC's oldest family farms. The Ruckle family retains its right to life tenancy within the park. Visitors can tour the historical farm buildings and learn about farming practices of a bygone age. Descriptive markers and photographs attached to the well-maintained historical buildings give details of a past life.

SAYSUTSHUN (NEWCASTLE ISLAND MARINE)

> ## Location

This 336-hectare park faces the Nanaimo waterfront and sits off the shore of popular Maffeo Sutton Park, where a ferry services foot-passengers to the island daily from 9:00 AM until 6:00 PM between May and September. During the rest of the year, ferry service ceases at 4:30 PM. Adult rates are $12 return and $5 for children. Bicycles can be transported for and additional $5, although for safety reasons electric and motorized bicycles are not permitted. Good trail maps can be accessed on the park website (newcastleisland.ca). As an alternative, another ideal way to explore the island is to take a walking tour featuring totems, a herring saltery, coal mine sites, and sandstone quarries, hosted by a Snuneymuxw Knowledge Keeper.

> Facilities

The park is a popular cruising destination for recreational boaters who can moor their boats near the ferry dock and spend their day exploring tidal pools or embracing the warm, shallow waters and the sandy beach. Food can be purchased in the tearoom located in the 1930s dance pavilion on the island. The 8-kilometre coastal hiking and biking trail hosts both local day users and campers, who can reserve one of the 18 designated camping spots, beautifully positioned at the edge of the forest. A vast grassland meadow can accommodate additional campers who prefer being closer to the water. There are flush and pit toilets, as well as two coin-operated showers, and the park is wheelchair-accessible. The pavilion offers food from 10:00 AM to 7:00 PM during the peak summer season. The campground is open year-round, but full services are only offered between April and October. Reservations are accepted for all 18 sites.

> Recreational activities

The island is rich in history; the Snuneymuxw people inhabited the area for centuries prior to the arrival of Spanish explorers in 1791. The Hudson's Bay Company later opened a coalmine on the island and named it after the famous British coal-mining town, Newcastle-upon-Tyne. Coal was extracted until 1887, and a sandstone quarry was in operation between 1869 and 1955. Evidence of the past can be seen when you take the 22 kilometres of hiking trails that zigzag their way around and across the park. Bikes are permitted on two of these trails. There are several beaches, caves, and bays to explore and a calm sea to swim in. Canoeing along the shoreline is a favourite pastime, and there is a children's play area. Deer can be seen grazing in the early evening, and the area is also noted for its shoreline bird life. Interpretive programs are offered in the summer.

> Additional information

I have fond memories of this park. When the CAMPA Big Band played the Newcastle Island Pavilion (now a visitor centre) in July of 1995, 1996, and 1997, we left Vancouver with rucksacks on our backs, caught two buses to the ferry at Horseshoe Bay, took the ferry from Horseshoe Bay to Nanaimo, and walked the 30-minute route from the BC Ferries terminal to the passenger ferry at Maffeo Sutton Park. We camped on Saysuthsun (Newcastle Island), hiked the trails during the day, ate on the verandas of the licensed tearooms during the evening, and then danced the night away to the sound of brilliant jazz music. On these occasions, I think we were the only couple wearing shorts, but we had great fun, and for under $20.00 each. This campground is not accessible by car and really should not be included in this book ... but it's one of my favourites and I believe everyone should know about it!

These days, a far faster but more expensive adventure is provided by Harbour Air seaplanes, who will store backpacks in their planes' pontoons and whose Nanaimo terminal sits less than a kilometre from the passenger ferry dock. The spectacular 20-minute journey across the Salish Sea often passes over Saysutshun and is truly memorable from takeoff until landing.

SIDNEY SPIT MARINE (NP)

> Location

Although it is effectively a marine park, Sidney Spit Marine Park on Sidney Island is a lovely camping facility that deserves a mention. There is no vehicle access; it is reached by taking a foot-passenger ferry that departs from Government Wharf at the end of Beacon Avenue in Sidney, a short drive from the Swartz Bay ferry terminal on

Vancouver Island. Services are found in Sidney and Victoria. The former provincial park is now part of the Gulf Islands National Park Reserve (see the Parks Canada website).

> **Facilities**

Once you take the 25-minute ferry from Sidney, you'll find the park has 29 formal walk-in camping spots in addition to group-camping facilities and plenty of space for spillover camping. There are pit toilets and picnic tables, but fires are not permitted and campers must bring their own water. Wheelbarrows for hauling gear, as the walk from the wharf to the campground is somewhat hilly and takes about 20 minutes, are provided. Reservations are strongly advised (via phone or the Parks Canada website; see page 7).

> **Recreational activities**

Sidney Spit has been described as "one of the most beautiful marine parks in the Pacific Northwest," as it features thousands of metres of white sandy beach backed by towering bluffs. Beyond these, the uplands contain a second-growth forest of fir, maple, western redcedar, and arbutus. One of its main features is a lagoon affording one of the best opportunities to explore intertidal life. These salt marshes and tidal flats attract both human and animal forms: ornithologists, naturalists, seals, killer whales, and dolphins all appear occasionally. Trails lead around the park, and the stunning beach provides opportunities to swim, sunbathe, and fish.

> **Additional information**

Some of the bricks used to build the famous Empress Hotel in Victoria and the Hotel Vancouver in Vancouver were produced by a brick factory that operated at the turn of the century near the southern wharf of Sidney Island. At its peak, this factory employed seventy workers. In 1924, the Todd family began purchasing land on Sidney Island and by 1968 owned all but the one tenth the provincial government had acquired in 1924. These 400 hectares form the marine park that's now part of the Gulf Islands National Park Reserve. The community of Sidney is an enjoyable place to take an afternoon stroll; in addition to shops that sell books, crafts, and antiques, there are inviting delis and cafes that offer an assortment of refreshments to revitalize a tired camper.

SMELT BAY

> Location

Located on the southern peninsula of Cortes Island, with stunning views to the south and west across a long pebble beach, 16-hectare Smelt Bay is the only provincial park on the island that permits camping. Cortes Island is not easy to reach but is well worth the effort. You must take two ferries, the first from Campbell River to Quadra Island (15 minutes), and the second from Quadra to Cortes (45 minutes). A well-signed 15-kilometre paved road leads from the ferry terminal to the campground. Services are available on the island at Whitecove, Manson's Landing, and Squirrel Cove.

> Facilities

Twenty-four camping spots are available in the woods, set back from the beach. Most are double sites. As one would expect, only the basic facilities are supplied (pit toilets, drinking water, picnic tables, fire pits). Reservations for 9 sites are accepted and advisable.

> Recreational activities

Leisure pursuits in the area include beachcombing, swimming, fishing for salmon and rock fish, and generally relaxing. At low tide, the pebble beach that leads to Sutil Point reveals a fascinating array of rock pools waiting to be explored. (Sutil Point is named after the Spanish ship Sutil on which Captain Galiano explored these waters in 1792.) Canoeing and kayaking are great in the calm waters of Smelt Bay, and there is a natural gravel boat launch. The immediate area of the park is rich in history. For example, the mounds behind the gravel beach were built centuries ago by Coast Salish First Nations as a form of defense. Cycling around the island is a pleasant, easy activity as the traffic is minimal and the roads are paved. Two other day-use parks—Manson's Landing and Hague Lake—are located nearby. Cortes is a quiet, remote island with a unique charm that is very different from nearby Quadra Island. The island has few settlements, with most of the development concentrated at the south end.

> **Additional information**

Smelt Bay was created in 1973 to offer camping facilities and to protect an Indigenous cultural site. In the early fall, tens of thousands of smelt spawn in this vicinity, hence the park's name. In turn, these small fish attract an array of other sea life to the area, including salmon, otters, seals, herons, and sea lions. Occasionally wolves and cougars are seen in the area. When this occurs BC Parks will convey the information at the campground noticeboard and on their website. A lovely, quiet getaway spot, Cortes Island is one of the more scenic islands and has an intricate coastline ideal for canoeing and kayaking.

SMONEĆTEN (MCDONALD) (NP)

> **Location**

If you have missed the last ferry to the mainland, you will be thankful for this park at the end of the Saanich Peninsula. Part of the Gulf Islands National Park Preserve since 2003, this former provincial park (renamed from McDonald to SMONEĆTEN in 2021, in collaboration with the W̱SÁNEĆ Leadership Council) has good views of the nearby islands and is geared to overnight stays. Located 2 kilometres from the Swartz Bay ferry terminal, the park primarily provides accommodation for travellers waiting to take the ferry from Swartz Bay.

> **Facilities**

This campground has 49 functional, treed drive-in camping spots suitable for RVs over 35 feet; there are also 6 walk-in sites. Despite being near considerable development, SMONEĆTEN Park has only the basic facilities (fire pits, picnic tables, pit toilets, drinking water), but it does have wheelchair access. Reservations can be made via the Parks Canada reservation system (see page 7).

> **Recreational activities**

As already mentioned, SMONEĆTEN is used primarily by people waiting to catch a ferry, or by those who have just taken a ferry and are only staying one night. The park therefore offers little in the way of recreational pursuits, but it is possible to cycle and hike there. The Lochside Regional Trail runs from the ferry to Downtown Victoria. There is more information on what to do in the Gulf Islands National Park Reserve at the Parks Canada website. The town of Sidney, which has a pleasant harbour, bookstores, craft shops, and cafes, is within easy access, and can be explored. In the summer, a small passenger ferry can be taken to Sidney Island, which contains a park with delightful scenery and campsites.

> Additional information

Victoria, only a 30-minute drive from Swartz Bay, offers a host of cultural and recreational activities for those who have time to explore. Victoria is the capital of British Columbia and houses the Provincial Legislature. Along streets lined with trees and flowers, the fascinating Royal British Columbia Museum, Empress Hotel, Parliament Buildings, Inner Harbour, and Chinatown are all within easy walking distance of one another. Shopping here is also a real treat. For those who have a choice and a vehicle, the provincial parks of Goldstream or Bamberton are preferable to SMONEĆTEN, but if you're tired after a long day of travelling and just want a place for the night, SMONEĆTEN delivers the goods.

SPROAT LAKE

> Location

Situated on the northern shore of Sproat Lake, just 13 kilometres west of Port Alberni off Highway 4, this is a popular family campground, but there is something for everyone here.

> Facilities

Excellent camping can be had at Sproat Lake, which has two connected campgrounds situated in a forested area straddling the highway. The more desirable are the "lower" 14 sites nearer the lake, but all 59 spots have access to showers, flush and pit toilets, and a sani-station. The park is wheelchair-accessible and reservations are accepted for all sites of both the upper and lower campgrounds.

> Recreational activities

Sproat Lake is noted for its warm water, which is fantastic for swimming. It is also possible to scuba dive. There is a large boat launch and good fishing, plus there are opportunities to paddleboard, water-ski, and windsurf. Trails lead through the forested area of second-growth Douglas fir, and the ground is littered with an attractive assortment of wildflowers at certain times of the year. The prehistoric petroglyphs found along trails at the southern end of the park are testimony to human presence in the area over the centuries and are considered some of the finest in BC. In addition, the town of Port Alberni, just 15 minutes away, is a pleasant community to explore.

> Additional information

Sproat Lake was home to a small fleet of huge Martin Mars air tankers, which took off from their lakeside base to extinguish fires. The world's largest water bombers, these planes were operated by a collective of five BC forest companies until 2015. Each plane could load 32 tonnes of water within 22 seconds by skimming across the lake at a speed of more than 110 kilometres per hour. The economy of Vancouver Island is dependent on the logging and tourism industries, and the threat of fires in this area and in the rest of BC peaks during the summer camping season. It is therefore imperative that all campfires be extinguished properly before a campsite is vacated. If the threat of fire becomes too great, fires are forbidden in provincial parks and sometimes parks can be closed to campers altogether.

STAMP RIVER

> Location

Formerly known as Stamp Falls, this park was renamed Stamp River when it was amalgamated with Money's Pool Provincial Park, increasing its area by 100 hectares. An angler's delight, this park is extremely popular with fishers, who visit the area for the excellent steelhead, coho, and cutthroat trout that can be caught in certain designated areas. Located 14 kilometres north of Port Alberni on a paved road off Highway 4, Stamp River has a lovely rural setting and yet is close to all of Port Alberni's amenities. It is also one of the closest provincial parks to Pacific Rim National Park, approximately 100 kilometres to the west.

> Facilities

There are 23 camping spots available here, some pleasantly located in a forested area near the river. Only the basic facilities exist (drinking water, pit toilets, picnic tables, fire pits). Reservations are accepted at 18 sites.

> Recreational activities

If you enjoy fishing, you'll love Stamp River, as the main attraction here is the fish. The campground is often used as a base camp for anglers who wish to explore the lakes and rivers in the vicinity. The park's unique feature is the fascinating display of salmon ascending the fish ladders in the summer and early fall. In July and August, some 30,000 sockeye salmon use this route; smaller numbers of chinook and coho follow in September and October (and sometimes into December). Two kilometres of trails lead visitors from the campground to the fish ladders and to the views of the waterfalls on Stamp River. As the park is a salmon hotbed, it also attracts bears. When bear activity is high, notices appear on the campground notice boards reminding visitors to be more vigilant.

> Additional information

This 327-hectare park was created in 1940 and is named after an early pioneer who built Port Alberni's first sawmill. It's a pleasant and interesting picnic spot for travellers heading along Highway 4. The highway between Port Alberni and Tofino is quite beautiful and follows the clear tumbling waters of the Kennedy River for half of its route. Upon reaching Pacific Rim National Park near Tofino, the traveller is rewarded with dramatic views of the Pacific.

STRATHCONA

> Location

Established in 1911, Strathcona is BC's oldest provincial park. Located in a majestic wilderness of old-growth forest, mountain peaks, clear rivers, waterfalls, and lakes, it encompasses more than 245,000 hectares. The main route to the park is from Campbell River on Highway 28, which runs through the park and connects to Gold River on the west side of the Island. All services are available in Campbell River, and there is a private lodge in the park that offers food, accommodation, and canoe/kayak rentals. Fuel is not available in the park.

> Facilities

In addition to wilderness camping, you can camp at two vehicle-accessible locations on Buttle Lake: Buttle Lake Campground, which has 86 spots (and the better beach), and Ralph River, 35 kilometres away, which also has 75. Facilities at both locations include wheelchair-accessible pit toilets, wood for sale, drinking water, fire pits, and picnic tables. There is no sani-station (the nearest one is at Elk Falls). Reservations are accepted for 96 sites at Buttle Lake and Ralph River.

> Recreational activities

As would be expected, there is a great deal to see and do in Strathcona Park, and it is easy to spend a week here. From Buttle Lake there are twelve hiking and walking trails that take explorers on a variety of hikes, and there are shorter nature walks too. There are climbing routes at Crest Creek Crags, and other areas of the park have developed trail systems. Swimming in Buttle Lake is good from both of the campgrounds, and there are two boat launches. Water-skiing is permitted on the lake, and the nearby lodge rents canoes and kayaks. A wealth of streams, rivers, and lakes provides angling opportunities, and there are excellent wildlife-viewing opportunities, as well. The southern section of the park contains Della Falls, one of Canada's highest waterfalls at 440 metres, and the tenth highest in the world. With the spring runoff in May and June, the falls are particularly spectacular. A working mine, the Myra

Falls Operation of Boliden-Westmin Resources Ltd., is located in the park, and guided tours are offered on weekdays during the summer. Details of these activities and the park's many other recreational options are listed in a leaflet produced by BC Parks or on the BC Parks website.

> Additional information

Strathcona is named after Donald Alexander Smith, First Baron Strathcona and Mount Royal, who was a Canadian pioneer and one of the principals involved with the construction of the Canadian Pacific Railway. Strathcona is an excellent location for those who enjoy hiking and the outdoor life, and is definitely worth more than a one-night stay. It is not particularly kid-friendly, especially if you have young children. Interestingly, the wildlife in the park differs from that on the Mainland: chipmunks, rabbits, coyotes, foxes, grizzly bears, skunks, and moose are not found here. The road from Campbell River to Gold River traverses much of the park and is a pleasant, quiet drive.

VANCOUVER COAST
AND MOUNTAINS

WITH THE HIGHEST population density in the province, south-western BC is undoubtedly the most popular region for provincial-park camping. Twenty provincial parks, all within a four-hour drive of downtown Vancouver, meet the demand for weekend getaways, and the spectacular scenery en route makes the commute enjoyable. Whether you head north on the meandering Sea-to-Sky Highway, east on Highway 7 to follow the mighty Fraser River, or to the Sunshine Coast via BC Ferries, your journey will include breathtaking views of mountains, clear rivers and streams, forests and fields, as well as the comforting knowledge that services are never far away.

Birkenhead Lake is surrounded by breathtaking snow-capped mountains.

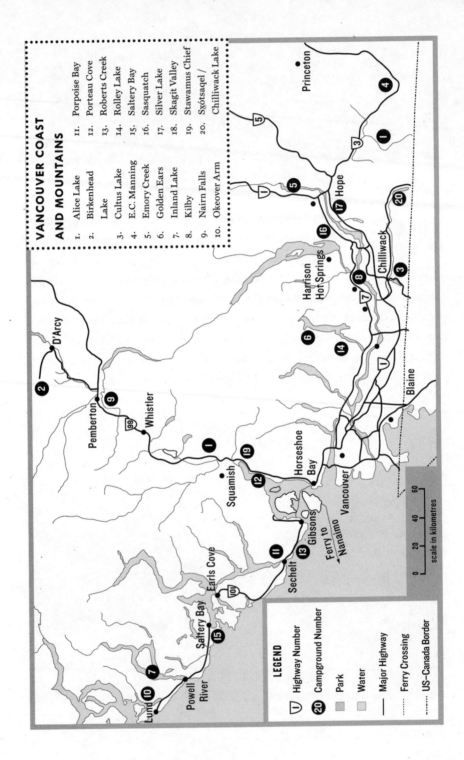

VANCOUVER COAST AND MOUNTAINS

1. Alice Lake
2. Birkenhead Lake
3. Cultus Lake
4. E.C. Manning
5. Emory Creek
6. Golden Ears
7. Inland Lake
8. Kilby
9. Nairn Falls
10. Okeover Arm
11. Porpoise Bay
12. Porteau Cove
13. Roberts Creek
14. Rolley Lake
15. Saltery Bay
16. Sasquatch
17. Silver Lake
18. Skagit Valley
19. Stawamus Chief
20. S<u>x</u>ótsaqel/ Chilliwack Lake

LEGEND

▽	Highway Number
● 20	Campground Number
(dark shade)	Park
(light shade)	Water
——	Major Highway
········	Ferry Crossing
- - - -	US–Canada Border

scale in kilometres
0   20   40   60

Princeton
Hope
Chilliwack
Harrison Hot Springs
Blaine
Vancouver
Horseshoe Bay
Squamish
Whistler
Pemberton
D'Arcy
Gibsons
Sechelt
Earls Cove
Saltery Bay
Powell River
Lund
Ferry to Nanaimo

ALICE LAKE

> Location

This is my second home. I have camped at Alice Lake more than at any other location and cannot get enough of this campground. I must have introduced about fifty friends and their families to this location and plan to camp here every year for the rest of my life! I adore this place. Alice Lake, easily accessible from Vancouver (71 kilometres away), is positioned in breathtaking mountain terrain and has every amenity campers require. The park is found on Highway 99—the Sea-to-Sky Highway—13 kilometres north of Squamish, which has all services.

> Facilities

Situated in a forest of western hemlock are 108 large, private, shady camping spots suitable for all camping vehicles; 55 camping spots have electrical hook-ups and ice is sold. The campground is equipped with two shower buildings, flush and pit toilets, and a sani-station. Many facilities are wheelchair accessible, and reservations during the summer months are a must. All sites are reservable.

> Recreational activities

There is never a dull moment here as the 396-hectare park has an abundance of activities to keep campers busy. One of the biggest attractions is a series of ten walking and hiking trails, ranging in length from half a kilometre to a day's hard walking. One of the most popular is the Four Lakes Trail, which takes hikers around the four warm-water lakes that dominate the area. Swimming, canoeing, kayaking (canoes and kayaks can be rented), and fishing for rainbow trout and Dolly Varden are popular pursuits, and large grassy areas provide venues for ball games. The two excellent lakeside beaches are perfect for children, and there's a safe swimming area and playground.

> Additional information

Alice Lake is a very popular campground even during the week, and it is almost always full during the peak summer months of July and August, so if you arrive without a reservation during these times, be sure you have other options available. A small concession stand selling drinks, ice cream, chips, sand toys, and many other things is open in the day-use area in July and August. It's a great addition to the park and useful for families. Bears are frequent visitors, but when they are around, BC Parks posts notices informing campers of the dates of sightings.

BIRKENHEAD LAKE

> Location

Six kilometres long, Birkenhead Lake is surrounded by breathtaking snow-capped Coast Mountains and blessed with beautiful clear waters. The 10,439-hectare park is located only a three-hour drive (210 kilometres) from Vancouver and is reached by taking Highway 99 to Pemberton, then turning off at Mount Currie to head toward D'Arcy. Just before D'Arcy, a 17-kilometre gravel road leads to the campground. Gas and restaurants are located in Mount Currie and Pemberton.

> Facilities

Ninety-one camping spots are available here, and all but a few are located in a beautiful wooded area with streams running adjacent to them (ideal for keeping your drinks cool on a hot summer day). There is a sani-station, but no flush toilets. The only wheelchair-accessible part of the park is a trail near the beach. The only other disadvantage is that some spots are near stagnant water pools, so mosquitoes can be a problem at certain times of year. Reservations are accepted for 72 sites.

> Recreational activities

Birkenhead Lake has a lovely beach and protected swimming area, although the waters themselves, which come directly from the surrounding mountain snow, can be cold. There is a boat launch and canoe rentals are available. Fishing for kokanee and rainbow trout is reputed to be good, as is wildlife watching for moose, black bear, mountain goats, and deer. Ospreys and bald eagles are often seen circling over the waters of the lake. Trails in the park total approximately 14 kilometres, and one good one leads along one side of the lake and is used by mountain bikers and walkers.

> ## Additional information
The tranquil location, spectacular scenery, and pleasant drive from the Lower Mainland make this my favourite provincial park for a weekend getaway from Vancouver. I have stayed here five times in different seasons. In June, the waters were so high I could not see the beach, but the hiking was excellent. In July, there were millions of flies and mosquitoes, and in late August, it was hot and perfect. When I stayed a few years ago, an enterprising couple had set up a really quaint "camper's store" in the back of their truck near the campground. Camping provides opportunities for a variety of entrepreneurs but challenges the travel writer—you never know if the same people will be in business in subsequent years.

CULTUS LAKE

> ## Location
On average, over 30,000 family groups stay at Cultus Lake per year, making it the fourth most popular campground in the province. The 2,729-hectare park includes both the east and west side of the 5-kilometre long Cultus Lake, from which a spectacular vista of mountains can be seen. Cultus means "worthless" in the Chinook language, but the lake's immense popularity suggests that many have found it anything but worthless. Cultus Lake is located 11 kilometres southwest of Chilliwack off Highway 1 on a paved access road. While Chilliwack provides all services, a number of small commercial facilities can be found adjacent to the park in the small community of Cultus Lake.

> ## Facilities
This campground is the third largest in the province (after E.C. Manning and Golden Ears), with 301 spaces spread across four locations: Maple Bay (106), Delta Grove (58), Clear Creek (85), and Entrance Bay (52). All campsites

are large and positioned well in wooded areas. There are a number of double camping spots, and 19 of the campsites at Delta Grove are close to the water's edge with their own section of beach. All amenities are found here, including flush toilets, a sani-station, showers, and various accessible facilities for campers in wheelchairs. Reservations are accepted for all sites. In addition, 25 "visitor cabins" are available to reserve.

> ## Recreational activities

Numerous recreational pursuits can be enjoyed. You can catch coho, chinook, chum, pink, and sockeye salmon, rainbow and cutthroat trout, and Dolly Varden if the powerboaters and water-skiers do not decide to disturb the tranquility of the lake. There is a boat launch and windsurfing is possible (if the jet skiers are not out in force), as is swimming from lovely sandy beaches. Canoes can be rented during the summer months. There are also several hiking trails. The most popular trek is to Teapot Hill, 5 kilometres return, where a good viewpoint rewards your efforts. Some trails permit mountain bikes and horses and have recently been extended and upgraded. The play area at the Entrance Bay Campground was dismantled after damage from winter storms in 2006–07, but it has now been rebuilt. Close to the park are golf courses, go-carts, canoe and Jet Ski rentals, trail rides, waterslides, laundromats, restaurants, and stores.

> ## Additional information

Although the setting and facilities here are perfect, the park can become very busy during the summer months, especially on weekends, and somewhat loud if too many powerboats congregate on the lake. Cultus Lake attracts a youthful summer crowd and, in my mind, represents the most commercial side of provincial park camping—not an aspect to which I'm particularly drawn. The best time to stay here is in the spring, when the trees are budding, wildflowers are blooming, and the woodlands are alive with birds attracted to the deciduous forest. Due to the floods of November 2021, many day-use areas, trails, and other facilities in the park were impacted and visitors are advised to watch for unidentified hazards and to avoid using the trails.

E.C. MANNING

> Location

E.C. Manning Provincial Park hosts the second most popular provincial camp-grounds (after Golden Ears). Within 3 hours of Vancouver (224 kilometres away) and covering over 83,671 hectares of the Cascade Mountains, this is a fantastic area for recreational use. The western park entrance is 26 kilometres east of Hope and the eastern park entrance is 52 kilometres west of Princeton, both off Highway 3, which runs through the park. Accommodation, gas, food, and other commercial facilities are located in the park, so if you decide not to cook breakfast or dinner, the bar/restaurant is only a short drive away.

> Facilities

In addition to wilderness camping (55 sites), there are four vehicle-accessible campgrounds with a total of 361 spots: Hampton (100), Mule Deer (49), Coldspring (66), and Lightning Lake (146). Lightning Lake has showers and flush toilets, and all of its campsites are included in the reservation system of BC Parks. It's a great place for children and has a playground. The other three campgrounds have reservable and non-reservable sites. All spaces are large and set among trees, offering privacy, although some campsites are close to the road, and Coldspring is a little sparse on vegetation due to a recent attack of pine beetles. There is a sani-station located at the park's visitor centre.

> Recreational activities

E.C. Manning Park offers an abundance of things to do and see. Upon arriving, visitors should go to the visitor centre located a kilometre east of Manning

Park Resort to pick up a detailed map of the area. The centre also has human and natural history displays of the park and area. E.C. Manning is a hiker's paradise; extensive trail systems meander through the mountains to alpine meadows, waterfalls, and rivers, and there are also self-guided interpretive trails. Eight trails are mountain-bike accessible, and there are also eleven trails open to horseback riding. Anglers can fish for Dolly Varden and rainbow and cutthroat trout in the Similkameen and Sumallo Rivers, and also in Lightning and Strike lakes. Lightning Lake has a beach with a swimming area, a boat launch, and good canoeing (rowboats, canoes, and kayaks can be rented in the day-use area). Powerboats are not permitted anywhere in the park, a rule that ensures a peaceful stay. Interpretative programs are offered in the summer.

> **Additional information**

E.C. Manning Park is named after the chief forester of BC from 1936 to 1941. In recent years, the park has suffered from devastation from the mountain pine beetle. The Lightning Lake Chain Trail is 24 kilometres round-trip, but there's no elevation gain. Fortunately, E.C. Manning provides a number of delightful shorter hiking options: for an easy 45-minute trail, try the Canyon Trail (2 kilometres); for a slightly longer walk, the Lightning Lake Loop (9 kilometres) is appealing. E.C. Manning Park is one of my personal favourites, but be warned that sometimes the campgrounds still have evidence of snow in early June. If you do not want to camp, the Manning Park Resort has cabins and rooms and is a delightful place to spend a few nights with access to an indoor pool, hot tubs, and weight room. In 2022, the resort also opened the new Skyview RV Campground next to the Lightning Lake day-use area, offering over 90 reservable sites in the summer and 60 in the winter.

EMORY CREEK

> **Location**

Emory Creek is located next to Highway 1, 18 kilometres north of Hope and 6 kilometres south of Yale. This beautiful campground on the banks of the majestic Fraser River is located on the site of Emory City, which in its 1880 heyday boasted thirteen streets and a population of over five hundred pioneers. Two decades earlier, the same number of people worked here after coming in search of gold. If you visit today, all you'll see is a lovely, serene wooded campground. A convenience store and restaurant are located opposite the campground.

> Facilities

Nestled in a mixed forest area of the 29-hectare park are 35 large private camping spots suitable for every type of recreational vehicle. Some spots have views of the water. One of the most distinctive features of this campground is the "flushing thunderboxes"—from the outside, these toilets look like pit toilets but they actually flush. During my first two stays in this park, the toilets not only flushed but the washroom also contained small containers of dried flowers and air fresheners. This park has no sani-station, showers, or wheelchair access. The transcontinental railway is adjacent to the park, and the sound of trains, while audible, can be quite soothing in the night.

> Recreational activities

Although there is not a lot to do at Emory Creek, the park seems to attract the retired folks looking for a tranquil spot in which to spend a few days. There is a small trail, and visitors can fish for salmon in the Fraser, which is easily accessible from a pebbled beach. When I last visited, two grey-haired gentlemen were busy panning for gold, an activity that struck me as an extremely pleasant way to spend an afternoon. There is a small beach that's ideal for children, but swimming isn't really an option. Visitors are encouraged to exercise caution around the water as the spring and summer run-offs can cause extreme water levels and currents.

> Additional information

Co-managed with the Yale First Nation, this provincial campground has a wonderful feeling about it. Its lack of defined or structured activities makes it particularly appealing to older campers, while the well-cared-for and unique washroom facilities are a welcome surprise to seasoned campers who often approach pit toilets with a deep dread, especially in the height of summer. The area was the site of one of the richest finds during the 1858 gold rush, before prospectors moved farther north. This attractive valley is part of the traditional territory of the Stó:lō People, who have hunted, fished, and lived in the region for centuries before Simon Fraser travelled here in 1808. A short drive north on the Coquihalla Highway is Coquihalla Canyon Provincial Park, where visitors can walk through a series of disused railway tunnels, which were blasted through the rock in the early years of this century.

GOLDEN EARS

> Location
Almost 40,000 camping parties regularly visit Golden Ears, making this large, well-appointed provincial park one of the most popular campgrounds in BC. Like Cultus Lake and E.C. Manning Park, Golden Ears is close to Vancouver. Although this proximity may dissuade some campers from visiting, let me add that whenever I have stayed here—even at the height of summer—the park has never felt crowded or busy, although the campground itself can get a little noisy. Named either for the twin peaks that shine golden in the sunlight or, as some locals claim, for a nesting place for eagles, "Golden Eyries" is located 11 kilometres north of Haney off Highway 7, on a paved access road, and is an easy 45- to 60-minute drive from Vancouver. All services are available at Haney, and there are a few additional stores close to the campground and a small concession stand in the park itself during the peak summer months.

> Facilities
Alouette, Gold Creek, and the newer North Beach campgrounds provide the camping options in Golden Ears, offering a combined total of 423 vehicle accessible and 20 walk-in spaces. All have large private spots within a forested area. There are showers, flush toilets, a sani-station, and wheelchair access. In the peak summer months, a security patrol operates. Reservations are accepted for all three campgrounds for all spaces.

> Recreational activities
The 62,540-hectare park is blessed with a number of trails suitable for both hikers and horses. Hiking options vary from 20-minute interpretive trips to overnight excursions up to the Golden Ears, and more than 20 kilometres of horse trails are available to those who love riding (horseback riding can be arranged from local facilities). Fishing for rainbow, coastal cutthroat, kokanee,

Dolly Varden, and freshwater trout is popular in Alouette Lake and Alouette River, Pitt Lake, Mike Lake, and Gold Creek. Good swimming beaches and a boat launch are available at Alouette Lake in both the day-use and camping areas. Boating and water-skiing are permitted on the lake away from the swimming area, and canoes can be rented in the park. An adventure playground keeps young ones entertained, and interpretive programs for children and adults operate during the summer.

> Additional information

The area around Alouette Lake was originally the hunting and fishing ground of the Xa'xtsa (Douglas-Lillooet) and Katzie Peoples. During the early 1900s, the area was the primary site for BC's railroad logging operations, and there are stories of loggers in the 1920s felling trees up to 4 metres in diameter. A huge fire that ripped through the area in 1931 stopped the logging operations. Today, Golden Ears is characterized by a second growth of western hemlock, western redcedar, and Douglas fir, but evidence of the earlier logging is everywhere. Be aware, this campground gets very busy, especially during the weekends in July and August, and may close when the parking lots get full.

INLAND LAKE

> Location

I love this place! A real gem of a campground, Inland Lake is located next to 1,065-metre-high Mount Mahony, 12 kilometres north of Powell River. Turn right off Highway 101 onto Alberni Street. Go up the hill to Manson Avenue, turn left and follow Manson to Cassiar Street. Turn right onto Cassiar (which becomes Yukon Street) and continue to Haslam Street. Turn right onto Haslam and follow the signs. A good gravel road leads to the campground. Services are available in Cranberry and Powell River.

> Facilities

Camping provisions at Inland Lake make this one of the choicest parks for campers with disabilities. It has ramps and larger toilets, and 13 kilometres of flat wheelchair-accessible trail around the lake, six piers jutting out onto the lake for easy fishing and a concrete ramp sloping into the water, plus five wheelchair-accessible cabins. The main campground is next to the day-parking area and accommodates 26 parties, with spaces for large RVs. Pit toilets, fire pits, garbage bins, and picnic tables overlooking the lake are in a lightly wooded area. Pumps are used to collect lake water, which should be boiled before using. Two wheelchair-accessible cabins are located here, and three are spaced along the lakeside trail and have their own wheelchair-accessible pit toilets. Four overnight camping spots are also located around the lake. Reservations are accepted for 15 sites.

> Recreational activities

The biggest draw at this 2,763-hectare provincial park is the 13-kilometre trail circling the lake. Convenient for cyclists, people in wheelchairs, or those with strollers, it has kilometre markers placed along it and wooden carvings of local pioneers, animals, and other subjects. You can take two paths from the trail: one to Lost Lake then on to Haywire Bay on Powell Lake, the other directly to Powell Lake. Or you can hike along the shoreline and then cross a small bridge to Anthony Island (which has 3 walk-in campsites). Inland Lake is great for canoeing and kayaking; although powerboats are permitted (there is a boat launch), they are limited to 10-horsepower engines. For fishers, the 349-hectare lake contains trout, and fishing is said to be best starting in April. Loons, eagles, ducks, ravens, grouse, blue jays, and hummingbirds can be seen, and sometimes beavers, otters, and bears. The lake water is calm, clear, and warm—ideal for swimming.

> Additional information

This campground and lake are wonderful. During our last visit, in September 2020, we started to walk around the lake at 9:00 AM. There was no one around, so we decided to go skinny dipping. Inland Lake is the best lake in the province to pursue this wonderful, slightly deviant activity.

KILBY

> Location

Kilby is now operated by the Fraser Heritage Society but retains ties to BC Parks. This 3-hectare provincial park is situated 15 kilometres from Agassiz, 1 kilometre off Highway 7 at Harrison Falls on the Fraser River. From the highway, follow the signs that will lead you onto School Road and then Kilby

Road, which leads into the park. Services can be found along the highway or at Harrison Mills, Agassiz, and Harrison Hot Springs.

> Facilities

Thirty-eight large campsites (33 reservable) on the river provide excellent spots from which to watch the Fraser meander on its course—however, high river levels have caused the campground to close on at least five occasions in the last few years. There are flush and pit toilets and water, but no sani-station, showers, or wheelchair accessibility. When I last visited, I found Kilby to be a little run down and not on par with other provincial parks, so my advice to anyone wanting to camp for more than one night would be to go somewhere else. To reserve a site, go to kilby.ca.

> Recreational activities

This campground is ideally located for those who want to explore the surrounding communities of Mission, Agassiz, Chilliwack, and Harrison Hot Springs. It also provides its own attractions in the form of a wide sandy beach and a river for boating, water-skiing, and swimming. As the campground is positioned near both the Fraser and Harrison Rivers, a variety of fishing spots in the immediate vicinity are available, where anglers can try their luck for cutthroat and Dolly Varden. There is a boat launch in the day-use area, and because the campground is a designated BC "Wildlife Watch" area, birdwatching is quite good.

> Additional information

One of the biggest attractions here is the Kilby General Store Museum, which is part of the adjacent 2-hectare historical site. The two-storey general store was built in 1904 and operated by the same family up until 1976. Guides dressed in period costume provide fascinating details of the development of the area at the turn of the century. The museum also boasts a gift shop and an excellent tearoom that serves traditional tea and scones. Both children and adults will find it is easy to pass the hours in the museum, reading and learning about the Fraser River's colourful past. Specifically, the photographs of huge sturgeon caught in the Fraser River should not be missed. The historic site also includes a small working farm (with pigs, goats, and hens—a delight for children) and an orchard, in addition to a number of buildings that have been faithfully restored. For hours and fees, check the website (kilby.ca).

NAIRN FALLS

> Location

One year, I stayed here in July, when the temperature was in the high 20s, so I really appreciated the shady canopy this wooded campground offers. Just 3 kilometres south of Pemberton off Highway 99, and considerably less popular than Alice Lake, its nearest big neighbour to the south, this is an exquisite, laid-back provincial park. Services are conveniently located at Pemberton or 32 kilometres south at Whistler.

> Facilities

Ninety-four spacious forested camping spots are available (all reservable). The best ones overlook the canyon, but the others are not bad. All sites will accommodate the largest recreational vehicle. Facilities include drinking water, fire pits, picnic tables, pit toilets, and a sani-station.

> Recreational activities

Travellers regularly use Nairn Falls as a picnic spot. An easy trail (3 kilometres round-trip) leads to the falls, which tumble down 60 metres into a beautiful canyon of Douglas fir, cedar, and hemlock. The park contains other trails, but when I visited, signage left a lot to be desired and some trails were washed out. Fishing is possible in Green River, while a short drive/walk from the park on Highway 99 toward Pemberton One Mile Lake is popular for swimming—a real luxury on a hot summer's day. The shady, peaceful campground is perfect for reading and relaxing, and Nairn Falls gives the impression of offering an almost sophisticated camping experience for those who want to escape from life's pressures.

> Additional information

When I stayed here, my calm camping environment was occasionally disturbed by the noise of powerboats ascending the rapids to take groups of visitors whitewater rafting. Excursions of this nature can be organized in Pemberton and Whistler. Nairn Falls is a good location from which to explore Whistler (and is also considerably cheaper than staying right at the year-round resort). The lack of recreational pursuits may put some people off; there is little to do in the park itself for those with young families, although the pretty lake just to the north of Nairn Falls has a small beach, despite there being a lot of reeds in the water. For the majority of people, though, Nairn Falls is a haven, and for those non-campers it is also a great location to stop and picnic.

OKEOVER ARM

> Location

In recent years, the waters and islands of this area have become known as a kayaker's dream. Consequently, Okeover Arm Provincial Park is a kayaker's campground. At the end of the Sunshine Coast Highway (Highway 101), overlooking Okeover Inlet on the eastern side of the Malaspina Peninsula, this small campground is ideal for campers who plan to kayak in Desolation Sound Marine Provincial Park. Okeover Arm is located 19 kilometres north of Powell River, 5 kilometres on a paved road from Lund. Powell River provides all services, but the small community of Lund 9 kilometres away has a store and accommodation.

> Facilities

Okeover Arm was upgraded a few years ago to ensure more camping spots were available for both vehicles and tents. There are now 14 vehicle-accessible camping spaces and 4 tent-only sites; some have tent pads and a few have views of the water. Only the basic amenities are available (pit toilets, drinking water, fire pits, picnic tables). The pit toilets are wheelchair accessible.

> Recreational activities

The main recreational activities here are walking in a lightly forested area, swimming, canoeing, kayaking, and boating; there is a boat launch adjacent to the park.

As mentioned, the campground is an ideal base for those who wish to explore Desolation Sound Marine Park, BC's largest marine park with more than 60 kilometres of shoreline, several islands, and a multitude of bays and coves.

> Additional information

Lund was originally settled in 1895 by two brothers from Sweden and is named after the Swedish city. The renovated hotel, which dates back to the turn of the twentieth century, is the hub of the community and has a great outdoor patio overlooking the calm waters. Watch the bald eagles soar while enjoying that well-earned beverage.

PORPOISE BAY

> Location

Reaching this 61-hectare park from the Lower Mainland requires a lovely excursion on BC Ferries to the Sunshine Coast. Take the ferry from Horseshoe Bay to Langdale, then Highway 101 to just north of Sechelt, where a 5-kilometre paved road leads to the campground. Services can be found in Sechelt, where the wide selection of restaurants, bakeries, and coffee bars offers a great alternative to campground food. On Saturdays, a farmers' market provides additional home-baked delights.

> Facilities

Campers here want for nothing. Porpoise Bay has flush and pit toilets, showers, a sani-station, good wheelchair access, and it accepts reservations. There are 84 large camping spots, including a few double sites, set among a second-growth forest of Douglas fir, western redcedar, western hemlock, and alder. Campfires at individual campsites are prohibited here, but group campfires are encouraged, so this integral part of the camping experience is not lost altogether. Reservations are accepted for 72 sites.

> Recreational activities

This popular park and campground offers a wide sandy beach, a protected swimming area, and two playgrounds, making it ideal for family camping. A large number of grassy areas great for ball games are a feature, and there are small trails, one of which leads to Angus Creek, a salmon-spawning waterway for chum and coho. The park is a base for kayakers who wish to explore the many coves and inlets of the surrounding area. At low tide, it is really pleasant to beachcomb and wander through the rock pools turning over the rocks to look for marine life. My children adored fishing with nets for "toe biters" and small crabs at this location when they were younger.

> **Additional information**

Porpoise Bay is near Sechelt Inlets Marine Provincial Park, which includes seven wilderness camping areas located among the sheltered waters of Sechelt Inlet—a paddler's delight. The area is also rich in marine life. This campground is perfect if you have young children and want the camping experience while still being near all commercial services.

PORTEAU COVE

> **Location**

The views from this campground off the fantastic Sea-to-Sky Highway (Highway 99) are stunning if the weather is good, and for this reason alone every attempt should be made to stop here. Although almost impossible to see from the road, Porteau Cove is an enchanting roadside campground with an astounding vista of Howe Sound, the most southerly fjord in North America. Thirty-eight kilometres north of Vancouver and a little over 8 kilometres south of Britannia Beach, Porteau Cove is a haven for campers and daytrippers. Britannia Beach has food; gas and other provisions are available in Squamish. A small concession has been set up at the entrance to the campground, but supplies are limited.

> **Facilities**

The campground has 44 vehicle camping spots, 16 walk-in sites, and all the amenities (showers, flush toilets, sani-station, wheelchair access, and reservations). Some spots overlook the water's edge with views of the mountains on Vancouver Island, and while the sites are not as large as those in other provincial parks, they are private thanks to the surrounding Sitka spruce trees.

Electrical hook-ups are available in all drive-in sites for an additional fee. The campground is set away from the road, so traffic noise is not a problem, but the railway runs close by and a number of trains pass during the day and night (if you're in a tent, it feels like the train is passing right over your head). Reservations are accepted for all spaces and are a must on weekends and during the summer months. Two furnished cabins can also be rented (seatoskyparks.com).

> Recreational activities

One of the biggest attractions of this location is scuba diving. There are man-made reefs and two ships have been sunk in the nearby waters to attract marine life and create a destination for diving enthusiasts. They also provide entertainment for those of us who just want to watch funny rubber-clad individuals plunge into the cool waters. Away from the diving area, it is possible to swim in the waters of Howe Sound. When I last camped here, I used Porteau Cove as my base but swam and sunbathed at Alice Lake, less than a 20-minute drive north. There are two public boat launches, but you can only fish outside of the park's boundaries.

> Additional information

The park is an extremely popular campground and picnic spot for people travelling along the highway. The mining museum at Britannia Beach is well worth a visit if you have time. Visitors are given hard hats and taken on a tour that includes a rail trip underground and a demonstration of past mining machinery. Britannia Beach also has a large number of arts and crafts shops and cafes to visit. Slightly farther north, check out the Squamish Adventure Centre—you'll recognize it by the huge sculpture of a logger—a must for any visitor to the area. Finally, this is a great location for stargazing and viewing the aurora borealis.

ROBERTS CREEK

> Location

If you want to spend your time relaxing, beachcombing, and staring out to sea to look for whales, stop at Roberts Creek. With fantastic views of the Strait of

Georgia and beyond to the mountains of Vancouver Island, this campground is found 14 kilometres west of Gibsons on Highway 101. From the Lower Mainland, visitors take a beautiful ferry ride from Horseshoe Bay to Langdale. Services are available at Gibsons or Sechelt, 12 kilometres to the north.

> Facilities

Camping facilities at this 40-hectare park are situated in a lightly forested area of second-growth Douglas fir and western redcedar. There are 21 spaces with wheelchair-accessible pit toilets and a sani-station, but no showers or flush toilets. The campground is quite near the main road, and traffic noise may be a problem for some people; it is quite unusual for a provincial park to be so close to residential houses. The day-use area is a short drive from the campground.

> Recreational activities

Beachcombing is a favourite activity here. At low tide a cobblestone beach reveals sea stars, mussels, oysters, and an array of other marine life. From the beach it is also possible to see whales, seals, and sea lions, but don't count on it—they were somewhat elusive when I visited. Although the waters tend to be cold, some people enjoy swimming and fishing.

> Additional information

The area of coastline between Langdale and Lund is called the Sunshine Coast because of its warm summers and mild winters. Annual precipitation here is almost 170 millimetres less than in Vancouver, making the Sunshine Coast a desirable place to live. Roberts Creek Campground is located on one of the busiest sections of the area. The park was established in 1947 and the campground in 1954. The community of Gibsons to the south is famous because the TV series *The Beachcombers* was filmed here. It also has a small maritime museum. To the north, Sechelt has a number of great bakeries and cafes—don't stop here if you are on a diet, but if you're not, it's a nice little community to wander through, and on Saturdays during the summer months, there is a farmers' market selling fresh produce and crafts.

ROLLEY LAKE

> **Location**

Some parks are criticized for being too big, some for being too small. In my opinion, 115-hectare Rolley Lake is the perfect size. It is also easily accessible from Vancouver, has a delightful setting, boasts a number of recreational activities, and is well equipped. It is located 23 kilometres northwest of Mission (70 kilometres east of Vancouver). Although well signposted from Highway 7, the location is a little hard to find. In Maple Ridge, turn off Highway 7 north at 287th onto the Dewdney Trunk Road, turn right onto Bell Street, then make a left turn toward the park. The road is paved all the way. Maple Ridge and Mission both have comprehensive services.

> **Facilities**

This popular campground has 64 spacious units set in a woodland area of western hemlock and mature vine maple, offering privacy and shade. The facilities are among the best provided by BC Parks and include showers, a sani-station, flush toilets, and good wheelchair access. Reservations are accepted at all sites.

> **Recreational activities**

Rolley Lake Provincial Park provides a relaxing environment for campers. The lake is surrounded by forest and, because powerboats are prohibited, it is a peaceful place to relax, canoe, swim, and fish (the lake is stocked with coastal cutthroat and rainbow trout). There are a couple of short walks: one leads to a waterfall, while another leads around the lake, includes a section of boardwalk, and takes about 60 minutes to complete. Children can have fun in the play area. Rolley Lake is also a good place for observing bird life, and there is a wildlife-viewing site for BC Wildlife Watch.

> **Additional information**

Rolley Lake takes its name from Fanny and James Rolley, who settled here in 1888. The park has played an active part in the logging industry of BC. In the early part of the twentieth century, the lake stored shingle bolts destined for a mill located at Ruskin, 5 kilometres away. In the 1930s, when all the old-growth forest had gone, it became home to a small Japanese-Canadian logging operation harvesting Douglas fir. BC Parks acquired it in 1961, and today it provides a tranquil environment for those who wish to escape the main centres of population. The only problems with this idyllic setting are the mosquitoes, which can be troublesome at times. During my first visit to Rolley Lake, the beach was littered with Canada goose droppings, but on subsequent visits, it was clean.

If you are camping here, you must visit the awesome Powerhouse at Stave Falls Visitor Centre, a brief 10-minute drive from the campground. This power-generating plant operated for over one hundred years and is now a fascinating museum run by BC Hydro. I cannot recommend this too highly, and few seem to know of it (see bchydro.com/community/recreation_areas/visitor-centres/stave-falls-visitor-centre.html).

SALTERY BAY

> ### Location

Saltery Bay Provincial Park is located about 27 kilometres south of Powell River on the north shore of Jervis Inlet. Visitors must take two delightful, short ferry rides, one from Horseshoe Bay to Langdale, the other from Earls Cove to Saltery Bay. The land and sea route from the Lower Mainland and the  ocean-view scenery at Saltery Bay make this camping excursion a real delight. The campground is just 1 kilometre north of the ferry terminal, and Powell River, 30 kilometres north, has all services. There is also a store at Black Point, 6 kilometres away.

> ### Facilities

This 69-hectare park has 42 large private camping spots in an evergreen forest. The campground is wheelchair accessible and has a sani-station, but only pit toilets and no showers. Reservations are accepted.

> Recreational activities

You can see Canada's first underwater statue at Saltery Bay, but remember to bring all the correct diving gear! In addition to the superb ocean-view scenery, the shallow offshore waters of the park are the biggest attraction here. Scuba divers are enticed to the area by the variety of marine life, underwater coves, and shipwrecks (there is also access for divers with disabilities). To the delight of many divers, a 3-metre bronze mermaid has been sunk at Mermaid Cove. For those who do not dive, the park offers beaches for swimming and sunbathing in the day-use area. There is also a 2-kilometre hiking trail to Little Saltery Falls, the chance to see killer whales, seals, and sea lions, who occasionally bask in the area, and salmon fishing from April to October.

> Additional information

Saltery Bay is named after the fish saltery that was located here at the turn of the century. The area is part of the traditional lands of the shíshálh Nation. This popular diving area has been featured in National Geographic and is an excellent spot from which to explore the Sunshine Coast. Even if you do not want to dive, this is a quaint campground and the journey to it is delightful.

SASQUATCH

> Location

With four pristine lakes, including the freshwater fjord of massive Harrison Lake, and 1,217 hectares of land, it is easy to see why this park is popular. The park offers a vast expanse of beautiful mountain scenery to explore. Sasquatch is located 6 kilometres north of Harrison Hot Springs off Highway 7. All services are found at Harrison Hot Springs.

> Facilities

The 178 camping spots here are set in an area of second-growth deciduous forest and are divided between Hicks Lake (72 spots, some close to the lake) and the campgrounds of Lakeside (42 spaces, and my favourite) and Bench (64 spaces), which are nearer to Deer Lake. Lakeside has some wonderful spots with access directly onto the lake, while the spaces at Bench are heavily shaded. There are flush and pit toilets and a sani-station but no showers. The park accepts reservations for 169 sites but is not wheelchair accessible.

> Recreational activities

The four lakes (Harrison, Hicks, Deer, and Trout) vary in size—and in the recreational pursuits they offer. Harrison and Hicks lakes allow powerboats, and at Deer Lake only boats powered with electric motors are permitted. Trout Lake prohibits powerboats completely and is therefore the best choice for canoeing and kayaking. Trout fishing in all the lakes is reputed to be excellent. A number of trails lead around the park. Two beach locations ensure sun-worshipping opportunities: one is at the southern end of Hicks Lake and the other is by the group-camping area, where you can swim over to two small forested islands to explore. A play area for children is located at the Lakeside Campground, and the day-use area on Harrison Lake has tons of picnic tables, plus sunbathing and swimming opportunities. Canoe rentals are also offered at Hicks Lake. Famous for its mineral pools, the nearby town of Harrison Hot Springs holds an arts festival in July and a sandcastle-building contest in September.

> Additional information

The name "Sasquatch" is an English corruption of the Hul'qumi'num word "sasq'ets," which means "wild man." In the traditions of some Coast Salish Peoples, including the Sts'ailes Nation, the sasquatch is an important and revered supernatural being that can move between the physical and spiritual realms and watches over the land—not a giant monster, but also not a being to be trifled with. Local people still report sightings of the sasquatch around Harrison River, so be warned! This area is spectacular in the fall when the colours are at their height; fall is also a good time to visit Harrison Hot Springs, which can become very busy during the peak summer months. This really is a great place to take the kids, but even for those without little ones, a lot of fun can be had at Sasquatch.

SILVER LAKE

> **Location**

Confession time: I do not much care for this campground. When I visited (on my way to Skagit Valley—a far superior campground), groups of teenagers from Hope were loud and boisterous and consequently shaped my impression. The relatively small lakeside campground is located 12 kilometres from Hope off Highway 1, the last 6 kilometres on a good gravel road. All services are available at Hope.

> **Facilities**

There are 25 sites at this 77-hectare park; some are little more than pull-ins at the side of the road, but the surrounding Fraser Valley scenery is great. Not surprisingly, only the basic facilities exist (drinking water, pit toilets, picnic tables, and fire pits). There are wheelchair-accessible pit toilets and reservations can be made for 20 sites.

> **Recreational activities**

One of the other problems I have with Silver Lake is that there is little to do here, in stark contrast to its neighbour, Skagit Valley. It is possible to swim in the lake and fish for trout. A small, 1-kilometre-long trail follows the water's edge, and there is a gravel boat launch. The town of Hope is an interesting place for a wander as there are a number of carved wooden sculptures downtown and a number of restaurants and eateries.

> **Additional information**

In a previous edition of this book, I wrote: "I cannot tell a lie: I would not want to camp here. Although the scenery is stunning and the campground's proximity to Hope is attractive, my advice to campers is to choose Skagit Valley—or, if you cannot face the gravel road, head to Emory Creek, or even to the Alaska Highway! Anywhere is better than Silver Lake—unless, of course, you are 18 years old, have a four-wheel-drive monster truck, love loud music, and want to hang out with like-minded people." While updating the book for this edition, I learned that wood ticks, which carry diseases and should be avoided, are here from March to June ... another reason to avoid Silver Lake!

SKAGIT VALLEY

> Location
Encompassing around 28,000 hectares, this park is in the Northern Cascades. West of Hope, a gravel road leads 32 kilometres to Skagit Valley, but the main camping area is an additional 26 kilometres on bumpy gravel. Once at Ross Lake (the main campground), the scenery is awesome. The nearest services are back at Hope, so stock up before making the journey.

> Facilities
Two campgrounds offer 131 sites: 43 are set among the trees at Silvertip, adjacent to the Skagit River near the park's entrance, and the remaining 88 are more out in the open at Ross Lake, where some sites are near the water's edge. Thirty-one sites are reservable. There is no sani-station or wheelchair access, and facilities are basic (drinking water, fire pits, picnic tables, pit toilets), although BC Parks says these facilities are soon to be upgraded. There is also space for 11 camping parties at a horse camp at Whitworth Meadows ... should you arrive on horseback.

> Recreational activities
At Silvertip, trails lead along the Skagit River, and Ross Lake has hiking trails in the immediate vicinity, but there are more than 50 kilometres of hiking trails in the park itself. Swimming, canoeing, and kayaking are possible from Ross Lake's sandy beach, and the lake is surrounded by fantastic snow-covered mountains. There is a boat launch at the Ross Lake Campground, which also has a new adventure playground for children and a large grassy field. While not suitable for canoeing or kayaking, the Skagit River is one of the best fly -fishing streams in North America and the most productive stream in the Lower Mainland. Fishing for Dolly Varden, char, eastern brook trout, and cutthroat trout is good. Wildlife here includes deer, black bears, cougars, coyotes, minks, and raccoons; there is also a wide array of birds.

> Additional information
In the 1970s, a public protest saved the valley from being flooded by a Seattle hydro company. Today, the water level at Ross Lake is controlled by a hydro

dam in Washington State and is subject to fluctuations. As I bounced along the 58 kilometres of gravel road, I cursed the fact that the park entrance is so far from the campground. But then I beheld the mountain scenery that surrounds the lake and suddenly the journey was worth it. Unfortunately, for me, the words "Skagit Valley" and "mosquitoes" are synonymous. Had I visited when these insects were not biting, it would probably rank as one of my top ten campgrounds, but I did not stay the night due to the bloodsuckers that were out in force that July day. However, it appears others have had the same experience, so be forewarned. The campground was upgraded a few years ago with a new playground, camping tables, and replaced toilets, and more recently the roads and bridges have been upgraded. In 2022, the park was partially closed and some access points unavailable due to impacts from increased wildfire activity and the floods of 2021. Check BC Parks advisories and plan ahead!

STAWAMUS CHIEF

> **Location**

Right next to Shannon Falls Provincial Park, this campground takes its name from the majestic piece of rock under which it is situated, and the primary reason for camping here is to scale it. The park is located on Highway 99, 5 kilometres south of Squamish, where all services are available.

> **Facilities**

There are 57 walk-in sites and 52 drive-in sites—the latter are unsuitable for larger RVs as they are very close together. Because the campground is relatively new, the ground vegetation is sparse, making the camping spots under the trees look quite dark and sad. Pit toilets and water are available but not fire pits because campfires are prohibited here (there is a shared shelter for cooking should you bring a stove). No reservations are available.

> **Recreational activities**

If you're a climber, this is the place to be; however, others may not find it so appealing. When I visited, the world-class climbing destination was dominated by skinny Lycra-clad individuals setting out to climb "the Chief," which is the second-largest granite monolith on Earth. Generally, the 700-metre-high rock is closed to climbers from March 15 to July 31 to protect nesting peregrine falcons. For those who do not wish to climb, it is also possible to hike up the rock, but be warned: this excursion is not for the faint of heart, and a sign at the outset reads "unsuitable for dogs." Upon reaching the top a few years ago, I discovered another small rock climb was required, after which it was necessary to walk a narrow pathway with dramatic crevices on either side. I turned back, believing this hike was not just difficult for dogs, but also for many two-legged individuals! However, there are other easier hiking trails, and less than 2 kilometres away is Shannon Falls Provincial Park, which is a great place for a picnic and a stroll to a platform for viewing BC's third-highest waterfall. The railway museum at Squamish and the mining museum at Britannia Beach are also well worth a visit.

> Additional information

This is not a picturesque campground as the views are minimal and the spaces small. There is also the distant sound of traffic. But if your passion is climbing, camp here and you will inevitably meet like-minded people. For all others, my advice is to stay at nearby Porteau Cove, Alice Lake, or Nairn Falls. The Sea-to-Sky Gondola, which I happen to think is better than the more famous Peak 2 Peak Gondola in Whistler, is a great nearby attraction and has easy trails awarding fantastic mountain views, including those of the Chief (seatoskygondola.com).

SX̱ÓTSAQEL / CHILLIWACK LAKE

> Location

Today it is rare to find areas of old-growth forest in BC. However, by undertaking a short walk from Chilliwack Lake, visitors can view majestic redcedar trees that are hundreds of years old. Southeast of Vancouver and situated in the magnificent Coast Mountains, this popular park was created in 1973 to protect an area of spectacular beauty and was recently extended to include the east side of the lake. The campground is 64 kilometres southeast of Chilliwack and can be reached by taking exit 104 from Highway 1 and following the signs for Cultus Lake until Cultus Lake Road. Rather than turning here, take Vedder Road across the bridge and turn right onto Chilliwack Lake Road, a paved/gravel access road leading to the lake—a distance of 40 kilometres. The nearest concentration of services is in Chilliwack; more limited provisions can be found at the Pointa Vista Store, 32 kilometres west of the park.

> Facilities
One hundred and forty-six camping spots are available in the 9,258-hectare park, divided among Radium Loop, Greendrop Loop, Lindeman Loop, and Paleface Loop. The majority of sites are large, private, and well positioned (about 10 of the Paleface ones are near the lake); the remainder are close, confined, and offer little privacy. Only the basic camping facilities are provided here (pit toilets, drinking water, fire pits, picnic tables). There are wheelchair-accessible pit toilets at Radium Loop. Reservations are accepted at all sites.

> Recreational activities
The park is a delightful place to visit if you enjoy hiking, as there are a variety of trails, starting from the campground and the Post Creek parking lot, covering over 40 kilometres. For instance, walkers can take an easy 6-kilometre return route to the Ecological Reserve with no elevation gain, or hike 14 kilometres to Flora Lake with a climb of over 1,000 metres. Chilliwack Lake is used for water-skiing, boating, and fishing for Dolly Varden, kokanee, rainbow, and cutthroat trout, and is equipped with a boat launch. The water, however, can be cold for swimming. A playground for children at the Paleface Loop camping area ensures the little ones are well entertained. Of interest to walkers, horseback riders, and cyclists, the Trans Canada Trail winds through the park (see tctrail.ca).

> Additional information
If the campground is full, which it frequently is, a notice will be posted on the park sign at the store on Chilliwack Lake Road, not far from the bridge. Almost 3 kilometres along a logging road that leads from the campground and follows the edge of Chilliwack Lake is the Chilliwack River Ecological Reserve. It was created in 1981 to protect a unique area of old-growth forest featuring large western redcedars; it is just one of a number of ecological reserves that exist in BC, which is geographically and biologically the most diverse province in the country.

THOMPSON OKANAGAN

THE THOMPSON OKANAGAN region includes a huge central area of land reaching from the US border in the south to the Canadian Rockies in the north. Pack the sunscreen if your plans include a trip to the southern portion, as summertime temperatures here are often the hottest in the province. This region features kilometres of orchards and vineyards, crystal-clear lakes, warm-hearted communities, and undulating countryside that gives way to beautiful mountains in the north. The southern Okanagan region incorporates Highway 3 from the Kettle Valley to Princeton, Highway 33, Highway 97, Highway 5A south of Aspen Grove to Princeton, and Highway 6. Farther north, three of the province's most spectacular provincial parks can be found: Mount Robson is named after its majestic mountain, the highest in the Canadian Rockies; Wells Gray is BC's fourth-largest park and is known as "the waterfall park"; and Shuswap Lake has over 1,000 kilometres of waterways and many sandy beaches. The northern region encompasses campgrounds accessible from Highway 16 from the border of Alberta to Route 5, Highway 5, Highway 5A, Highway 1 as far as Lytton, and the northern section of Highway 23. With such diversity, there is something for every camper in this area of BC.

Fish and swim in the Similkameen River at Bromley Rock Provincial Park.

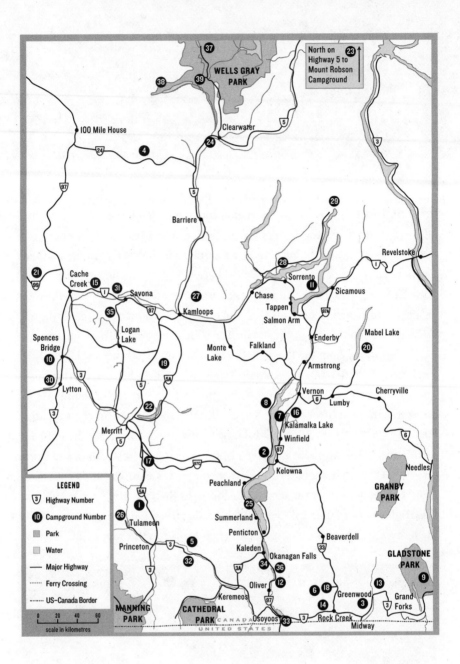

North on
Highway 5 to
Mount Robson
Campground

WELLS GRAY
PARK

100 Mile House

Clearwater

Revelstoke

Barriere

Cache
Creek

Savona

Sorrento

Sicamous

Chase
Tappen
Salmon Arm

Spences
Bridge

Logan
Lake

Kamloops

Enderby

Mabel Lake

Monte
Lake

Falkland

Armstrong

Lytton

Vernon

Lumby

Cherryville

Merritt

Kalamalka Lake

Winfield

Needles

Kelowna

GRANBY
PARK

Peachland

Tulameen

Summerland

Beaverdell

Princeton

Penticton

Kaleden

GLADSTONE
PARK

Keremeos

Oliver

Greenwood

Grand
Forks

MANNING
PARK

CATHEDRAL
PARK

Okanagan Falls

Osoyoos

Rock Creek

Midway

CANADA
UNITED STATES

LEGEND

3 Highway Number

10 Campground Number

▩ Park

▨ Water

— Major Highway

..... Ferry Crossing

----- US–Canada Border

0   20   40   60
scale in kilometres

THOMPSON OKANAGAN

1. Allison Lake
2. Bear Creek
3. Boundary Creek
4. Bridge Lake
5. Bromley Rock
6. Conkle Lake
7. Ellison
8. Fintry
9. Gladstone (Texas Creek)
10. Goldpan
11. Herald
12. Inkaneep
13. Jewel Lake
14. Johnstone Creek
15. Juniper Beach
16. Kekuli Bay
17. Kentucky–Alleyne
18. Kettle River Recreation Area
19. Lac Le Jeune
20. Mabel Lake
21. Marble Canyon
22. Monck
23. Mount Robson
24. North Thompson River
25. Okanagan Lake
26. Otter Lake
27. Paul Lake
28. Shuswap Lake
29. Silver Beach
30. Skihist
31. Steelhead
32. Stemwinder
33. sẁiẁs (Haynes Point)
34. sx̌ʷəx̌ʷnitkʷ (Okanagan Falls)
35. Tunkwa
36. Vaseux Lake
37. Wells Gray (Clearwater)
38. Wells Gray (Mahood Lake)
39. Wells Gray

Campgrounds in the Okanagan are very busy in peak summer months, so book ahead to avoid disappointment.

ALLISON LAKE

> ## Location

On the relatively quiet Highway 5A, at the southern end of Allison Lake, is an enchanting little 23-hectare park, perfect for those with time on their hands. Services can be found at Princeton, 28 kilometres south.

> ## Facilities

Twenty-two large, well-positioned camping spaces are found in a lovely forested area of mature Douglas fir, not lakeside. The sites are suitable for every type of vehicle, and although some are quite close to the road, there is not a lot of traffic. All the basic amenities exist (fire pits, drinking water, picnic tables, pit toilets). No reservations are taken.

> ## Recreational activities

The primary recreational activities here centre on beautiful Allison Lake and include swimming (although there are quite a few reeds), fishing (the lake is stocked with about 15,000 blackwater rainbow trout), canoeing, and kayaking. Water-skiing is also possible. A single-width gravel boat launch is located in the day-use area. Aspen trees border the lake, and the area is particularly attractive during the fall when the trees turn golden and red, presenting fantastic photography opportunities.

> ## Additional information

This is one of the better roadside campgrounds used primarily for overnight camping. Highway 5A between Kamloops and Princeton is a lovely quiet route, suitable for appreciating the scenery of the Okanagan. And for those who have the time, it is a far more pleasant way to travel than the busy Coquihalla Highway. The route is 118 kilometres longer than the main highway but avoids the long, steep hills of the Coquihalla. Be prepared for little development and a scenic drive if heading south from the campground as the road follows Allison Creek to Princeton. The area is rich in mining history; information is available from the newly renovated and very well stocked visitor centres in Princeton and Merritt.

BEAR CREEK

> Location

Go to sleep to the sound of tree frogs at this popular 178-hectare park. Bear Creek exhibits a variety of geological features, including sandy beaches and spectacular canyons and waterfalls. These features are supplemented with a diversity of vegetation, which encourages wildlife populations. The park is
situated to the north of the Okanagan, 9 kilometres west of Kelowna (where all services are found) on the western side of Okanagan Lake, off Highway 97 on paved Westside Road.

> Facilities

Bear Creek provides 143 camping spots and every type of camping service, including flush and pit toilets, a sani-station, showers, and wheelchair access. Sites accommodate all recreational vehicles, and there are a number of double spots. Some of the more desirable spots overlook Lambly ("Bear") Creek, where campers can be lulled to sleep by the sound of the trickling waters (not recommended for those with weak bladders). Fourteen sites have 30-amp power, seven 50-amp. The park administrators operate a small concession selling ice cream, juice, coffee, ice, pop, and some groceries. Reservations are accepted and strongly advisable.

> Recreational activities

This stunning location facilitates a variety of recreational pursuits. The beach is over 400 metres in length, ideal for swimming and sunbathing. The lake has rainbow trout, whitefish, and kokanee, as well as boating potential. There is a boat launch and a private company offers canoe and paddle boats for rent in the summer. In addition to a number of smaller interpretive trails, over 15 kilometres of well-maintained hiking trails exist, some of which lead to views of the lake and canyon. Remember to pack your camera, as there are excellent photographic opportunities. Children can enjoy an adventure playground, recently updated for kids aged 2 to 12, and there is also a horseshoe pit. An adjacent grassy area is ideal for parents to watch their offspring play. Bear Creek is home to an array of wildlife, including swallows, hawks, and owls. Tree frogs can be heard in the spring, and rattlesnakes live in the vicinity but are rarely seen. There is also an amphitheatre where interpretive programs are conducted during the summer. There are numerous wineries in the Kelowna area, many offering fine meals and panoramic views of the lake.

> Additional information

In the early fall, kokanee can be seen spawning in the lower reaches of the creek. This park is extremely popular in the summer months and is particularly appealing for those with children. I strongly advise making a reservation if you hope to camp in July or August.

BOUNDARY CREEK

> Location

If you are debating whether to spend the night at Boundary Creek or at another location, my advice would be to choose the alternative. Though it does have the advantage of being the only campground in the immediate area and is conveniently situated 4 kilometres west of Greenwood (where all services are found), this 2-hectare park has little to recommend it.

> Facilities

The 17 camping spots of this roadside campground are quite large, but the lack of dense vegetation makes them open and without privacy. The campsites adjacent to the creek are somewhat more private, as cottonwood trees line the banks of the creek itself, and the sound of the creek drowns out the noise of the road. In 2016, this location was upgraded to accommodate larger RVs. All the basic facilities offered by BC Parks are available (picnic tables, flush and pit toilets, drinking water, fire pits), but there is no wheelchair accessibility. No reservations are taken. As the campground is close to the main road, it can be quite noisy.

> Recreational activities

This is very much an overnight campground and therefore offers little recreational activity. It is possible to catch rainbow and brook trout in the creek. The mining industry developed the area adjacent to the campground. A nearby slag heap and crumbling stack are evidence of the BC Copper Company's smelter, which employed over four hundred men during its years of operation in the first part of the twentieth century. The historic town of Greenwood contains some beautiful turn-of-the-century buildings, including a courthouse and post office, and is a pleasant place to stroll around. We visited in 2008 with a 7-year-old and a 9-year-old and found a great playpark at the eastern end of the town; I drove past in 2021 and noted this playpark still exists. I did not stop there, but I did visit a couple of very good bakeries in the town. How life changes ...

> Additional information

Out of necessity, I stayed at Boundary Creek in late September one year. The proximity to the road coupled with the openness of the sites themselves mark this as one of BC Parks' less desirable spots; however, it does have the advantage of being the only campground in the immediate area. I visited Greenwood during the late afternoon and enjoyed it, so I went back in the evening, only to find it extremely quiet. Despite its claim to be Canada's smallest city, little occurs in Greenwood after 6:00 PM, but during the day it's a pleasant little town to explore. The visitors centre and quaint adjacent museum are worth a visit.

BRIDGE LAKE

> ## Location

This area, known as the "Interlakes District," is an angler's paradise, as hundreds of lakes offer fishing for eastern brook and lake trout, burbot, and kokanee. It was recently expanded from 11 to 405 hectares and now protects an area of undeveloped shoreline in addition to a number of islands. Bridge Lake Provincial Park was established by BC Parks in 1957, and there are two main ways to reach it. The first entails turning off Highway 97 east of 93 Mile House onto Highway 24 (the campground is 51 kilometres east of 100 Mile House); the second is to turn off Highway 5 at Little Fort and travel west on Highway 24. Full services are available at 100 Mile House.

> ## Facilities

Thirteen vehicle-accessible and 3 walk-in campsites are available at the south end of the lake. The sites are large, set among trees, and have views of the lake. Facilities are basic and consist of picnic tables, fire pits, drinking water (see below), and pit toilets. There is no sani-station.

> ## Recreational activities

Activities at this location include fishing for burbot and lake and rainbow trout, water-skiing, boating (there is a boat launch), and swimming. The lake is also ideal for canoeing and kayaking. A small hiking trail skirts the lakeside, and there is an archaeological site in the park itself. The Douglas fir and spruce trees adjacent to the lake have several bald eagle nests and there are beaver colonies in the lake. River otter, black bears, red foxes, mule deer, and mink all inhabit the area, so there are numerous wildlife viewing opportunities.

> ## Additional information

Recently a number of resorts have developed in the area, and these now offer holiday excursions. The easy access from two main highways means that this campground is a convenient stop-off for the traveller during the busy peak months of July and August. The location seems to be particularly popular with anglers. In 2016, there was no drinking water in the park because of "arsenic concerns."

BROMLEY ROCK

> Location

Set astride a rock bluff on the
Similkameen River, 21 kilometres
east of Princeton on Highway 3,
is the riverside campground of
149-hectare Bromley Rock Provincial Park. By staying here, campers
trace the footsteps of the early pioneers who came in search of gold
and other minerals. The area was

also a traditional Indigenous fishing site. Services are located in Princeton
(21 kilometres west) or Hedley (15 kilometres east).

> Facilities

The campground has 17 spots set in a forested area on the Similkameen River.
All the basics are here (fire pits, drinking water, picnic tables, pit toilets), and
two of the pit toilets are wheelchair accessible. The campground is located
near the road so there is the noise of traffic, as Highway 3 is quite busy. Bromley Rock accepts reservations for all its camping spots and is very popular.

> Recreational activities

The river offers swimming in delightful cool swimming holes, and there
is fishing potential. Be careful when swimming, though, as the current is strong. When I visited, local young male adventurers were tubing
downstream to Stemwinder Provincial Park, a popular activity not recommended for the uninitiated. Just outside the park, hiking trails lead to
fantastic views of the Similkameen Valley. The nearby town of Princeton
was named in 1860 to commemorate the visit of the Prince of Wales that
year. Princeton has a pioneer museum with displays of clothing, mining
items, and furnishings. Artifacts from Indigenous communities, including
the Lower Similkameen Indian Band, and Chinese immigrants, who played
a major role in the early development of mining and the railway, are also
on display.

> Additional information

This campground is only 14 kilometres from Stemwinder Provincial Park, which is slightly larger in capacity and may provide an alternative should Bromley Rock be full. Bromley Rock is a great place to stop for a picnic even if you do not want to camp. The area is traditional territory for the Nlaka'pamux, Syilx Okanagan, and Secwépemc Peoples, and was explored by miners and trappers in the last two hundred years. Anyone travelling west along Highway 3 should make time to visit the nearby Grist Mill and Gardens at Keremeos. Even if you do not have time to tour this BC Heritage site, just call in for coffee and the wonderful home cooking.

CONKLE LAKE

> Location

If you are looking for a backcountry retreat to get away from the crowds, and you can endure a bumpy road and navigate around herds of cows, this is the place for you. The campground is in a beautiful location amidst the Okanagan Highland, but BC Parks warns that the access route along twisting gravel roads is not suitable for large motorhomes or towed trailers. Consequently, those travelling in these types of vehicles may wish to choose another spot. The park can be reached by gravel access roads from three points, but BC Parks recommends only one of these: from Highway 3, 6 kilometres east of Bridesville, a 26-kilometre gravel road leads to the site. The alternative access points—either 16 kilometres down a gravel road from Highway 33 at Westbridge, or a very challenging route 35 kilometres down from Highway 97 at Okanagan Falls—are not recommend by BC Parks as the routes follow forestry roads that are not well marked or well maintained, and therefore not suitable for vehicle traffic. Services are available at Westbridge and at the junction of Highways 3 and 33.

> Facilities

There are 34 private camping spots located in a lightly forested area of western larch, lodgepole pine, alder, and willow on the northwest corner of the 3-kilometre-long lake. Some spots overlook the lake. Only the basic facilities are provided by BC Parks (pit toilets, picnic tables, pump water, cooking pits). There is no sani-station and no reservations are taken.

> Recreational activities

Secluded Conkle Lake has a beautiful beach, where you can sunbathe, swim (although the lake tends to be cold), or fish for rainbow trout. A steep drop-off, however, means non-swimmers and children should be cautious. There is a boat launch, but the park has a motorboat size restriction. A number of hiking trails lead from the campground, one of which goes halfway around the lake. The 2-kilometre Falls Trail includes a beautiful multi-tiered waterfall and leaves from between campsites 31 and 32. For rainy days, a covered picnic shelter is available.

> Additional information

The park is named after an early settler to the Kettle Valley, W.H. Conkle. The fact that this park is relatively difficult to access by the RV population may suggest it is a campground only for four-wheel-drivers and their passengers to enjoy. When I visited, quite a few large recreational vehicles had obviously managed the routes, and their owners were enjoying the beautiful Okanagan scenery. However, the roads should not be attempted by those with low-loaders or long vehicles because of the number of tight switchbacks.

ELLISON

> Location

If diving is your game, then Ellison Provincial Park should be your aim. In addition to the diving opportunities it provides, Ellison is an excellent spot for a family vacation, perfect if you have children to entertain. Set on the north-eastern shore of Okanagan Lake and encompassing 200 hectares between  the Thompson Plateau and the Monashee Mountains, the park is reached from Highway 97 by heading south for 16 kilometres on 25th Avenue from Vernon's main intersection. All services are available in Vernon.

> Facilities

The park has 71 spacious, well-appointed sites set in a natural forest of Douglas fir and ponderosa pine and is suitable for every size of recreational vehicle. There are wheelchair-accessible flush toilets, pit toilets, and a sani-station. Reservations are accepted at 61 locations.

> Recreational activities

Ellison Provincial Park is home to Canada's only freshwater dive park, located at Otter Bay. A number of objects and artifacts have been sunk here to attract fish and create a diving haven for the rubber-clad enthusiasts who explore the dark, cold waters. If diving is not your passion, there is a wide array of other activities to enjoy, including 6 kilometres of hiking trails that take visitors to many of the park's natural features and viewpoints. (Watch out for porcupines, often seen on the popular Ellison Trail.) Two protected beach areas ideal for swimming and sunbathing are equipped with changing facilities and an outdoor shower. A little farther away is a third beach, which allows dogs. Fishers can try their luck for large carp, burbot, kokanee, and trout, and while there is no boat launch in the park, one is located 6 kilometres to the north. A number of the camping spaces overlook the playground and are ideal if you have young children. There is also an almost manicured green field, which many golf courses would be envious of, for ball games.

> Additional information

Ellison is in the heart of the fruit-growing region of the province, and orchards, ranches, and farms dominate the area, as they have since the 1800s. This park provides an excellent base from which to explore the North Okanagan and savour the produce of the region. A great family campground.

FINTRY

> Location

This is a wonderful provincial park to explore. It has so many facets and is one of my favourites in the area. Ideally situated for exploring the Okanagan and found in one of the region's few remaining natural areas, Fintry started to register campers in 1996. The park is on the northwest side of Okanagan Lake, 32 kilometres north of Kelowna and 37 kilometres south of Vernon. It is clearly

signposted from Highway 97 and accessed by 3 kilometres of paved road. Services are available in Kelowna and Vernon.

> Facilities

Camping facilities here include recently renovated flush toilets and showers. Most of the camping spots are in a large open area. Some are shaded by pine trees, and others have views of the lake. One hundred and fifty-eight camping spots are available and reservations are accepted for 80 percent of them.

> Recreational activities

Close to the campground is a beautiful 2-kilometre sandy beach, ideal for swimming, sunbathing, and family activities. For paddlers and boaters, there is a paved boat launch and a floating dock in the park. Fishing in the warm waters of Okanagan Lake can be rewarding, and hiking the Shorts Creek Canyon Trail provides opportunities to view white-tailed deer, bighorn sheep, and a variety of birds. BC Parks warns that caution should be exercised on sections of the trails; in places it is quite narrow and near steep cliffs. In 2021, a new playpark was constructed. I visited this park in 2007 and was amazed at the newly renovated Manor House, which has numerous rooms open to the public, including a trophy room full of stuffed animals and birds, such as a huge white bear, a giraffe head, a warthog, and numerous other animals. It's one of the best small museums in BC that I've seen. I revisited in 2021 and took a tour, and it has only got better. Tours are offered in July and August. The Friends of Fintry Provincial Park Society has a good website with a calendar of park events and list of things to do (fintry.ca).

> Additional information

The park is a heritage site occupying the former Fintry Estate. Its history dates to the nineteenth century, when fur dealers traded with the Indigenous inhabitants of the area. In 1909, James Cameron Dun-Waters, originally from Scotland, purchased the land and called it Fintry. He built many of the buildings that can be toured today, including the manor house and farm buildings. Fintry has the advantage of being located in a popular area of BC, and it is one of my personal favourites.

GLADSTONE

> Location

Gladstone (formerly Texas Creek) Provincial Park is located at the north end of Christina Lake, 20 kilometres northeast of Grand Forks. To reach the campground, take Highway 3, then turn onto East Lake Drive and drive for 4 kilometres on a paved road. Residents of Christina Lake boast that the waters here are the warmest in BC; however, Wasa Lake and Osoyoos Lake residents make the same claim. Whatever the truth, Christina Lake is an immensely popular recreational place where all services can be found.

> Facilities

Sixty-two large camping spots are set in an open pine forest in this 39,387-hectare provincial park, and many are shaded. Facilities include fire pits, drinking water, picnic tables, pit and flush toilets, and showers. Some park facilities are wheelchair accessible and reservations are accepted for all sites.

> Recreational activities

Nineteen kilometres long, but only 55 metres deep, Christina Lake supplies a wealth of leisure pursuits, including swimming from delightful, secluded pocket beaches and boating and fishing for kokanee, rainbow trout, and small-mouthed bass in the clear waters. There is a boat launch. Gladstone has 48 kilometres of trails, including one that leads north along the lakeshore and another that heads to Deer Point Lookout (26 kilometres return); details of all trails can be found on the park's notice board. The nearby popular holiday centre also has golf courses and country clubs to enjoy.

> Additional information

For years, I avoided staying here, as I found the community of Christina Lake very busy and commercialized and envisaged the campground having similar traits. How wrong I was! This is a wonderful quiet camping spot where very lucky campers gain sites overlooking the water. I spent a gorgeous summer night here and cursed my previous preconceptions about the place, which were grounded in the knowledge that the population of Christina Lake swells from 1,000 to 6,000 in the summer months. More recently the community of Christina Lake has grown even more, but the campground away from the centre of population provides a tranquil camping experience.

GOLDPAN

> Location

Watch out for river rafters and gold prospectors if you plan to sojourn here. Goldpan is a 5-hectare roadside provincial park conveniently located on Highway 1, 10 kilometres south of Spences Bridge, where services are located. There is also a restaurant just down the road.

> Facilities

There are just 14 camping spots available here beside the mighty Thompson River. Facilities are basic (drinking water, fire pits, picnic tables, pit toilets). Railway trucks and the noise of road traffic can be heard from the campground. No reservations are accepted.

> Recreational activities

Goldpan's main draw is fishing, with 600 metres of accessible river, and the park attracts steelhead anglers, especially in October, November, and December. Because the Thompson is very fast-moving, swimming in the river is not recommended, but it is popular for kayaking and river rafting. We picnicked here one year, and during our brief visit witnessed six different whitewater-rafting excursions glide past our beach spot. The area is heavily used during the peak summer months by commercial river-rafting companies looking for a resting place for their downriver trips. As one would surmise, gold panning can be undertaken here. Ospreys also frequent the area—so keep looking up.

> Additional information

Spences Bridge, named after Thomas Spence, who built the original bridge in 1865, is where the Thompson and Nicola Rivers meet. This area has been fished for hundreds of years by the Nlaka'pamux Nation, whose people continue to fish here today, as indeed do many others. For those who want a taste of adventure by whitewater rafting, the area is ideal. Be warned: in summertime the area is prone to very high temperatures (often the highest in the country), so remember the sunscreen. The campground was established in 1956 and is primarily a one-night stop for travellers on Highway 1. Trains passing at night are easily audible. I believe this park serves well as a picnic spot for breaking the journey on Highway 1, rather than an ideal place to camp. Skihist Provincial Park, a short drive south, is far superior and not as noisy, and it also offers much-needed shade.

HERALD

> Location

A variety of flora and fauna and easy access to the calm waters of Shuswap Lake are just two of the many attributes of Herald Provincial Park. The vegetation is attributable to the park's distinctive position amid steep uplands and flat deltas. It includes Douglas fir, juniper, dryland shrubs, redcedar, hemlock, cottonwood, aspen, and paper birch. A naturalist's delight, Herald is found on the Salmon Arm of Shuswap Lake, 14 kilometres east of Tappen off Highway 1. Services are available at Tappen.

> Facilities

On the calm lakeside are over 120 beautiful wooded camping spaces with all the services required for a comfortable camping experience, including showers, flush and pit toilets, and a sani-station. Some facilities are wheelchair accessible. The campsites are at three locations: Reineker, Bastion Mountain, and Homestead. Reineker's 36 sites are closer to the water, Bastion's 15 sites are larger and more secluded, while the 68 sites at Homestead do not have much shade. Reservations are accepted for all sites.

> Recreational activities

Shuswap Lake is a relatively warm lake and therefore a delightful place to swim, water-ski, or scuba dive. The park has sand and fine-gravel beaches ideal for sunbathing. Fishing and boating are pursuits enjoyed by many, and there is a boat launch in the day-use area (1 kilometre from the campground). There are also a number of trails in the park, including a recently rebuilt and enhanced 20-minute route through an area of cedar growth to the beautiful Margaret Falls. Reineker Creek runs through the park near the campground, and evidence of Secwépemc pit houses is visible west of the creek. Birding is reputed to be fantastic, as more than seventy species frequent the park.

> Additional information

The lake is named after the Secwépemc (Shuswap) Nation, who recognized it as a bountiful hunting and fishing ground. Cliff faces around the lake display pictographs (rock paintings) that provide evidence of humankind's long residency in the region. Although the lake is named after the area's first inhabitants, the park takes its name from the Herald family, who were early settlers of the area. The remains of the family's farm buildings can still be seen today. Herald Provincial Park is very popular with both locals and tourists as it offers every facility yet is not tremendously large. It's a delightful place to camp. The sani-station here has the best view of any sani-station in the province, so even this most mundane camping chore becomes a delight. The BC Parks website warns that theft from vehicles can be a problem in this area.

INKANEEP

> Location

Inkaneep Provincial Park is an ideal spot from which to experience the excellent local fruit and wine. However, the campground here offers little else: it's primarily geared to overnight camping. On the shores of the Okanagan River, this 21-hectare park is 6 kilometres north of Oliver on Highway 97. Services are found in Oliver, or at the gas station at the junction of Highway 97 and the turnoff to the campground. The park was established in 1956 and plays a role in protecting old cottonwood trees.

> Facilities

Inkaneep offers 7 camping spots, more suitable for tents than RVs, set in a shady oasis of cottonwood trees on the edge of the Okanagan River. Only the basic facilities are available here (pit toilets, picnic tables, drinking water, cooking pits). The campground is very close to a group of houses, and in this respect it is quite suburban.

> Recreational activities

From this campground it is possible to fish in the Okanagan River and to canoe (although it is quite a trek from the campground to the water). The arid desert habitat around the park is home to many species of wildlife; consequently, one of the main activities here is birdwatching. A small path through old-growth cottonwood trees leads from the campground to a small dike on the Okanagan River, where there are birdwatching opportunities. The area is home to black-headed grosbeaks, northern orioles, yellow warblers, blue-listed Lewis's woodpeckers, and warbling vireos. An ecological reserve is also located nearby. Over the recent past, biking in the vicinity has gained in popularity.

> Additional information

The town of Oliver was established in 1921 under a land grant by then-BC premier John Oliver as a settlement for veterans from the First World War. Now it is known for housing some of the best wineries in the country, which can be toured by visitors. Be sure to make time to explore the local caves and perhaps purchase a bottle of wine for savouring around the campfire. Just south of Oliver is a "pocket desert." When I first visited in 1999, it was somewhat difficult to find, as there were no signposts. However, in 2001 it was designated as a provincial park and now has lovely boardwalks with interpretive signs and information. The area supports subtropical flora and fauna, such as cacti, horned lizards, rattlesnakes, and burrowing owls. Remember to take along drinking water, as it can be very hot.

JEWEL LAKE

> Location
Somewhat off the beaten track, Jewel Lake provides a get-away-from-it-all camping experience, and if campers are keen on fishing, then this place could be heaven. I don't think I have seen a lake with so many fish jumping! Found 12 kilometres east of Greenwood off Highway 3, the park is accessed by travelling on a paved road, steep in places, toward Jewel Lake Resort. All services are available at Greenwood, but the resort also has some provisions and boat rentals.

> Facilities
There are 26 large, well-spaced, vehicle-accessible spots here, plus the basic facilities (drinking water, picnic tables, fire pits, and pit toilets); the pit toilets are wheelchair accessible. All sites are in a forested area of Douglas fir, hemlock, birch, and larch, and are suitable for larger RVs. The BC Parks website describes Jewel Lake as providing "an old-fashioned camping experience in a natural setting"—which could be translated by the cynical to "we haven't done anything here for years." No reservations are accepted.

> Recreational activities
Like so many out-of-the-way places in the province, Jewel Lake is primarily a location for fishing. Stocked with brook and rainbow trout from the Summerland Trout Hatchery, the 3-kilometre-long lake attracts anglers by the score. Fly-fishing is also popular. There is a car-top boat-launch location, and boats can be rented at Jewel Lake Resort. Motors are restricted to 10 horsepower, making canoeing a delightful alternative. Swimming is also possible from a small beach. The historical town of Greenwood has a number of interesting

buildings and a small museum, but be warned that everything seems to close early—even at the height of summer.

> Additional information

Now for my confession: I have only visited this campground once in my 30 years of camping in BC: June 2021. But when undertaking the research on this location and speaking to people who have visited, the words "fish" and "mosquito" always punctuate their sentences. I found it small, quaint, and very quiet. This is very much an "away from it all" camping location more suitable for the older camper than those who have children.

JOHNSTONE CREEK

> Location

Established in 1956 for day use only, this small, 38-hectare roadside provincial park started offering camping recently. It is located near Bridesville on Highway 3, about 5 kilometres west of Rock Creek and 45 kilometres from the town of Osoyoos, where all services are available.

> Facilities

Situated in an area of Douglas fir, pine, and aspen are 16 campsites a little distance away from the road. No reservations are taken. The trees make a good sound barrier, so noise from traffic is not a huge issue. The spots seem to be evenly split between those that are quite open with only a few shrubs dividing them and those with more privacy, thanks to the trees. There are four pit toilets, picnic tables, fire pits, and drinking water. I stayed here in the springtime, so the smell of blooming spring vegetation was an added bonus.

> Recreational activities

A pleasant waterfall where the waters of Johnstone Creek and Rock Creek converge is the main attraction here. There are also good photography opportunities at Rock Creek Canyon. According to BC Parks information, white-tailed deer and woodpeckers are often seen in the park. The campground is geared toward the overnight camper, and hiking and fishing opportunities are very limited. There are, however, hiking trails leading to three beaches, which offer views of the surrounding geography (and maybe sightings of the white-tailed deer) and fishing potential in the immediate vicinity.

> Additional information

On the drive from Osoyoos to Johnstone Creek, look out for huge sculptures of bald eagles, moose, pumas, ravens, deer, and even a Yeti, which make for great photo opportunities. For those interested in prospecting for gold, a visit to the ghost town of Camp McKinney is a must. Situated 11.5 kilometres northwest of Highway 3 on Mount Baldy Road are the ruins of the mining town, which yielded more than 80,000 ounces of gold between 1887 and 1903. A stop at the Osoyoos Visitor Centre provides more details. For those who plan to camp in the area longer than one night (and have a vehicle that can take the terrain), Conkle Lake is the preferred option; for others, Johnstone Creek is a superior roadside campground.

JUNIPER BEACH

> Location

Situated 19 kilometres east of Cache Creek on Highway 1, Juniper Beach is distinct from many other provincial parks because of its dry desert setting. Services are available at Cache Creek or Kamloops (53 kilometres to the west).

> Facilities

On the banks of the Thompson River, 32 camping spots are yours for the taking. The vegetation consists of sagebrush, prickly pear cactus, juniper, and cottonwoods. Although the camping spots accommodate every type of recreational vehicle, they are somewhat open. A special area has been designated just for tents, and some of the vehicle sites have the advantage of being close to the water. The campground is wheelchair accessible and has pit toilets, a sani-station, electrical hook-ups, and pay-to-use showers. Located a fair distance from the road, the campsites are not affected by the noise of road traffic, but two railway lines are close by. This is not the place to stay if you hate trains, as there is considerable rail traffic. When I stayed here, there were quite a few trains to lull me to sleep. Reservations are accepted for 21 sites.

> Recreational activities

Juniper Beach provides one of the few access points to the Thompson River between Savona and Spences Bridge. The easy river access makes this provincial park a pleasant place to stay and fish, and picnics on the shoreline are a delight. BC Parks says this is a good place to view sockeye salmon and to witness the summer migration of chinook and coho, although when I stayed here, there was no evidence of fish, either in the river or being caught by the patient anglers. A large natural pool separated from the river is perfect for swimming when the river's not too high, and canoeing and kayaking are also possible. There are lots of prickly pear cactus plants, so be careful if you're camping with little children. And, as mentioned above, if you are a train enthusiast, this is the place for you as both Canadian National and Canadian Pacific railway tracks run adjacent to the park.

> Additional information

This campground is located in the desert area of the Thompson–Nicola region and so looks quite barren compared to BC parks in more fertile regions. Do not expect to find much shade here on a hot summer day! I came here on one occasion directly from a waterlogged Alice Lake Campground and really appreciated the fantastic hot, dry climate.

KEKULI BAY

> Location

This is one of BC Parks' newest additions, but unlike many other recent arrivals, it is not small in capacity. Although only 57 hectares in size, it has space for 73 camping parties, and all sites have fantastic views of the lake, where rose bushes and flowering shrubs enhance the ambiance. It is located on a gorgeous bay on the west side of Kalamalka Lake, 2 kilometres from Highway 97 and 11 kilometres south of Vernon, where services are available.

> Facilities

Kekuli Bay has flush and pit toilets, drinking water, showers, and all the other amenities. The toilets and showers are wheelchair accessible. Recently four electrical hook-ups were added in the overflow area. Traffic noise may be an issue for some, and a railway line, though not much used, is also close to the campground. There are 73 spots shaded by trees that were planted when the park was established in 1990. Reservations are accepted at all sites.

> Recreational activities

The boat launch at this location is reported to be the best on Kalamalka Lake. Kayaking and canoeing are also pleasant here. Water-skiing is also popular. With a sandy beach close by, those who don't want to ride on the waters can certainly have fun splashing in them. A small 2.6-kilometre trail circles the campground, and there is a great kids' play area. If the weather isn't accommodating, a host of activities awaits in the town of Vernon. Kalamalka Lake Provincial Park, just to the north, provides a habitat for a variety of birds and wildlife (including rattlesnakes), while the high rodent population at Kekuli Bay ensures a healthy population of birds of prey, including ospreys and vultures. Yellow-bellied marmots run around the campground and are great fun for preschoolers to watch. This campground is the closest one to the Predator Ridge Resort and golf course, which reputably has some of the best greens in the Okanagan.

> Additional information

Kekuli Bay Provincial Park takes its name from semi-subterranean homes built by Interior Salish people. I visited this campground for the first time in June 2002 and loved the views but hated the intense heat and the lack of shade. Now well established, this provincial park is becoming very popular and the trees are providing that much needed shade.

KENTUCKY–ALLEYNE

> Location

Campers from the Lower Mainland looking for a weekend getaway cannot go wrong in choosing Kentucky–Alleyne, a real gem of a park situated 38 kilometres south of Merritt. To reach the campground, turn off Highway 5A just south of the Okanagan Connector and follow the marked 6-kilometre paved road; from the east, follow the signs from the Coquihalla for 11 kilometres. Services are available in Merritt.

> Facilities

The 190-hectare park has 87 camping spots. Although most spots do not have the advantage of vegetation to afford privacy, they are well spaced and suitable for every type of recreational vehicle, and some are right on the lake. Facilities are basic (pit toilets, fire pits, picnic tables, drinking water). The campground accepts reservations for a proportion of the sites.

> Recreational activities

This is a stunningly beautiful area of undulating glacial hills and grasslands surrounded by forests of pine and fir in the heart of cattle country. Lakes are re-stocked annually so there is good fishing potential for rainbow trout, and I love the way there are two "ponds" between the lakes restricted to "children only" fishing. There is a boat launch, and canoeing is a delight here, as is swimming, although accessing the water is tricky because of the reeds. In 2004, when we were camping with our children, our 4-year-old went running to the children's pond, straight through mud that resembled sand, and sank in it almost up to his waist. So, be warned of sand that is actually mud, especially if you have little ones! A number of trails take visitors around the lakes to different areas of the park where it is possible to see beaver lodges. As the campground is spread out, cycling on the many gravel roads and trails is an enjoyable activity for all ages; however, there are a number of private roads displaying no trespassing signs.

> Additional information

I love this park. Although the camping spots themselves are not stunning, the size of the camping area, the many dirt trails and roads around the park, and the glacial topography make Kentucky–Alleyne a pleasant place to explore. The sunsets are gorgeous—it is magical to cook dinner on an open fire while watching the beautiful red sunset over the water, as ospreys circle above. We stayed here a few years ago, when my husband and I escaped for a few days, camping with just our tent, some alcohol, and a plastic bag of sandwiches. The BC Parks attendant, on collecting our fee and seeing our meagre provisions, asked if this was my first camping trip ever.

KETTLE RIVER RECREATION AREA

> Location

On August 13, 2015, a devastating fire tore through this area. It was the largest single fire in the SE Forest Districts in thirty years, burning at a rate of 55 metres per minute. Evidence of the blackened, burned trees is everywhere as you drive to this campground. Named after the river that runs through it, Kettle River Recreation Area is located 5 kilometres north of Rock Creek on Highway 33. Services (pub, gas, store, accommodation) are located at Rock Creek, and they have improved tremendously over the last ten years.

> Facilities

At a bend on the west bank of the river are 114 well-spaced camping spots nestled in an area of ponderosa pine and birchgrass, with sites suitable for every size of recreational vehicle. In addition to the basic facilities offered, in 2013 a new toilet block and showers were added in addition to a new sani-station. Site 78 is completely wheelchair accessible. Reservations are accepted at 85 sites and strongly advised.

> Recreational activities

The Kettle Valley Railway discontinued its service in the early 1970s, and the track between Midway and Penticton was removed in 1980. The abandoned route runs through the park and is an excellent hiking and biking trail (see kettlevalleyrailway.ca). It is now part of the Trans Canada Trail. There is also fishing, swimming, and canoeing in the park, and a playpark for children; tubing is another river-based activity popular with locals and regular campers. On the eastern banks of the river, remains of gold and silver mines can be seen—evidence of the pioneers who travelled and worked in the area at the turn of the twentieth century. Excellent opportunities exist for the photographer and artist in this locale, and many people resurrect the past by having a go at panning for gold. Really, there is something for everyone here.

> Additional information

For those who decide not to cook, there is an interesting collection of eateries at Rock Creek, including a pub and some good breakfast cafes. Between 1860 and 1864 this region was worked by more than five hundred miners who scoured for gold. A prospector called Charles Dietz started a gold rush here, but there were never large quantities of gold found, only copper. Thankfully, the wildfires that damaged sections of the park, and which are clearly visible, spared the majority of the campground and the day-use area. A delightful place to camp.

LAC LE JEUNE

> Location

If you are looking for a base from which to explore the region, this 180-hectare lakeside provincial park, easily accessible from Kamloops and Merritt, is an excellent bet. It is situated just off the Coquihalla Highway, 37 kilometres south of Kamloops and 47 kilometres north of Merritt, and a full range of services can be found at these locations, and at Logan Lake, 26 kilometres away.

> Facilities

Set among a forest of pinegrass and lodgepole pines at the cool elevation of 1,280 metres are 144 large, well-positioned, wheelchair-accessible campsites. A few of these spots have the added advantage of being close to the lake. There are flush toilets and a sani-station in the day-use area. Reservations are accepted for 60 percent of the spaces (91 actual sites). In addition to firewood, the park also sells ice.

> Recreational activities

Lac Le Jeune is equipped with a boat launch (powerboats are limited to a speed of 20 kilometres per hour), and swimming is possible in a protected swimming area. All the literature on the park states that Lac Le Jeune is famous for "fighting rainbow trout," so go win a battle! To facilitate this, a 250-foot-long fishing wharf is on offer in the day-use area. There is also an adventure playground, a horseshoe pit, and interpretive programs in the summer. The Gus Johnson Trail rings the lake and is an easy 8-kilometre hike, and another trail connects the park to the adjacent McConnell Lake Provincial Park and the extensive Stake Lake trail system, which has 160 kilometres of trails for hiking, mountain biking during the summer, and cross-country skiing in the winter. Walloper Lake Provincial Park, a short drive from here off Highway 5, has only wilderness camping, but it does provide canoe and boat rentals and access to the beautiful waters of the area.

> Additional information

During the hot, dry days of summer, this campground offers a welcome respite from the heat, as it is at a higher elevation than the Thompson Valley to the north and the Nicola Valley in the south. Lac Le Jeune is an excellent base from which to explore the towns of Merritt, Kamloops, and Logan Lake. When I visited, we took a short 20-minute trail to a trout-spawning stream that the camp host had told us about. My only criticism of this park is the lack of information boards or maps detailing the trails in the area. Hopefully, this will have been addressed by the time you visit.

MABEL LAKE

> Location

Mabel Lake is perfect for those who want to appreciate the Okanagan from a cooler vantage point. Somewhat off the beaten track, it is a lovely 182-hectare provincial park between the Thompson Plateau to the west and the Monashee Mountains to the east. Temperatures here tend to be lower than in many other areas of the Okanagan, providing a pleasant respite from the summer heat. The campground is 60 kilometres northeast from Vernon. Travel east on Highway 6 to Lumby, then take a paved road for 36 kilometres followed by 1 kilometre on gravel. Services are available at Lumby; there is also a small marine store by the campground, which sells candy, milk, propane, and other supplies.

> Facilities
You can camp here at one of three campgrounds: Monashee (which has been recently updated), Trinity, and Taylor Creek. Together, they provide a total of 114 well-situated spaces in a wooded setting, some with great views of the lake. Monashee's sites are smaller but more private. There is a sani-station, but no flush toilets or showers. Some park facilities are wheelchair accessible. Reservations are accepted at 46 sites. Recently, an overflow camping area was created to accommodate those who arrive without a reservation and find the campground full and for those who wish to prolong their stay longer than their reservation allows.

> Recreational activities
A 2,100-metre shoreline that includes two lovely beaches (and a pet beach) with safe swimming areas provides access to the waters of Mabel Lake, 35 kilometres long. Fishing is good both from the shore and in the deeper waters where anglers hope to catch rainbow trout, Dolly Varden, lake trout, kokanee, and chinook salmon. Numerous fishing competitions are held here. Water-skiing and boating are popular, and the nearby marina offers boat rentals. The area is attractive to canoeists, who paddle down the Shuswap River just south of the park. For those who like to see more unusual wildlife, painted turtles can be observed in Taylor Creek. The park also has a one-hour interpretive trail, tons of grassy areas, and a wonderful kids' playground. When our children were 3 and 5, we really enjoyed staying here.

> Additional information
The surrounding area offers interesting alternatives to the recreational activities found in the park. The road between Lumby and Mabel Lake takes travellers through the distinctive landscape of ranches and farmland—quite beautiful and somewhat "un-Okanaganish." Wilsey Dam has a picnic spot with trails leading to the awe-inspiring Shuswap Falls. I adore this park and highly recommend it. The 36-kilometre approach road is a lovely drive, and

the reward at the end is well worth the effort. Bears and deer are often seen in the vicinity. My only note of caution: there can be mosquitoes.

MARBLE CANYON

> Location

Established in 1956, 355-hectare Marble Canyon Provincial Park is popular with rock climbers, who are attracted to the area for its rugged terrain. It is not difficult to see why mountaineers and others choose to visit this park, nestled on a lakeside below towering limestone cliffs and amid the beautiful scenery of Marble Canyon. The campground is found by travelling 40 kilometres north-west of Cache Creek on Highway 99. It is about 35 kilometres northeast of Lillooet. Services are available at Cache Creek or Lillooet, or at the Butterfly Creek Store, 2 kilometres from the campground.

> Facilities

There are 30 relatively small gravel campsites with little privacy, some directly overlooking the lake and some with tent pads. The services provided are limited to the basics (pit toilets, picnic tables, drinking water, fire pits).

> Recreational activities

Leisure activities include fishing, swimming, rock-climbing, kayaking, and canoeing. Only electric motors are permitted on the lake and there is no boat launch. A trail along the side of the lake leads to a waterfall and is an easy 30-minute trek. There are two archaeological sites where there are pictographs that are spiritually important to the Ts'kw'aylaxw (Pavilion) First Nation. The park was established in 1956, but in April 2001, Pavilion Lake was added to the park to preserve unique freshwater stromatolite features (fossilized remains of microorganisms considered to be among some of the oldest life forms on Earth). People interested in fauna and flora will find the vegetation and the bird and animal life here fascinating.

> Additional information

Reaching this campground is a beautiful and scenic drive. Close to Lillooet, travellers see some of the ginseng farms for which BC is known, easily spotted by looking for vast expanses of black plastic. At the junction of Highway 97 and Highway 99, the historic 1861 Hat Creek Ranch, an original stopping place on the Cariboo Wagon Road, offers guided tours. The area is noted for its rock formations, scenery, and the beautiful lake. The disadvantage to camping here is the campsite's proximity to the road; although the route is not tremendously busy, campers may be kept awake by the sound of traffic. When I stayed here in 2015, noise was not a problem, and we enjoyed an evening meal cooked at the lakeside, as our campsite was on the water's edge. Wasps can also be a problem, but they have not bothered me on the six separate occasions I have camped there. As always, black bears inhabit the vicinity. One of the better roadside campgrounds.

MONCK

> Location
With fantastic views of the Nicola Valley south of Kamloops, and within easy reach of Merritt, the nearest large settlement, this 118-hectare park has a great deal to offer. Monck Provincial Park is reached by taking Highway 5A to Nicola, then following a paved road to the campground, situated 22 kilometres north of Merritt (where all services are available).

> Facilities
With the exception of showers, this 120-space campground has all the necessary requirements for camping, including a sani-station and wheelchair-accessible flush toilets. The cheery camping spots, set among a lightly forested area of ponderosa pine and fir on the north side of Nicola Lake, are suitable for every type of recreational vehicle. Most have views of the water. Reservations are accepted for 85 sites.

> Recreational activities
Monck Provincial Park is an ideal family vacation spot. There is a playground and a sandy beach leading to the beautiful waters of Nicola Lake, where a cordoned-off swimming area and two change houses are provided. The beach shelves quickly, so you do need to use caution. Fishing for kokanee is reputed to be excellent, and twenty-five other species of fish, including rainbow trout, can be caught in the waters. There is a recently upgraded concrete boat launch

to facilitate boating and sailing pursuits. A number of trails lead from the campground through a forest to various vantage points. Indigenous pit house depressions can also be found here, and a walk along an old road to Second Beach leads to a fine example of Nlaka'pamux petroglyphs. Interpretive programs are offered during the summer and birdwatching in the spring and fall is reported to be excellent.

> Additional information

The Nicola Valley is rich with green fields and marshland. Originally settled by the Nlaka'pamux Peoples and later by European ranchers in the 1860s, the area is now home to Canada's largest working cattle ranch, the Douglas Lake Ranch, which offers horseback riding and ranch tours. The land that now includes Monck was donated by Major Charles Sidney Goldman in honour of his son, Lieutenant-Commander Penryn "Pen" Monck, a British soldier in the Second World War who changed his name to "Monck" to improve his chances of survival should he be captured by the Germans. Goldman moved to the Nicola Valley in 1919, purchased 2,650 hectares of land, and built up a cattle ranch with over 5,000 head. It's a good location for family camping, but it is becoming very busy as its reputation grows.

MOUNT ROBSON

> Location

Mount Robson Provincial Park provides a camping experience that should not be missed. Mount Robson, "the monarch of the Canadian Rockies," is the highest peak in the Rockies, at almost 4,000 metres high. In 1913, a special act was passed by the BC legislature to preserve this 225,285-hectare area of exceptional beauty for all to encounter and enjoy. It is the second oldest provincial park in BC. The park is about 4 hours north of Kamloops and is easily accessed from the Yellowhead Highway (Highway 5). A gas station and a store are located at Mount Robson Motor Village.

> Facilities

There are three wheelchair-accessible campgrounds in the park, and two of them are located at the western end: Robson Meadows has 125 spots and

Robson River has 19 spots. Both have flush toilets and showers, and Robson Meadows also has a sani-station. The third campground is Lucerne, 10 kilometres west of the Alberta border, which has 36 spots on Yellowhead Lake. Most sites are large, private, and well situated in the evergreen forest, but Robson River is my favourite campground: it's smaller than Robson Meadows but has all the amenities and is adjacent to services. All three campgrounds are open from mid-May to the end of September. Lucerne and Robson Meadows both have reservable sites, totalling 94. Electrical hook-ups are available in 20 locations in Robson Meadows.

> Recreational activities

The spectacular scenery, which consists of lakes, waterfalls, rivers, glaciers, and mountains, makes this a paradise for hikers, climbers, canoeists, and anyone who loves the outdoors. There are over 200 kilometres of hiking trails within the park, one of the most popular being the Valley of a Thousand Waterfalls, which takes explorers past the fantastic azure brightness of Berg Lake and on to views of Tumbling Glacier's spectacular waterfalls. I believe this to be one of the best hikes in BC. Boat launches are available at Moose Lake and Yellowhead Lake, but fishing tends to be poor, as the glacial waters yield only small populations of fish. The Mount Robson Visitor Information Centre at the Mount Robson Viewpoint has details of all the park's activities, and staff there can advise on the weather and camping conditions. Because of significant impacts caused by severe floods in July 2021, the entirety of the Berg Lake Trail was closed for all of 2022 while BC Parks assessed the damage and carried out repairs, including campground upgrades. See also the BC Parks website, where you can access the numerous maps and guides produced by the park.

> Additional information

The Texqakallt Nation calls Mount Robson "Yexyexéscen" (or "Yuh-hai-has-hun"), meaning "Mountain of the Spiral Road." It is unclear whether the park is named after Colin Robertson, a Hudson's Bay Company factor and later member of Parliament, or John Robson, premier of BC from 1889 to 1892. This is one of my favourite BC parks, as there is so much to do and the scenery is breathtaking. When you're arranging a holiday tour of BC, Mount Robson is a lovely destination to include on your itinerary.

NORTH THOMPSON RIVER

> Location

The most amazing feature of this 126-hectare provincial park is the meeting of two distinctly individual water systems. North Thompson River is located where the Thompson and Clearwater Rivers meet, 5 kilometres south of the town of Clearwater, just off Highway 5. Clearwater has services such as gas, propane, food, and accommodation, as well as a number of commercial tour operations.

> Facilities

The campground is on the banks of the Thompson River in a mixed forest of Douglas fir, pine, cedar, and spruce. There are 69 camping spots in total, the more desirable ones being closer to the river. These are not suitable if you have young children as the riverbank is steep. Some park facilities are wheelchair accessible and there is also a sani-station. A railway line runs close by, so expect the noise of trains. Reservations are accepted at 53 sites.

> Recreational activities

A number of short trails lead through the campground. All take less than 30 minutes to complete. A small wading and swimming area is located on a back eddy where the Clearwater River flows into the North Thompson. BC Parks cautions that during the flood season of June and July, currents can be powerful. Canoeing, kayaking, and fishing for rainbow trout and chinook salmon are also possible here. In addition to the recreational activities available in the park itself, there is the fantastic "poggy playground" for kids, one of the best playgrounds I've seen anywhere—and I've seen more than my fair share of these! The nearby community of Clearwater has bikes and canoes for rent, horseback trail rides, and rafting trips. Nearby Dutch Lake has swimming. Bald eagles and ospreys can be seen fishing for Dolly Varden, rainbow trout, and chinook salmon.

> Additional information

From a viewpoint in the park, you can take in the vista of the distinctive green waters of the Clearwater River meeting those of the muddy brown Thompson.

It was once the site of a Secwépemc Nation encampment, and there are two archaeological sites in the park. The campground is very sedate and peaceful (ideal for the older RV crowd and for family camping), and is a good spot from which to explore Wells Gray Provincial Park. That park's visitor centre in Clearwater is worth a visit: my kids liked the life-sized moose outside, and there is excellent tourist information inside.

OKANAGAN LAKE

> Location

Okanagan Lake Provincial Park is the most popular camping location in the Okanagan. Like sẅiẅs (Haynes Point) and Bear Creek, 98-hectare Okanagan Lake is very busy in the peak summer months of July and August. This park has fantastic panoramic views of the mountains and lake. It is located 11 kilometres north of Summerland and 24 kilometres from Penticton. Services are available in these

communities, but there is also a fruit stand close to the park entrance and the south park gatehouse sells ice, frozen treats, cold drinks, and some groceries.

> Facilities

The park has 176 vehicle/tent campsites: 80 in the north campground and 96 in the south campground, some with views of the lake. I prefer the camping spots in the north campground, which are better spaced and less confined than those in the south. Both are set in an unusual forest area and have showers and flush and pit toilets. The south campground shower building is wheelchair accessible. Reservations are for all sites in the north campground and 94 of the sites in the south.

> Recreational activities

With over a kilometre of beach (some of it pebbly), Okanagan Lake Provincial Park is a paradise for swimmers, sunbathers, anglers, and water-sports enthusiasts. There is a boat launch at the south campground, and the lake is popular for windsurfing and sailing. For those who prefer other activities, there are interpretive programs in the summer and a number of small hiking trails to explore. One of the unique features of the park is an arboretum of more than 10,000 exotic trees, including Russian olive, Chinese elm, Norway, Manitoba and silver maples, and red, blue, and mountain ash. This woodland enhances the birdlife, so keep your eyes peeled for hummingbirds, larks, and woodpeckers, which can be easily seen. Fantastic photography opportunities abound.

> Additional information

Due to its popularity, you may well be disappointed if you arrive at this park without a campsite reservation in the peak summer months. Summerland's Kettle Valley Steam Railway operates a quaint steam train during the summer months. Each year this attraction employs wonderful volunteers and enthusiastic employees, dressed in period costume, who provide tons of information for tourists (kettlevalleyrail.org). BC Parks warns of rattlesnakes living in the park.

OTTER LAKE

> Location

BC Parks suggests that 49-hectare Otter Lake is ideal for old-fashioned camping, a provincial park where campers can find privacy in a natural setting. This park is 33 kilometres northwest of Princeton off Highway 5A. From Princeton, drive to Coalmont and Tulameen on Coalmont Road, then to Otter Lake, which is well marked with signs. The park can also be accessed from Highway  97C by turning at Aspen Grove (which is Highway 5A) and following the signs. Services are available in the small towns of Coalmont and Tulameen.

> Facilities

Otter Lake boasts 45 beautifully spaced, large camping spots on the northwest shore of the lake, some with views of the water. Large trees provide much-needed shade in an area of the province that can become very hot in the summer. Some park facilities are wheelchair accessible and there are flush and pit toilets, but no sani-station or showers. Reservations are accepted at all sites and strongly advised.

> Recreational activities

Five-kilometre-long Otter Lake provides the main venue for recreational activities, which include fishing for rainbow trout, swimming from a warm beach in the day-use area (5 kilometres from the campground), and boating (two boat launches are provided). There is also a horseshoe pit. The surrounding area is home to a variety of animals, including otters, beavers, red squirrels, mountain goats, cougars, and grizzly bears—but don't expect to see them all on your first visit! Across the lake, but visible from the campground, is the now disused Kettle Valley Railway, part of the Trans Canada Trail linking Princeton and Merritt that offers a fantastic mountain bike or hiking route amid some spectacular scenery.

> Additional information

Otter Lake is an ideal base from which to explore the mining history of the Tulameen region. The town of Tulameen (which means "red earth" in Nlaka'pamuctsin, language of the Nlaka'pamux Peoples) is located 5 kilometres south of the campground and was first used by Indigenous Peoples for hunting and fishing and then explored by gold miners in the nineteenth century. The Hudson's Bay Company used a road that passed through Tulameen and labelled the settlement "Campement des Femmes," as it was populated primarily by women waiting for their men to return from trapping and hunting for furs. The town of Coalmont, also south of the park, sprang to life during the gold rush; in 1925 it produced 100,000 tonnes of coal, making it the region's largest producer. By 1940, the mine was exhausted, and most residents moved away. Today, Coalmont contains a cafe, a general store, and a hotel dating back to 1912 (you won't be able to miss the hotel—it's painted bright pink).

PAUL LAKE

> Location

Provincial parks near populated areas often offer the best amenities for family camping, whether you're staying in a tent or an RV. Paul Lake is one such park. Residents of Kamloops and visitors are regular patrons of this popular provincial park, conveniently located 24 kilometres northeast of Kamloops. Access Paul Lake by turning off Highway 5 and following a well-maintained twisting road across a meadow landscape for 17 kilometres. Gas and food are available at the turnoff from Highway 5; all other needs can be accommodated in Kamloops.

> Facilities

The 728-hectare park has 90 large, well-maintained, private camping spots suitable for every type of recreational vehicle, making the park popular with RVers. The campground is set in a lightly forested area of Douglas fir and aspen, and there is a sani-station and flush and pit toilets; some park facilities are wheelchair accessible. Reservations are accepted in 47 sites.

> Recreational activities

The lake provides a host of activities, including swimming in a protected area from a 400-metre sandy beach, boating (with canoes and paddleboats available for rent), and good fishing since Paul Lake is stocked with rainbow trout. Over 7 kilometres of trails lead from the campground and a pleasant hike, with over 900 metres in elevation gain, leads up Gibraltar Rock (the last section is the steepest). The park is particularly appealing to people with young children; it has a playground, horseshoe pits, and wide grassy areas, plus a maze of paved roads connecting the camping facilities that ensures fun for young cyclists and rollerbladers. In 1996, 268 hectares were added to the park to protect the habitat of ospreys, falcons, bald eagles, coyotes, and mule deer. The area is popular with the birdwatching community.

> Additional information

At certain times of the year, the park is blessed with an array of beautiful wildflowers. (Remember, visitors are forbidden to pick vegetation in the provincial parks.) For good views of the vicinity, campers with stamina are advised to climb Gibraltar Rock. The park's proximity to Kamloops means it is often filled to capacity. It is also in a high-risk forest fire area that is often subject to campfire bans. Signs are posted if a ban is in place. For some reason, though, I find this park to have little atmosphere and not as much character as most others. In some respects, it appears too ordered and regimented, almost clinical. This is a purely personal observation and clearly not one shared by everyone, for when I visited, a number of campers, especially family groups, seemed to be well established. I just find it to be one of BC's more formal parks.

SHUSWAP LAKE

> Location
For people who love water-based activities, Shuswap Lake, with over 1,000 kilometres of waterways, is a real magnet. The provincial park is conveniently located 90 kilometres east of Kamloops on Highway 1 at Squilax. A 20-kilometre paved road leads to the campground. Some supplies can be found at a store adjacent to the entrance of the park, while more comprehensive supplies are found in Sorrento, 35 kilometres away.

> Facilities
Because Shuswap Lake is one of BC's largest provincial parks, the facilities offered here are comprehensive. There are 330 camping spots suitable for every type of recreational vehicle, flush and pit toilets, a sani-station, showers, and full access for those in wheelchairs. Reservations are accepted at all sites and electrical hook-ups are provided at some. BC Parks describes Shuswap Lake as operating "at capacity" from mid-July to Labour Day. An extremely popular location.

> Recreational activities
Shuswap Lake is perfect for water sports like paddling, water-skiing, and windsurfing, and the 1-kilometre-long beach has a designated swimming area. There is also a boat launch, and 2 kilometres offshore is Copper Island, which has a 2.8-kilometre hiking trail and lookout. Anglers can fish in the lake for nineteen different species. Another popular recreational pursuit here

is cycling, as there are over 11 kilometres of paved road in the 149-hectare park itself, plus trails that permit bikes. To entertain the entire family there is an adventure play area and a nature house with summertime interpretive programs, and this facility now rents kayaks. Other commercial recreational activities (boat rentals, para-sailing, mini-golf, horseback riding, and go-carts, for example) are easily accessible in the North Shuswap and surrounding area.

> Additional information

The park was established in 1956 and named after the Secwépemc (Shuswap) People, whose artifacts were found here. Although there is no overnight boat mooring at Shuswap Lake, the nearby Shuswap Lake Provincial Marine Park offers this option, as well as six developed and eight undeveloped camping locations along all four arms of the lake. As already noted, this area is extremely popular during the summer months and may not be to everyone's taste at that time, as it presents the more commercial side of camping in BC parks. For those who want to experience the delights of the lake from a quieter vantage point, Herald and Silver Beach provincial parks are tranquil alternatives.

SILVER BEACH

> Location

Campers who wish to enjoy the waters but not the crowds of Shuswap Lake should head for Silver Beach. This somewhat remote provincial park is located 65 kilometres from Scotch Creek. Turn off Highway 1 just east of Squilax and

take the paved road to Scotch Creek. The road to the park from Scotch Creek is only partially paved (expect approximately 42 kilometres on gravel). Gas and limited provisions are available near the campground.

> Facilities

Silver Beach has 35 vehicle/tent campsites located in a forest of Douglas fir and aspen at the head of the Seymour Arm of Shuswap Lake. The campground offers the basic amenities (pit toilets, picnic tables, drinking water, fire pits).

> Recreational activities

As this quiet campground is at the northern end of Shuswap Lake, all activities involving the lake can be enjoyed here: swimming at a delightful sandy beach, fishing (for trout, and nineteen other species, according to BC Parks literature), boating, canoeing, windsurfing, water-skiing, etc. In August and September, it is possible to view sockeye salmon spawning in the Seymour River, which runs into the lake near the campground. Wildfowl observation is good, and there is also a short trail along the top of the beach.

> Additional information

The remains of Ogden City, an old gold rush town of the late nineteenth century, can be seen here if you are prepared to navigate a somewhat overgrown trail. An old graveyard and archaeological sites are also in the park. With its beautiful sandy beaches, the Silver Beach area is popular with sailors and houseboaters exploring the lake, so expect to share your tranquility with more than just your fellow dry-land campers. Houseboating is a very popular activity on the four arms of Shuswap Lake: at the height of the season, as many as 350 houseboats can be navigating its waters. Silver Beach provides a quieter and less commercialized view of Shuswap Lake than Shuswap Lake Provincial Park, but it does not have all the facilities the larger park offers.

SKIHIST

> Location

Anyone stopping here will be rewarded with brilliant views of the Thompson Canyon, but be sure to remember the sunscreen, as Skihist is situated in an area prone to very high summer temperatures. This quaint 33-hectare provincial park is found 8 kilometres east of Lytton on Highway 1. Services are available in Lytton. (Note: This park is temporarily closed for the foreseeable future while BC Wildfire Services work to restore the area in the aftermath of the Lytton Wildfire in the summer of 2021.)

> Facilities

Fifty-eight well-positioned, quiet camping spots (including 4 walk-in ones for tents only) are available, set in a lightly forested area high above the Thompson and Fraser Rivers with great views of the Coast Mountains. The park has both pit and flush toilets, a sani-station, and wheelchair accessibility (there is one wheelchair-accessible pit toilet). Reservations are not available. There is also a large day-use area, which is a popular resting place in the summer.

> Recreational activities

Recreational activities in the park including picking saskatoon berries, which are plentiful at a certain time of year, taking photographs, admiring the fantastic views and looking for the elk that have been introduced to the area. The campground is a good base for those who wish to try white-water rafting; trips are easily arranged through commercial businesses in Lytton and Spences Bridge. Hiking is possible from the trailhead in the campground. One trail leads to Gladwin Lookout, a 90-minute hike that rewards hikers with excellent views of the mountains. Another loop includes portions of the Cariboo Gold Rush Trail. Remember to take along lots of water, as this area can be very hot in the summer. Although there is no fishing in the park, along Highway 1 it is possible to catch trout, steelhead, and salmon.

> Additional information

Skihist Provincial Park includes part of the old Cariboo Wagon Road used by the early pioneers of the province. Its main attraction must be the fantastic views of the Thompson Canyon, where water gushing over thousands of years has cut into the pre-glacial valley floor. (The fact that the park has flush toilets is another attraction!) Lytton, at the junction of the Fraser and Thompson Rivers, claims to be Canada's official "hot spot," although its northern neighbour, Lillooet, disputes this claim. As neither community has a weather station, the debate continues, but be prepared for some hot days if visiting Skihist in the peak summer months. The campground was recently updated to ensure it could easily accommodate even the largest RVs.

STEELHEAD

> Location

Set in an almost desert environment, Steelhead, which began operating in 1997, really is the baby of provincial parks. The 37-hectare park is located on the site of one of the oldest homesteads in the Interior, which was also a ferry stop and a stagecoach depot. Steelhead is an excellent base for exploring the city of Kamloops, Kamloops Lake, the mighty Thompson River, and the surrounding plateau scenery. The campground itself is rather spartan and is found 40 kilometres west of Kamloops on Highway 1, just west of Savona, which has food, gas, and supplies.

> Facilities

The campground is situated at the outflow of Kamloops Lake. Forty-four camping spots are available, all quite open, but half of them overlook the lake. There are flush toilets, showers, and wheelchair-accessible pit toilets. Steelhead is also one of the very few BC parks with water and electricity hook-ups (10 sites). In addition to firewood, ice can be purchased onsite.

> Recreational activities

Campers can enjoy swimming from a good 240-metre beach and canoeing in Kamloops Lake. There is also fishing here and in the many plateau lakes in the region. There is only a cartop boat launch in the park, but Savona has a public boat launch a short drive away. Naturalists will appreciate the wildlife in the area, which includes deer, elk, and mountain sheep, plus migratory waterfowl, shorebirds, and songbirds. The city of Kamloops is only a short drive away and is the major centre of the region. Just south of the campground is the community of Logan Lake, where fascinating tours of the Highland Valley Copper mine can be taken.

> **Additional information**

BC Parks should be sincerely thanked for establishing a number of additional campgrounds in the High Country Region twenty years ago. Steelhead is the most developed; other recent additions are Momich Lakes, Tunkwa, and Roche Lake, but they have only primitive camping facilities. All were once forestry campsites, but BC Parks became responsible for their administration in 1997. On a personal note, I do not find the Steelhead Campground very appealing, probably due to the lack of vegetation and the near-desert surroundings. I prefer Juniper Beach, just down the road, which is more spacious and offers better views. If staying in this region, be prepared for some very high temperatures, and remember to put on some sunscreen.

STEMWINDER

> **Location**

Between 1904 and 1955, $47 million in gold was extracted from the mountains adjacent to 4-hectare Stemwinder Provincial Park, and rumour has it that there is still some left. So what are you waiting for? There's gold in them thar hills! The park's small roadside campground is very much geared toward overnight stops and is located 35 kilometres east of Princeton on Highway 3, next to Hedley. Services are available in Hedley and at a store adjacent to the campground.

> **Facilities**

The campground of pine trees offers 27 spots on the banks of the Similkameen River. Only the basic amenities are available (drinking water, pit toilets, picnic tables, fire pits). One of the pit toilets is wheelchair accessible. A number of the camping spots are quite close to the road, so expect the noise of traffic. Reservations are accepted for all sites.

> **Recreational activities**

Because this campground is geared toward overnight camping, there are limited recreational activities. The waters of the Similkameen River can be fished but are fast-flowing. Caution must be taken by those who wish to swim; only strong swimmers should consider it. A number of people try tubing from this location, and you can try your luck at panning for gold, an activity that began here at the turn of the twentieth century. Be careful to avoid the poison ivy found along the riverbank. If you drive 25 minutes along Highway 3, the Grist Mill and Gardens at Keremeos cannot be too highly recommended. This BC Heritage site is the last remaining pioneer flour mill in western Canada, dating back to 1887. When I visited, a man on a penny-farthing cycled around the wonderful gardens. My children delighted in feeding chickens and collecting eggs, and the tearoom served delicious pastries and desserts. Well worth a visit (oldgristmill.ca).

> Additional information

When visiting this area, it is worth turning off Highway 3 to explore the museum, the older architecture, and the back roads in and around Hedley. The quaint Similkameen community dates to the early 1900s, when the Nickel Plate Mine, one of BC's first hardrock mining operations, was established 1,200 metres above the town. The mine operated from 1904 to 1956, extracting gold, silver, and copper. The remnants of the Mascot Mine's buildings can be seen perched on a cliff high above the town.

sẁiẁs (HAYNES POINT)

> Location

In 2015, this extremely popular provincial park, formerly known as Haynes Point, was renamed sẁiẁs to reflect its cultural and archaeological heritage following the discovery of two important archaeological sites in the campground. It is a great shame that this popular campground is not larger than its 38 hectares. For the longest time, whenever I attempted to stay in this idyllic setting, it was full. I finally succeeded in September 2002—my one and only overnight visit—and got the last remaining space, even at that supposedly quiet time of the year. It is located at the southern end of the Okanagan River Valley, in the rain shadow of the Cascade Mountains on Osoyoos Lake, just 2 kilometres from Osoyoos on Highway 97. In 2021, it was not well signposted.

Sweeping views on Pender Island.

The jade glacial waters of Muncho Lake are but one of the many wonders along the Alaska Highway.

Majestic mountain views at Sx̱ótsaqel / Chilliwack Lake.

Newcastle Island offers scenic walks under arbutus trees just a stone's throw away from Nanaimo. PHOTO COURTESY OF TORI ELLIOTT

The subalpine waters of Nancy Greene Lake are a
lovely spot for swimming, fishing, and sailing.

Majestic mountains and mirror lakes of are among the wonders
of Strathcona, BC's oldest provincial park.

A railway line snakes long the water's edge in beautiful BC. PHOTO BY TREVOR AND RICHARD JULIER

The national parks along the BC–Alberta border are a wildlife watcher's paradise. PHOTO BY TREVOR AND RICHARD JULIER

ABOVE Two Jack Lake Campground, Banff National Park. PHOTO BY TREVOR AND RICHARD JULIER

OPPOSITE Driving East on Highway 1 into Yoho National Park. PHOTO BY TREVOR AND RICHARD JULIER

Fintry Provincial Park and beach on Okanagan Lake. PHOTO BY TREVOR AND RICHARD JULIER

Take a journey into the past at Fort Steele. PHOTO BY TREVOR AND RICHARD JULIER

ABOVE Paddling on Emerald Lake, Yoho National Park. PHOTO BY TREVOR AND RICHARD JULIER

OPPOSITE Driving to Moraine Lake, in Banff National Park. PHOTO BY TREVOR AND
RICHARD JULIER

The Langham Hotel in Kaslo, BC, one of the historical sites that can be visited from nearby Kootenay Lake and Kokanee Creek provincial parks. PHOTO BY TREVOR AND RICHARD JULIER

BC Ferries *Osprey*, the longest free ferry ride in the world, which takes travellers across Kootenay Lake. PHOTO BY TREVOR AND RICHARD JULIER

The Railway Museum at Revelstoke. PHOTO BY TREVOR AND RICHARD JULIER

A grizzly bear at home under the Rockies in Alberta. PHOTO BY TREVOR AND RICHARD JULIER

Waterton Lake, village, and townsite campground at twilight. PHOTO BY TREVOR AND RICHARD JULIER

OPPOSITE TOP Park your RV for the night at Lockhart Beach, one of the province's better roadside campgrounds. PHOTO BY TREVOR AND RICHARD JULIER

OPPOSITE BOTTOM Enjoy beautiful coastal sunsets from Saltery Bay.

ABOVE Mt. Robson, resplendent under the sun.

Wells Grey Provincial Park, aptly known as "the waterfall park."

The climb up Stawamus Chief offers a fun challenge to hikers and rock climbers, with rewards of breathtaking views from the top. IMAGE COURTESY OF BC PARKS

ABOVE Historic cabins just off the Alaska Highway north, in Silver City.
COURTESY OF THE GOVERNMENT OF YUKON

BELOW Sun, sand, and surf in Canada's north. COURTESY OF THE GOVERNMENT OF YUKON

> Facilities

It is little wonder this is a popular retreat, as all of the 41 camping spots are located on a narrow sandspit with over half of them having direct access to the beach. There are both flush toilets and pit toilets (one flush toilet is wheelchair accessible), but no sani-station or showers. Reservations are accepted but only for a maximum of seven nights for all 41 sites.

> Recreational activities

The deep Okanagan River Valley, formed by glacial erosion, receives less than 35 centimetres of rain per year and is classified as a "semi-arid shrubland." (It is frequently mislabelled as being a part of the Sonoran or Great Basin Deserts, though neither of those regions reach BC.) The lake is reputed to be the warmest in the country, making it a magnet for swimming, boating (there is a boat launch), and fishing for rainbow trout and bass. Forty-three different varieties of fish can be found in the lake. The fish are huge here and can easily be seen from a trail in the park. There are short trails, which have boardwalks and interpretive boards. The warm climate and lack of precipitation promote desert-loving plants such as ponderosa pine, bear cacti, sagebrush, and grease-wood, which in turn provide a habitat for a wide array of bird, animal, and reptile life (including species unique to this area of BC, such as the Great Basin spadefoot toad, burrowing owl, and desert nightsnake).

> Additional information

The Sylix People have lived, hunted, and fished in the area for millennia; two archaeological sites in the park provide evidence of this long history. It is an extremely popular location during the peak summer months, although it can be extremely hot at this time. The area's climate ensures a pleasant stay for those who visit in the spring and fall. Some of the Okanagan's finest vineyards and fruit farms are found in this region. From May to November, fresh fruit and vegetable stands at the side of the highway provide produce for campers to enjoy around an open fire. Besides the high summer temperatures, the only disadvantage to this campground is that at certain times it can be a little noisy, as the sound of traffic and music is easily audible from the town of Osoyoos across the water. The park is now administered by the Osoyoos Indian Band.

sx̌ʷəx̌ʷnitkʷ (OKANAGAN FALLS)

> Location

In 2015, the Okanagan Falls park was renamed "sx̌ʷəx̌ʷnitkʷ," the traditional name of this area, meaning "little falls," and its management taken over by the Osoyoos Indian Band. It is found at the town of Okanagan Falls, which is off Highway 97, south of Skaha Lake, 20 kilometres south of Penticton. All services can be found in "OK Falls" and in Penticton.

> Facilities

The picturesque campground with 25 spacious camping spots is set among a forest of deciduous trees just above the Okanagan River. It has an extremely neat and tidy feel about it, and when I last visited, in June 2021, all the spots were taken by large RVs whose owners seemed as if they'd been there for years. The campground is wheelchair accessible and provides flush and pit toilets, but no sani-station or showers. The campground is 100 percent reservable but is closed the third weekend in September for the Okanagan Alliances Salmon Festival (see syilx.org).

> Recreational activities

Like the two other provincial parks in the immediate vicinity (Vaseux Lake and Inkaneep), the area is rich in bird and animal life and therefore makes a good location for nature study and photography. A species of small sonar-equipped bats is found here, in addition to a wealth of other birds and animals. Fishing is possible in the Okanagan River, and the park has horseshoe pits. The area is rich in grapevines, and visitors can tour the local wineries. The community of Okanagan Falls has an excellent ice cream store and fudge shop, which campground research has required me to evaluate in depth for all nine editions of this book. I would also recommend a visit to Linden Gardens, home to over 3 hectares of gardens and a lovely tea house in the nearby community of Kaleden.

> Additional information

Anyone looking for spectacular waterfalls will be disappointed as the falls here have been reduced to rapids due to rock blasting for water control in the area.

The museum at Okanagan Falls is housed in a restored 1909 prefabricated building that was ordered from a catalogue, shipped in pieces, and assembled here. It contains artifacts and memorabilia of the pioneer Bassett family. I really have the impression that this is a campground geared to the retired RV owner who wants to put down roots for weeks and do little other than sit in the shade, listen to the river, and pass the time with fellow campers. It's a campground geared more to adults than to children.

TUNKWA

> Location
Tunkwa Provincial Park covers a massive 5,138 hectares of land not far from Logan Lake, a town established in 1970 for the 1,000 employees of the Highland Valley Copper Mine. The park is situated 16 kilometres north of the town, off Highway 5, but can also be accessed off Highway 1 at Savona or from the Coquihalla Highway. All access roads are good gravel routes. The nearest services are at Logan Lake; Kamloops is 40 kilometres away.

> Facilities
Tunkwa, Leighton, and Leighton North are the three campgrounds here, offering a total of 275 spaces, some with excellent views of the lake. The vast majority are informal "cluster" sites that allow up to four groups to camp together; 55 sites are of the kind traditionally found in BC Parks. Only the basic amenities are available (pit toilets, picnic tables, fire pits, and drinking water). Reservations are not accepted and the park boasts itself as a year-round recreational area.

> Recreational activities
Trout fishing is popular not only at this location but also in the multitude of lakes in the vicinity. Tunkwa and Leighton Lakes are known for their excellent trout fishing, with Tunkwa voted one of the top ten provincial rainbow-trout locations. (I have a firm mental image of the individuals involved in this research!) There is a boat launch at each lake, but it is also possible to swim, canoe, and kayak here. Logan Lake has a nine-hole golf course, and tours of the copper mine can be arranged. Horseback riding is available at a few of the corrals in the area and is

an excellent way to experience the rugged landscape. BC Parks says that wild horses can be seen grazing in meadows adjacent to Tunkwa Lake. Be advised that ATV use is also popular here, so noise can be a problem.

> Additional information

Formerly the site of a forestry campground, the park was initially established to protect an area of fragile grassland and wetland. It is popular in winter for ice fishing, snowmobiling, and cross-country skiing, but in the summer it is really a venue for the fishing community. Sites 54–66 and 70–79 have been designated "long-stay" sites. In 2022, these could be rented for a minimum of four consecutive weeks for a fee of $70.00 per week. Like other parks in this area of the province, it can become extremely hot during the peak summer months, so come prepared. A major wildfire swept through Tunkwa during the deadly summer of 2021, so while the park is once again open for use, it is being managed with post-wildfire recovery as a priority and visitors are advised to be cautious of the potential long-lasting hazards resulting from wildfires.

VASEUX LAKE

> Location

"Vaseux" is French for "silty," and this shallow, weedy lake is one of Canada's foremost birding areas and a real magnet for ornithologists. Between Highway 97 and the lake sits 12-hectare Vaseux Lake Provincial Park, located just 4 kilometres south of Okanagan Falls and 25 kilometres south of Penticton.

> Facilities

Surrounded by cliffs, this 12-spot roadside campground contains all the basic amenities found in BC Parks (pit toilets, picnic tables, drinking water, fire pits) and is wheelchair accessible. There is no sani-station. As the highway is close to the campground, noise from traffic is audible and constant, but the advantage is that the camping spots are right on the lake.

> Recreational activities

A variety of grasses, weeds, and willow vegetation provide a home for birds and animals, so this area attracts ornithologists and wildlife enthusiasts. Waterfowl and birds calling the park home include trumpeter swans, widgeons, Canada geese, wood ducks, blue-winged teal, chukar partridge, wrens, swifts, woodpeckers, and dippers. California bighorn sheep inhabit the cliffs near the park, and smaller animals in the area include beavers, muskrats, deer, mice, rattlesnakes, and turtles. Vaseux Lake is excellent for fishing in both winter and summer and yields largemouth bass, rainbow trout, and carp. The park also has a beach for sunbathing and swimming. There is no boat launch and powerboats are prohibited, but canoeing and kayaking are permitted on the lake.

> Additional information

Just north of the park is the Vaseux Lake Bird Observatory, in addition to two wildlife management units operated by the federal and provincial governments. If you are an ornithologist, Vaseux Lake really is the place to be, as over 160 species of birds can be seen. Anyone interested in gardens should visit Linden Gardens in Kaleden. There is a great cafe, and the gardens are inspired by English country and coastal gardens. There are also numerous wineries in the region.

WELLS GRAY

> Location

BC Parks previously called Wells Gray a "vast, untamed, and primitive wilderness." The 541,000-hectare park displays a landscape formed by volcanoes and water and contains two large river systems, five huge lakes, numerous small lakes, streams, waterways, rapids, and waterfalls. The main entrance to Wells Gray is 40 kilometres from the community of Clearwater on a paved access road. The road from Helmcken Falls to Clearwater Lake is gravel. The park can also be reached by travelling

88 kilometres on a secondary road from 100 Mile House, and there is also access from Blue River. Services are located at Clearwater and 100 Mile House.

> Facilities
In addition to numerous wilderness camping spots, Wells Gray has three vehicle-accessible campgrounds. Two of them are accessed from the Clearwater approach road: Pyramid has 50 campsites while Clearwater Lake/Falls Creek has 80 campsites, divided between two campgrounds. Reached from the 100 Mile House entrance off Highway 97, the Mahood Lake Campground has 39 splendid, huge sites. Clearwater Lake and Falls Creek have a sani-station and some park facilities and trails are wheelchair accessible. There are only pit toilets and no showers. Reservations are accepted at Clearwater Lake (20 sites), Falls Creek (41 sites), and Mahood Lake (34 sites).

> Recreational activities
How do I even begin to describe one of the best provincial parks in BC? There are hundreds of things to see and do at Wells Gray, BC's fourth-largest provincial park. Fortunately, BC Parks publishes informative leaflets on all the recreational activities, and this information is a must for anyone wanting to gain maximum benefit from a holiday. Numerous trails run through the park and lead to waterfalls and creeks; some of the trails are open to mountain bikes. Boat launches are provided at Mahood and Clearwater Lakes, and canoeing and kayaking are very popular in the park (especially on Murtle Lake, which prohibits powerboats). Fishing is reputed to be good in Canim River, Mahood Lake, Murtle Lake, and Murtle River, and the best swimming is at Mahood Lake. It is impossible to count the number of waterfalls in the park, but two of the best known are Helmcken Falls (three times higher than Ontario's Niagara Falls) and Dawson Falls. Down the road at Spahats Creek day-use area is the magnificent Spahats Creek Falls. From a lookout, visitors can view the 122-metre-deep canyon carved by Spahats Creek to the 61-metre waterfall that cascades down the volcanic precipice to the Clearwater River below. Be sure to bring a camera, as I think these falls are more spectacular than the more popular Helmcken and Dawson falls. The park was affected in 2021 through 2022 by floods, so check the BC Parks website for updates on closures and ongoing restoration work, and plan accordingly.

> Additional information

This massive provincial park is named after the Honourable Arthur Wellesley Gray, minister of lands for BC from 1933 to 1941. A travel information centre at the junction of Highway 5 and Clearwater Valley Road has all the information you need to know about the park and has a wonderful, huge moose outside that makes for a good photograph. This area of the North Thompson is becoming increasingly popular with outdoorspeople, who come to explore the hectares upon hectares of undisturbed forest, abundance of lakes, rivers, and streams, fantastic mountain scenery, kilometres of trails, and moderate summertime temperatures. Over the course of the last thirty years since I have been visiting and writing about Wells Gray, the amount of detailed information available about this park has grown tremendously, as indeed have the number of tour companies and guiding businesses that provide excursions into the park. Anyone visiting has a wealth of well researched, detailed resources to draw upon in planning their trip. A park that demands more than just an overnight visit.

Kikomun Creek Provincial Park is beautiful and varied; it is home to a large population of western painted turtles.

Illecillewaet Campground is one of the camping areas in spectacular Glacier National Park.

BC ROCKIES—PROVINCIAL

JUST MENTIONING THE famous Canadian Rockies conjures images of high snow-capped mountains, icefields, glaciers, huge lakes, fertile valleys, rushing rivers, and dramatic waterfalls. When you travel in this region of BC, you won't be disappointed—you will see all these splendid features and more. Despite its great beauty, this part of the province is not densely populated.

This chapter provides details of the provincial parks situated in the Rocky Mountain/Kootenay area of the province accessible from Highways 1, 93/95, 95, 3, 3A, 31, and 6. There are few large camping spots here; instead, the accommodation tends to consist of campgrounds with fewer than 100 camping spots but they are nestled in some of the most breathtaking scenery you'll ever see.

Peckham's Lake, in Norbury Lake Provincial Park.

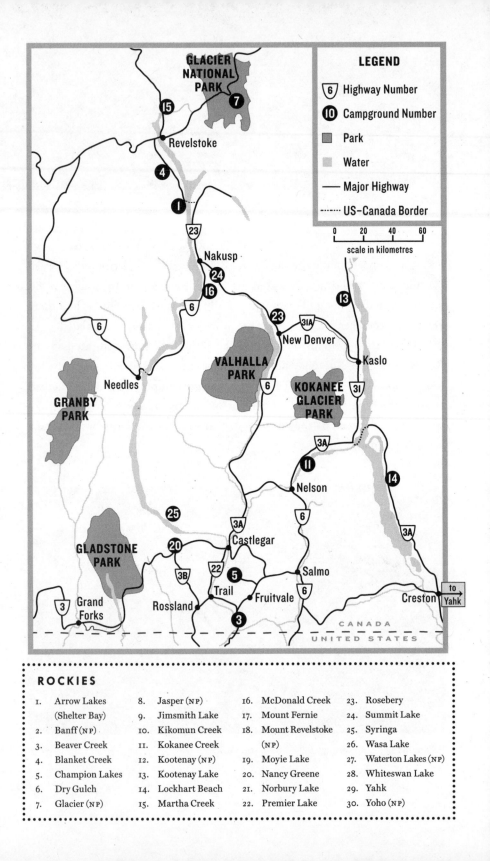

LEGEND

6 Highway Number
10 Campground Number
■ Park
■ Water
— Major Highway
⋯ US–Canada Border

0   20   40   60
scale in kilometres

GLACIER NATIONAL PARK
15
7
Revelstoke
4
1
23
Nakusp
24
16
6
6
23
31A
New Denver
13
VALHALLA PARK
6
KOKANEE GLACIER PARK
Kaslo
31
GRANBY PARK
Needles
3A
11
Nelson
14
6
25
3A
GLADSTONE PARK
20
3A
Castlegar
3B
22
5
Trail
Salmo
6
Rossland
Fruitvale
3
Grand Forks
3
Creston
to Yahk

CANADA
UNITED STATES

ROCKIES

1. Arrow Lakes (Shelter Bay)
2. Banff (NP)
3. Beaver Creek
4. Blanket Creek
5. Champion Lakes
6. Dry Gulch
7. Glacier (NP)

8. Jasper (NP)
9. Jimsmith Lake
10. Kikomun Creek
11. Kokanee Creek
12. Kootenay (NP)
13. Kootenay Lake
14. Lockhart Beach
15. Martha Creek

16. McDonald Creek
17. Mount Fernie
18. Mount Revelstoke (NP)
19. Moyie Lake
20. Nancy Greene
21. Norbury Lake
22. Premier Lake

23. Rosebery
24. Summit Lake
25. Syringa
26. Wasa Lake
27. Waterton Lakes (NP)
28. Whiteswan Lake
29. Yahk
30. Yoho (NP)

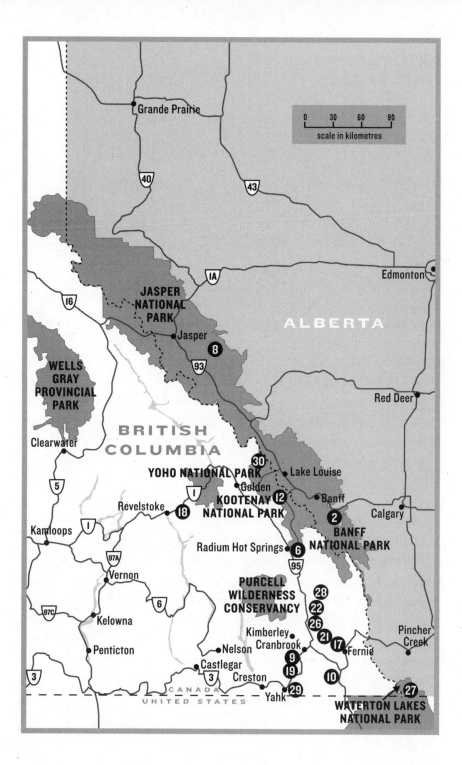

Grande Prairie

40

43

1A

Edmonton

16

JASPER
NATIONAL
PARK

Jasper

8

93

ALBERTA

WELLS
GRAY
PROVINCIAL
PARK

Red Deer

Clearwater

BRITISH
COLUMBIA

5

Revelstoke

1

30

YOHO NATIONAL PARK

Golden

Lake Louise

12

KOOTENAY
NATIONAL PARK

Banff

18

2

BANFF
NATIONAL PARK

Calgary

Kamloops

1

97A

Vernon

Radium Hot Springs

6

95

PURCELL
WILDERNESS
CONSERVANCY

97C

6

Kelowna

28

22

26

Kimberley

21

Pincher
Creek

Penticton

Nelson

Cranbrook

17

Fernie

3

Castlegar

3

Creston

9

19

10

CANADA
UNITED STATES

Yahk

29

27

WATERTON LAKES
NATIONAL PARK

0   30   60   90
scale in kilometres

ARROW LAKES
(SHELTER BAY)

> Location

Pack a camera and marvel at the sunsets from the quaint little 97-hectare roadside campground located on the western side of Upper Arrow Lake. This park is reached by taking Arrow Park Ferry from Galena Bay, just south of Nakusp, or by travelling 50 kilometres on Highway 23 south of Revelstoke (which has all services).

> Facilities

Seventeen camping spots are positioned quite close together and, as there is no vegetation, they afford little privacy. Some do, however, overlook the lake, providing beautiful views of the water and the landscape beyond. Only the basic amenities found in BC parks are available (pit toilets, picnic tables, drinking water, fire pits). Those who prefer flush toilets and sinks can find them a short walk away at the Shelter Bay ferry terminal.

> Recreational activities

This campground is primarily for overnighters. The lake is excellent for swimming (though the water is not that warm) and fishing for rainbow trout, Dolly Varden, and kokanee. There is a boat launch, and it is possible to canoe and kayak from the park.

> Additional information

This is a pleasant place to stop because of its proximity to the lake and for the views of the rugged Selkirk Mountains that reach over 3,000 metres. Although the campground is near the road, traffic ceases around 9:30 PM when the ferries stop, so the location is very peaceful at nighttime. The five-minute ferry ride from Shelter Bay to Galena Bay is free and provides a beautiful break from driving to enjoy the scenery. I stayed here in August, and the campground was barely half full. With no traffic noise and a beautiful lake in which to bathe, this is definitely one of the better roadside camping spots.

BEAVER CREEK

> Location

Beaver Creek is a Class C provincial park, jointly administered with the Kiwanis Club of Trail. As a result, the services provided may differ slightly from other BC parks. The park is found on the eastern side of the Columbia River, close to Trail Airport (which isn't very busy, so noise shouldn't be a problem). Access is from Highway 22A, 10 kilometres from Trail where all services are located. The nearest local store is 4 kilometres north of the park at Waneta Junction.

> Facilities

This 89-hectare park's campground has 19 vehicle-accessible, semi-shaded camping spots beautifully situated along the Columbia River. About half are suitable for the largest RVs. The campground only has pit toilets, but, unusual for this type of park, there is also a shower building with flush toilets, which are wheelchair accessible. Reservations are possible by calling the Kiwanis Club of Trail at 1-250-367-9165.

> Recreational activities

The popular day-use area has a huge picnic shelter, as well as a grassy area for ball games, a softball area, a concrete basketball court (very unusual for a BC park!), and bocce ball court. There is also a boat launch in the park, but it is only recommended for four-wheel-drive vehicles. Because of the Columbia River's very swift currents, BC Parks recommends it only to experienced and able canoeists and kayakers. Fishing is possible for rainbow trout, walleye, and whitefish. A hiking trail popular with locals meanders along the banks of the river at the south of the campground and there is a play park for children.

> Additional information

The park is very popular with day-trippers from the Kootenays, and I have the impression this is very much a locals' campground. The campground host lives at the entrance to the campground to collect fees and ensure everyone remains a happy camper. For those with children to entertain and who want to leave the campground for a few hours, there is a great outdoor pool and water slide on Highway 38 just before Rossland when approaching from Trail. The gold mine in Rossland is also well worth a visit and has something for every age group.

BLANKET CREEK

> Location

In its former life, Blanket Creek was a busy homestead, and it is easy to see why the original pioneers chose to settle here. Created in 1982, this delightful 318-hectare provincial park is located at the point where Blanket Creek enters the Columbia River, 25 kilometres south of Revelstoke on Highway 23. The nearest services are available at Revelstoke.

> Facilities

With the addition of two new campgrounds and many new campsites in 2017, the number of sites at Blanket Creek increased from 63 to 105—large, well-positioned camping spots for every size of vehicle. They are set in a lightly forested area and all have spectacular views of the Monashee Mountains. Some of the better spaces are adjacent to meadow areas. There are flush and pit toilets, showers, and a sani-station at the park's entrance. Reservations are accepted for 67 spaces. Long-stay camping (four consecutive weeks or longer) is available here, but only early in the season.

> Recreational activities

In the day-use area of Blanket Creek, a large beach-rimmed lagoon ideal for swimming has been constructed and a trail leads from the campground to the pool. There is a playground here and a dog beach a 10-minute walk away. A 5-minute walk along Old South Road takes campers to the beautiful 12-metre-high Sutherland Falls. Fishing in both the creek and Upper Arrow Lake can yield Dolly Varden, rainbow trout, and kokanee, and in the fall, kokanee can be seen spawning in the mouth of the creek. The nearby town of Revelstoke is a lovely place to visit, offering a golf course, a railway museum, a piano museum, and a local history museum, as well as a number of cobbled streets and turn-of-the-century buildings to explore. Nakusp Hot Springs are also worth a visit (nakusphotsprings.com).

> Additional information

The site contains the remains of the Domke homestead, one of the few properties unaffected by the flooding of the Arrow Reservoir. The land was abandoned in the late 1960s when the Hugh Keenleyside Dam near Castlegar was completed and the Arrow Reservoir flooded. Blanket Creek supplies a pleasant quiet camping experience suitable for every age group.

CHAMPION LAKES

> Location

Situated in the Selkirk Mountains east of Trail at an elevation of 1,067 metres, this chain of three lakes set in a 1,422-hectare provincial park provides a taste of the true Kootenay experience. Champion Lakes is an 18-kilometre drive from Fruitvale and is reached by turning off Highway 3B after 6 kilometres and taking a paved road. There are services at Fruitvale and at Trail.

> Facilities

The facilities at this 95-spot campsite include drinking water, a sani-station, and flush and pit toilets. There is also a large day-use area with wheelchair-accessible flush toilets. The campground itself is located between Second and Third lakes, with trails leading to the water. All spots are large, shady, and private, set in a forest of Douglas fir, pine, and spruce. Reservations are accepted at 44 sites.

> Recreational activities

Described as a canoeist's dream, this park supplies a ribbon of lakes and portages and offers brilliant paddling potential. Development is concentrated around Third Lake, which has a boat launch, playground, picnic area, and change house, but Second Lake also has a rustic gravel boat launch. All three lakes prohibit powerboats. There are two good beaches, so swimming is a popular pastime here, and there is a buoyed swimming area for kids. Another popular pursuit is angling for rainbow trout, which are stocked in the lakes. Onshore, more than 6 kilometres of hiking and walking trails lead from the campground: the Third Lake Trail is a 1.5-kilometre trek and is a popular stroll between the Main and Campers beaches on Third Lake, while the Second Lake Trail is about 2.5 kilometres long and has sections of boardwalk and good views.

> Additional information

The trio of lakes is named after James W. Champion, who was an early settler and orchardist in the area. First Champion Lake is about 1,500 metres long, and Second and Third are each about 800 metres long. The park's location between the coastal and dry biotic zones results in a diversity of plant species, as well as more unusual animals such as beavers, porcupines, minks, and muskrats. Painted turtles also frequent the lake. If canoeing is your passion, you should definitely include Champion Lakes on your list of prime paddling locations. Families are also big winners here, as there is a wonderful beach and the waters are relatively warm. We stayed here once when Syringa Provincial Park was full. My children were in the water until 8:00 at night, and I marvelled at the way the beach was free of goose poop. We loved it so much that we returned on two other occasions. Another wonderful BC provincial park.

DRY GULCH

> Location

If hot springs are your passion, you'll love Dry Gulch. This beautiful little campground is less than 5 kilometres south of Radium Hot Springs, at the foot of Redstreak Mountain amid steep-sided gullies eroded by glaciers. All amenities can be found at Radium Hot Springs, just a short drive away (radiumhotsprings.com). The campground is one kilometre from Highway 93.

> Facilities

Dry Gulch Provincial Park consists of 27 campsites set in a lightly forested area of Douglas fir and ponderosa pine. It's one of the better small campgrounds: all sites are large, private, and able to handle every type of recreational vehicle; some have tent pads. There are flush and pit toilets but no sani-station or showers. The park is wheelchair accessible and there are wheelchair-accessible flush toilets. The campground is located just far enough from the main road that traffic noise is not a problem. Reservations are accepted at 18 sites.

> Recreational activities

Bighorn sheep are often observed on the grassland behind the campground, but one of the biggest attractions of staying here is your proximity to the world-famous Radium Hot Springs, which are located in Kootenay National Park. Prior to their formal development in 1911, the springs had been used for centuries by the Ktunaxa, Secwépemc, Kainai, Stoney Nakoda, and Piikani Peoples. Dry Gulch is an excellent, quiet campground for enjoying the mineral waters. In addition to the springs, the resort has a cafe and shop. Other recreational activities in the vicinity include golf courses and the towns of Invermere (where there is a boat launch) and Radium. There's also easy access to the Panorama Mountain Resort, which is a great place to hike, golf, and take children (panoramaresort.com).

> Additional information

As this 29-hectare park is adjacent to Kootenay National Park on the western slope of the Continental Divide, the campground is often used as an overspill location when the national park campgrounds are full. In addition to the hot springs, Kootenay National Park has more than 200 kilometres of hiking trails and features alpine meadows, snowfields, lakes, and mountains.

JIMSMITH LAKE

> Location

It's easy to see why this park is popular with both visitors and locals. Although Jimsmith Lake Provincial Park is relatively small (14 hectares), it is well situated at the western end of the Rocky Mountain Trench and surrounded by a forest of Douglas fir, spruce, western larch, aspen, and lodgepole and ponderosa pines. The campground is reached by taking

Highway 3/95 south from Cranbrook, then heading west on a paved road. All services are available in Cranbrook, which is just 5 kilometres away.

> Facilities

Thirty-five large, private, well-spaced campsites suitable for every type of vehicle are available here (as long as you can navigate a gravel road with a few potholes). The park has all the basic amenities (drinking water, fire pits, picnic tables, pit toilets) and a couple of sites have views of the lake. There is no sani-station.

> Recreational activities

Campers can enjoy a lovely sandy, developed swimming beach, grassy picnic area, canoeing and kayaking, and fishing for jumbo rainbow trout and large-mouth bass. Powerboats are not allowed and the 14-hectare park is frequently used for picnics and day trips by locals who relish the tranquility it offers. The nearby town of Cranbrook houses the Cranbrook History Centre, where trains from an earlier era are shown and tea can be taken. Cranbrook also boasts a self-guided heritage tour that highlights buildings dating from 1898 to 1929. Sixteen kilometres from Cranbrook is the heritage town of Fort Steele, where more than sixty buildings from the turn of the twentieth century have been restored to recreate a bygone era, and an awesome bakery delivers wonderful baked goods.

> Additional information

This 14-hectare park is a popular destination in the wintertime for ice fishing, ice-skating, cross-country skiing, sledding, and tobogganing. The economy of Cranbrook has been built on mining, fishing, and the railway. It is the largest town in the region and five provincial parks are within a 30-minute drive. Jimsmith Lake has a very "local" feel about it, and the campground offers a rather urban (although pleasant) camping experience. When I last visited the park, there were several groups of teenagers in the day-use area, which made me presume this area was used well into the evening. Fortunately, the day-use area is located far enough away from the campsites that noise from adolescents is not a problem.

KIKOMUN CREEK

> Location

Sometimes human influence is beneficial. Such is the case at Kikomun Creek Provincial Park in the southern part of the Rocky Mountain Trench by Lake Koocanusa. This human-made lake was created by the construction of Libby Dam on the Kootenay River in Montana. The park is reached by turning off Highway 3 at Elko and travelling 8 kilometres west, or by turning  off at Jaffray and travelling 16 kilometres south. Jaffray has a store/gas station, coffee shop, and pub, and there is a marina 4 kilometres from the campground selling gas, propane, and food. A concession stand also operates in the park.

> Facilities

This campground has recently created additional campsites as well as a new shower block. Located in three campgrounds (Surveyors, Ponderosa, and Kalispell Trail) are 171 sites that can accommodate every type of recreational vehicle, though some of the newer sites are the "stall" type and offer little privacy. There are flush and pit toilets, a sani-station, and showers, and some park facilities are wheelchair accessible. Surveyors Campground has the older shower building and the best location. Reservations are accepted at 140 sites, and cabins are available to rent. Fourteen locations at Ponderosa have hook-ups. Ponderosa and Kalispell Trail are closer to the lake.

> Recreational activities
Fishing in this park is varied and good. The smaller lakes (especially Hidden Lake and Surveyors Lake) offer potential for catching bass, eastern brook, rainbow trout, and Dolly Varden, while the 144-kilometre-long Koocanusa Reservoir has cutthroat trout and Rocky Mountain whitefish (and a boat launch). Powerboats are not permitted on the smaller lakes, thus ensuring a peaceful time for paddlers, and canoes can be rented in the park. There are two beaches, and picnic areas are found at Surveyors Lake. Hiking trails around the smaller lakes (30 to 90 minutes) offer opportunities to see elk, deer, badgers, and ospreys. Old roads and railway beds give hikers and bikers easy access to the 682-hectare park. For young campers, there is an adventure play-ground, and interpretive programs are offered.

> Additional information
Kikomun Creek Provincial Park has one of BC's largest painted turtle populations, so-called because of the bright pattern underneath their shells. The turtles can often be seen soaking up the sun. Kikomun Creek is a beautiful and varied place, ideal for a family vacation. It reminds me of an English country estate.

KOKANEE CREEK

> Location
It is difficult to imagine anyone not enjoying a visit to Kokanee Creek— especially if you have children—as this popular provincial park has a wealth of activities for campers of all ages. I think it's one of the best in BC. The 260-hectare park is situated amidst the beautiful scenery of the Slocan Range of the Selkirk Mountains on the west arm of Kootenay Lake, 19 kilometres east of Nelson on Highway 3A. Services are conveniently located in Nelson or Balfour (15 kilometres away).

> Facilities

Kokanee Creek has 189 wooded camping spots in four locations—Osprey Point, Sandspit, Friends, and Redfish—off paved lanes and suitable for every size of vehicle. Redfish is closer to the road, and Friends is quite tightly packed, making Sandspit my personal preference. The site is home to the Kokanee Creek Nature Centre and the facilities here are good and include flush toilets, showers, and a sani-station. Sandspit also has a wheelchair-accessible campsite, flush toilet, and shower stall. Reservations are accepted at 132 sites; 13 sites have electrical hook-ups.

> Recreational activities

You can easily spend a week at Kokanee Creek. There is a wealth of things to see and do, both in the park itself and in the immediate vicinity. Activities linked with the water include swimming from wide sandy beaches (over 1 kilometre of beach is on offer here), boating, water-skiing, and wind-surfing. The fishing is reported to be excellent for both rainbow trout and kokanee, and the park has a boat launch. There is a large children's play area, a visitor centre that has exhibits of natural and human history and hosts interpretive programs, and there are a number of trails. The nearby town of Nelson boasts the largest concentration of heritage buildings in BC, and farther north on Highway 3, visitors can explore the Cody Caves near Kaslo or relax in the therapeutic mineral pools at Ainsworth Hot Springs (ainsworthhotsprings.com).

> Additional information

The spawning channel and visitor centre here make this a truly educational place to visit. The word kokanee is derived from the Sinixt word "kekeni," the name given to the landlocked salmon that spawn here in large numbers (the average is 2,000 to 4,000, but the number has been as high as 20,000). When I first stayed here, it was late August and the spawning was at its peak. At dusk, bald eagles and ospreys can be seen diving for salmon, and although it is sad that a few of these fish who have come so far with the sole thought of spawning will meet their demise so close to their destination, the spectacle is straight from a National Geographic television program. The salmon, together with the many other activities and the beautiful location, make this provincial park well worth a visit in August or September. I last visited in September 2020 when many trails were closed due to bear activity, so we walked the one which wasn't closed, which was also where we saw the black bear ambling in front of us.

KOOTENAY LAKE

> Location

Kootenay Lake Provincial Park has two beautiful, quiet campgrounds located on the west side of Kootenay Lake, north of Kaslo on Highway 31, in the heart of Kootenay country. There is little to distract the camper other than mountain scenery and bald eagles flying overhead. Services can be found in Kaslo, a 30-minute drive south.

> Facilities

Forty-two campsites are available at two locations: Davis Creek and Lost Ledge. Some sites are very close to the lake and afford fantastic views of the Purcell Mountains. There is no sani-station and the facilities are the basic ones found in BC Parks (pit toilets, drinking water, fire pits, and picnic tables). There is a wheelchair-accessible campsite and pit toilet at Lost Ledge. Reservations are accepted at 10 sites at Davis Creek.

> Recreational activities

Leisure pursuits include swimming (but take it from one who knows—the water here is very cold; BC Parks describes it as "refreshing"), boating (there is a boat launch at Lost Ledge), paddle boarding, windsurfing, kite boarding, and fishing for kokanee, bull, and rainbow trout. In addition, the quaint town of Kaslo is well worth a visit. In Kaslo, you can rent canoes, kayaks, and bikes to explore the lake and surrounding area, or just enjoy exploring this characterful town of the Kootenays. To the south, Ainsworth Hot Springs provides a relaxing afternoon activity where you are invited to enter a cave and experience the hot waters (ainsworthhotsprings.com).

> Additional information

The campgrounds are located on a very quiet section of Highway 31. When I stayed, I cycled north to Duncan Dam, then on to Howser, which has a small cafe. The highway follows the lake and has excellent views. There is another provincial park children and adults will adore located a short distance from Kootenay Lake: Cody Caves has no camping facilities and is located in the Selkirk Mountains just above Ainsworth Hot Springs, 11 kilometres down a good forest road off Highway 31. Visitors to this provincial park are treated to a full array of spectacular cave formations, including stalagmites, stalactites, waterfalls, draperies, rimstone dams, and soda straws. You must wear protective clothing and hard hats (the necessary equipment is provided) when taking the highly informative tours offered by BC Parks.

LOCKHART BEACH

> Location

This quaint lakefront provincial park, established in 1939, covers just 8 hectares and is therefore one of the smallest in the province. It's located on the east side of the south arm of Kootenay Lake, 19 kilometres south of Crawford Bay. Food and lodging are available at Crawford Bay; more comprehensive services are located at Creston, an hour's drive south (40 kilometres).

> Facilities

The campground, primarily used for overnight stops, has 18 camping spots across the road from the lake that are suitable for every type of camper. It features the basics (pit toilets, pump water, fire pits, and picnic tables). There is no sani-station or access for those in wheelchairs, and campers are advised to boil their drinking water for at least 5 minutes. Traffic noise from the road is audible, but a couple of sites are close to the creek, where you'll hear the babble of water instead.

> Recreational activities

The park has a lovely, quiet beach area where you can swim, canoe or kayak, or fish for rainbow trout and Dolly Varden. You can also catch rainbow trout in the Lockhart Creek. A trail leads from the park and through a forest of Douglas fir, redcedar, and ponderosa pine along the creek. It takes about 3 hours to hike the trail, which has an elevation gain of 800 metres.

> Additional information

Highway 3A from Creston to Kootenay Bay is a lovely drive that takes tourists past small stores, galleries, and an amazing circular glass house that a retired funeral director constructed out of 500,000 square embalming-fluid bottles. Definitely the only one like it in Canada, if not the world, the house is 7 kilometres south of the campground. At Kootenay Bay, travellers can take the Kootenay Lake Ferry—the world's longest free ferry ride—across the lake to Balfour (kootenaylake.bc.ca). If you take the Osprey, you will be able to experience the excellent little cafe onboard. Be sure you're hungry when you embark: the breakfast is very good, as is watching the lake go by as you eat. This boat trip offers excellent photography opportunities and is recommended to everyone holidaying in the area. Lockhart Beach is definitely one of the better roadside campgrounds.

MARTHA CREEK

> Location

The views from this 71-hectare park, which overlooks the Revelstoke Reservoir, stretch on to the Monashee Mountain Range and provide fantastic photography opportunities. In June, a blanket of colourful wildflowers covers the campground. For these reasons alone, Martha Creek is a delightful place to sojourn, and it is located just 20 kilometres north of Revelstoke on Highway 23. All services are available in Revelstoke.

> Facilities

Located on an old river terrace on the western shore of Revelstoke Reservoir, Martha Creek has recently been developed and now offers 75 campsites, almost half with access directly onto the beach, although some are quite close to each other, restricting privacy. There are flush and pit toilets, showers, and a sani-station. There are 9 wheelchair-accessible campsites. Reservations are possible for 52 sites.

> Recreational activities

A 300-metre swimming beach is located near the campground, and you can fish in the Revelstoke Reservoir for rainbow and bull trout (there's a boat launch at the southern end of the park). An enchanting 7-kilometre hiking trail leads walkers through wildflowers, cedar, and hemlock and on to flowering meadows and alpine lakes within the Sleeker Mountains. There is a children's playground and a large grassy field with a volleyball net. The historic town of Revelstoke has been restored over the last few years and is an appealing place for shopping and wandering. In the summertime, the bandstand in the town's plaza has evening entertainment for visitors. I spent a lovely August evening dancing to a local band as the sun went down—just the sort of light exercise needed before retiring to the tent or RV.

> Additional information

When staying in this vicinity, you must visit the Revelstoke Dam, one of North America's largest and most modern hydroelectric developments, located 5 minutes from Revelstoke on the road to Martha Creek. Mica Dam, 2 hours north of Revelstoke on Highway 23, is also worth a visit. Both offer fascinating tours of their facilities and interesting programs on how and why they were constructed. In 1999, as we travelled toward Revelstoke over Robson Pass with the rain pouring, I called in to the hotel to inquire about a room for the night: $125.00 plus tax! We travelled on to Martha Creek, and the skies cleared and the sun shone. We spent much, much less to camp in a field full of wildflowers and wonderful smells! A few years later, we returned and discovered Canyon Hot Springs, about 20 kilometres east of Revelstoke on Highway 1. Here there are two wonderful hot mineral pools where you can soak in therapeutic waters while surrounded by mountains. Recently renovated and worth a visit (canyonhotsprings.com).

MCDONALD CREEK

> Location
Ten kilometres south of Nakusp on Highway 6, this 468-hectare provincial park occupies land on both the eastern and western shores of Upper Arrow Lake. Camping facilities are situated adjacent to the highway on the eastern side of the lake. It's a perfect location for an evening's beach barbecue or lunchtime picnic. All services are found in Nakusp.

> Facilities
Over the recent past, the McDonald Creek park has expanded considerably. Seventy-three relatively private campsites are available in a lightly forested area, some overlooking the lake. There are flush and pit toilets, showers, a sani-station, and electrical hook-ups for 18 sites. There is access for the disabled. Reservations are accepted for all spaces.

> Recreational activities
Massive Arrow Lake is the central source of activity. You can swim, sunbathe, sail, and fish for kokanee, bull, and rainbow trout. The water levels in the lake fluctuate: in June, there is mud, but a sandy beach is revealed in July and August. A boat launch is available in the park. The nearby town of Nakusp is renowned for its hot springs, located north of the town, 12 kilometres down a gravel road. The pools are high in the Selkirk Mountains; one is 38°C, the other 41°C. The views from these outdoor pools to the Selkirk Mountains are quite spectacular, and if you visit at the right time you could have this facility all to yourself. A 20-minute drive farther north of Nakusp on Highway 23 is Halcyon Hot Springs Resort. The original world-famous hotel was destroyed by fire in 1955 but rebuilt in 1999. Today, the timber-frame day lodge offers a licensed

restaurant, two mineral hot pools, and a heated swimming pool, all situated on a steep hillside next to Upper Arrow Lake.

> Additional information

Arrow Lake, like Kootenay Lake, holds Gerrard trout, the world's largest rainbow trout. When I visited, I had to stay at the overspill site, but even so, I had a wonderful time cooking dinner by the lakeside on a hibachi and watching the sun go down. Although it was full, the campground did not appear crowded, and it has a good ambiance. As with other communities in the Kootenays, the economy of Nakusp has depended on the logging industry since 1910 and, notwithstanding some diversification, remains so today. There are a number of stores, restaurants, and coffee shops in this quiet town, which provides an ideal location to break a journey. Evidence of the logging industry is never far away from the traveller vacationing in the Kootenays.

MOUNT FERNIE

> Location

Rich in legends of unrequited love, broken promises, and catastrophes, this 259-hectare park in the shadow of Mount Fernie has been described as the eastern gateway to the Kootenays. It is located 3 kilometres south of Fernie on Highway 3. Services are provided at Fernie.

> Facilities

The campground has 64 vehicle-accessible sites set among a parkland of diverse vegetation including western larch, Douglas fir, black cottonwood, trembling aspen, western redcedar, and spruce. Campsites here can accommodate all sizes of RVs. There are flush and pit toilets, as well as showers, but no sani-station. Reservations are accepted at 36 sites.

> Recreational activities

The main attraction of this park is a 3-kilometre interpretive trail that winds its way through the park and takes visitors to picturesque Lizard Creek and waterfalls. The walk from the parking lot to the falls also makes a pleasant short trip for those people not intending to spend the night here. The trail continues on past the falls, but when I was last here it was badly signposted and no maps were available, so I couldn't explore it to the extent I would have liked. Hopefully, BC Parks will have updated the signposting when you visit. The park has areas of old-growth forest, and there are wildlife-viewing opportunities: you may see black bears, elk, or deer, which are common here. The town of Fernie, just 3 kilometres from the park, has a historical museum, buildings dating back to 1904, a historical walking tour, and a cultural centre and restaurant on the site of the former Canadian Pacific Railway station. It also has an array of individualistic shops that I had a wonderful time exploring in 2020. Mountain biking is popular in the area, and there are lots of trails at Fernie Alpine Resort, but this activity is not permitted within Mount Fernie Provincial Park.

> ### Additional information
Fernie is named after William Fernie, who was instrumental in the development of coal mining in the area. Over the history of the town, a fabricated legend spread that William Fernie found out about the coal deposits from the Ktunaxa People by promising to marry the Chief's daughter. After gaining this information, he rejected her, thereby provoking her father to place a curse on the name "Fernie." The town subsequently suffered many calamities that were blamed on this curse: a mine explosion killed 128 men in 1902; there were two fires in 1904 and 1908, the latter leaving 6,000 people homeless; and several floods. Although there is no veracity in this story, in 1964, Mayor James White of Fernie and the Ktunaxa Nation performed a ceremony to "lift the curse" as a gesture of goodwill. Some people still believe that on summer nights the ghost of William Fernie rides across the face of Mount Hosmer with the Ktunaxa woman and her father in pursuit.

MOYIE LAKE

> ### Location
A restful, relaxing time awaits campers at this beautiful 90-hectare provincial park. Adjacent to the eastern fringe of the Purcell Mountains near the northern end of Moyie Lake, the campground is a wonderful retreat, especially for

folks with young children. Established in 1959, the park is 20 kilometres south of Cranbrook (where all services are available) and 5 kilometres north of the community of Moyie on Highway 3/95. Moyie got its name from the French word "mouillé," which means "wet."

> Facilities

The 111 camping spots are all large and private, but do not have views of the water. The campground has a sani-station, plus flush toilets, and showers (including facilities exclusively for those in wheelchairs). The only downside here is the railroad near the campground, which may cause problems for light sleepers. Reservations are accepted at 59 sites, and long-stay camping (four weeks at a time) is also available.

> Recreational activities

A wealth of activities can be enjoyed at Moyie Lake. Campers can hike the Meadow Trail or the Kettle Pond Trail, which offer interpretive signs describing the forest typical to the area (both are 2 kilometres long, 45 minutes return). Swimming is easy from a protected swimming area, and there are 1,300 metres of beach. For anglers, the lake contains ling cod, kokanee, burbot, rainbow trout, and eastern brook trout. A boat launch is available and windsurfing is possible, weather permitting. Children can be kept busy at the adventure playground. For those who enjoy mountain biking, a half-day trip up a gravel road to Mineral Lake, formally a forestry recreational site, is a fun excursion.

> Additional information

Moyie Lake is a delightful place to set up camp and an ideal place to spend time if you have a young family, although the campground is not just for those with children. The nearby town of Cranbrook supplies all services should you have forgotten any basic camping items. When I last stayed here, the only drawback was the three jet skiers who shattered the calm of the afternoon and made me appreciate the lakes on which powerboats are prohibited. My advice to those who prefer a smaller, quieter experience is to try Jimsmith Lake instead.

NANCY GREENE

> Location

This lovely 203-hectare park is just as popular in the wintertime as it is in the summer. Named after Canada's world-famous Olympic skier Nancy Greene, who came from the Rossland–Trail area, this provincial park is nestled in the  Rossland Range of the Monashee Mountains, 29 kilometres north of Rossland on Highway 3, at the intersection of Highway 3B. Services can be found at either Rossland or Castlegar; both communities are about a half-hour drive from the campground.

> Facilities

There are 14 formal campsites here, primarily geared to tenters and smaller recreational vehicles. These sites are not great, being closely packed and adjacent to the car park. Larger RVs are allowed to camp in the parking lot. All the basic facilities exist (pit toilets, picnic tables, pump water, fire pits). There is no sani-station or wheelchair access. Noise from traffic is audible, but the road is not tremendously busy, especially at night.

> Recreational activities

The park itself and the adjacent recreational area of the same name contain the subalpine Nancy Greene Lake, and there's a lovely beach area where you can swim, fish for rainbow trout, or sail (powerboats are not allowed). A self-guided, 5-kilometre nature trail leads around the lake, and the recreational area offers more than 20 kilometres of hiking trails. The area is popular in the winter for both downhill and cross-country skiing. The park has a covered picnic shelter and an old log cabin with a wood-burning stove.

> Additional information

The picturesque town of Rossland dates back to the turn of the century. More recently, it has gained a reputation for mountain biking. Just outside Rossland is the Le Roi gold mine, where visitors are taken underground to become acquainted with the life and work of a hard-rock miner. Between 1900 and 1916, the Le Roi mine produced 50 percent of BC's gold and swelled the population of Rossland to 7,000 before its demise in the 1920s. The mine is a great place to visit and tour, as is the adjacent museum (rosslandmuseum.ca). Both Trail and Rossland are delightful communities to spend time in. I was here in the summer of 2020, and a local author had set up a table to sell her self-published work, which detailed the history of the area and its characters. The best thing about camping is undoubtedly the wonderful characters you meet at these breathtaking locations.

NORBURY LAKE

> Location

Norbury Lake is nestled in the Hughes Range of the Rocky Mountains and supplies excellent views of the Steeples— a distinctive feature of the Hughes Range and the Purcell Mountains. The 97-hectare provincial park is easily found 13 kilometres southeast of Fort Steele on a paved road from Highway 93/95. Services are available at Fort Steele. The campground is approximately 1 kilometre away from the day-use area at Peckham's Lake.

> Facilities

This is a secluded location, with 46 gravel camping spots set among a lightly forested area of Douglas fir, lodgepole pine, ponderosa pine, and western larch. The number of trees decreased considerably in June 1998 when a strong wind blew through the area, causing the campground to close for more than two weeks (fortunately the two families camping at the time were not hurt). Facilities are restricted to the basics (pump water, fire pit, picnic tables, pit toilets). There is no sani-station or wheelchair access. Long-stay camping (minimum four weeks) is permitted at 2 sites.

> Recreational activities

Recreational pursuits within the park include fishing for rainbow trout in Peckham's Lake, swimming, and boating (there is a boat launch but powerboats are prohibited). Two trails are available to lead explorers through a diverse area of lightly forested landscape where it is possible to see elk, deer, and Rocky Mountain bighorn sheep. Norbury Lake is close to the historic town of Fort Steele, a fascinating example of early twentieth-century life in Canada and a real delight to visit. In 1961, the provincial government recognized Fort Steele as a place of historical significance. A perfect example of a pioneer town, it contains some sixty buildings, including an original North West Mounted Police camp, excellent bakery, restaurant, theatre, and museum (fortsteele.ca).

> Additional information

Norbury Lake is named after F. Paget Norbury, a magistrate who served in Fort Steele in the late nineteenth century. This park is situated within the traditional lands of the Ktunaxa Nation. An informative display giving details of Ktunaxa culture and history is found at the Peckham's Lake entrance.

PREMIER LAKE

> Location

This region, on the traditional lands of the Ktunaxa Nation, attracts visitors for its splendid views. Premier Lake is in the Hughes Range of the Rockies, about 45 kilometres northeast of Kimberley. It is reached by turning off Highway 93/95 at Skookumchuck (which is a Chinook word meaning "strong or turbulent water") and travelling 9 kilometres on a paved road, then 5 kilometres on a gravel road. (Watch for logging trucks, which frequently travel along this route.) A gas station, shop, and restaurant are available at Skookumchuck.

> Facilities

Set among Douglas fir, western larch, cottonwood, and aspen trees are 57 campsites suitable for all vehicles, some with tent pads and some adjacent to a bubbling creek. Facilities are the basics (pump water, fire pits, picnic tables, pit toilets). Some facilities in the park (including a pit toilet and picnic site) are wheelchair accessible. An unusual, manually operated, solar-heated shower is available here; plastic shower bags are no longer supplied by the park, so make sure you bring your own. Reservations are accepted and advised for 20 of the sites.

> Recreational activities

Seven lakes—Premier, Canuck, Yankee, Turtle, Quartz, and the two Cat's Eye lakes—exist in this 837-hectare park, which has gained a reputation as a good spot to fish for eastern brook trout and Gerrard rainbow trout. A short walk from the campground, there is a spawning and viewing area together with an interpretive display to explain enhancement procedures, including how eggs are collected for the Kootenay Trout Hatchery. Forty percent of rainbow trout eggs required for the provincial egg hatchery system come from here and are distributed to over 350 lakes and streams in the province. Premier Lake has a boat launch, and swimming is available. The park also contains a number of trails that cover a variety of distances and take between 20 minutes and 5 hours to complete. For children, there is an adventure playground.

> Additional information

The area is rich in wildlife—watch for elk roaming on the cleared hills near the highway. Premier Lake is yet another BC provincial park located amidst spectacular, breathtaking scenery. It is a little off the beaten track and offers a very adult camping experience. When I last visited, the campground was very busy. A gorgeous location, but the camping spaces are quite tightly packed.

ROSEBERY

> Location

Rosebery Provincial Park has undoubtedly one of the better campgrounds dedicated primarily to one-night stops. The scenery here is lovely: visitors can gaze across Slocan Lake to the majestic Valhalla mountains. The 32-hectare park is situated on Highway 6, between Nakusp and New Denver, where services are available.

> Facilities

Campers can take their pick of 33 large, private, shady camping spots suitable for every type of recreational vehicle. Some overlook the rushing Wilson Creek, while others are closer to the road (although the road is not busy at night). There is no sani-station or wheelchair access, and the facilities are basic (pit toilets, drinking water, fire pits, and picnic tables). Long-stay camping is available and reservations are accepted for some sites.

> Recreational activities

There are few activities to pursue in the park itself. Wilson Creek runs through the park and has a short trail leading along its edge. Fishing for rainbow trout is possible. By crossing nearby Slocan Lake you can explore and hike the much larger Valhalla Provincial Park. There are also a number of private golf courses in the area. New Denver is a delightful place to wander around, and a number of lovely coffee shops have recently sprung up to entice tourists to linger. This early twentieth-century community has some wonderful buildings that are currently being restored to their former glory. Unfortunately, the town's summer season is quite short.

> Additional information

Located directly across Slocan Lake from Rosebery is Valhalla Provincial Park. This is a region of dramatic and diverse wilderness that includes lakes, alpine meadows, and the impressive New Denver glacier. Despite limited road access, the park offers 50,000 hectares of beautiful, unspoiled land to explore. Observant sailors heading toward Valhalla can spot pictographs painted by the forefathers of the Arrowhead First Nation on the western shoreline of Slocan Lake. There are also a lot of hot spring resorts in the area to explore.

SUMMIT LAKE

> Location

Although this tiny 6-hectare provincial park was established in 1964, the campground only opened in 2001, making it one of BC's newer provincial park campgrounds. Situated at the southwestern corner of Summit Lake, it is one of only two campgrounds in the Slocan Valley (Rosebery is the other) and therefore a much-needed addition to the area. It can be found on Highway 6 between New Denver and Nakusp. The nearest services are at Nakusp, 18 kilometres north.

> Facilities

Summit Lake is one of the better roadside campgrounds. Some of the 35 vehicle-accessible sites are quite closely packed together, but a number have wonderful views of the lake and are set in a lightly forested area of hemlock and cedar. Although the campground is quite near the road, noise is not much of a problem, as traffic is not heavy. There are flush and pit toilets, drinking water, and fire pits, as well as a picnic shelter with a wood stove. Reservations are accepted.

> Recreational activities

When my family visited, the biggest attraction for us was skimming stones on the fantastically calm waters of Summit Lake. The lake has 100 metres of pebbly beach and is quite warm and attractive for swimming. There is a small trail that meanders from the day-use area to the campground. The campground has a boat launch, and canoeing and kayaking are popular pastimes. Fishing is also reputed to be good, as the lake is stocked with over 10,000 rainbow trout annually (do you ever wonder whose job it is to count them?), and the local fly-fishing championships are held here. New Denver and Nakusp are pleasant places to wander through and stop for coffee in, and you'll find the wonderful Nakusp Hot Springs to the north of Nakusp.

> Additional information

This park could easily have been named Toad Provincial Park. It houses an important breeding ground and migration habitat for western toads.

Information boards in the park describe these primarily nocturnal creatures. In the fall, thousands of toads emerge from the lake and head for the adjacent forest to hibernate. Each year in August the park hosts Toadfest—an event to help toads cross the road and to encourage education about these creatures. It is worth camping here just for this event. Other wildlife includes eagles, kingfishers, hawks, bears, and mountain goats. Summit Lake is a delightful addition to the campgrounds of the province, but it can be quite cool early in the season.

SYRINGA

> Location
On a creek on the eastern side of Lower Arrow Lake, Syringa Provincial Park covers 4,499 hectares below the Norns Range of the Columbia Mountains. The lake, on the Columbia River, resulted from the construction of the Keenleyside Dam. The campground is reached by turning off Highway 3A just north of Castlegar and travelling 19 kilometres on a paved road. All services are available in Castlegar, a 25-minute drive away, while a nearby marina and store offer more limited supplies.

> Facilities
Eighty-six large, private spots, some overlooking the water and others adjacent to a grassy meadow, are available in a forest of redcedar, western hemlock, and ponderosa pine. In addition to the basic facilities, Syringa has a sani-station, showers, flush and pit toilets, and wheelchair access (including wheelchair-accessible flush toilets). Reservations are accepted at 54 sites and 9 sites have electricity connections.

> Recreational activities
Syringa boasts a fantastic rocky beach from which to view the Columbia Mountains and Monashee Range. Though water levels fluctuate, all forms of aquatic activity are possible, including swimming, boating, water-skiing (the park provides the only public boat launch in the area, but be warned—the waters can be rough when there is a wind), and fishing for kokanee salmon and rainbow trout. For those who prefer non-water-based pursuits, a number

of trails lead from the park for walking and mountain biking. The 4-kilometre Yellow Pine Nature Trail is a particularly pleasant hour-long interpretive trail. There is also an adventure playground and a beautiful grassy area by the beach that's perfect for ball games. When I stayed here, I got chatting with parks staff Pam and Debbie, who told me that the mosquitoes were never a problem here as the wind tends to keep them away—information well worth having.

> Additional information

The park's namesake, Syringa Creek, is named after the syringa (a.k.a. mock orange), a regional white-flowered shrub that blooms in early spring. Nearby Castlegar is rich in Doukhobor history; a heritage museum near the airport details this culture and is worth a visit. Although the paved road ends at the park, an unpaved road carries on to an area known as Deer Park, where there is an attractive waterfall. A few years ago, my family and I made a great boat in the sand here out of driftwood, and my children still talk about it. Along with Alice Lake, this is one of their favourite sites.

WASA LAKE

> Location

This gem of a provincial park provides a comprehensive range of facilities and activities. The campground, one of the largest in the region, lies at the northern end of Wasa Lake, a glacier-formed kettle lake, reputed to be one of the warmest in the east Kootenays, if not the province. Wasa Lake Provincial Park is situated 40 kilometres north of Cranbrook on Highway 93/95. The community of Wasa, 1 kilometre away, has stores, a gas station, restaurants, laundry facilities, and a neighbourhood pub.

> Facilities

With the Rocky Mountains to the east and the Purcells to the west, the views from the Wasa Lake Campground are staggering. There are 104 well-appointed camping spots set among pine and aspen trees, which can accommodate every type of recreational vehicle. There are flush and pit toilets, a sani-station, and showers. The flush toilets (and some other park facilities) are wheelchair accessible. Reservations are accepted at 69 sites.

> Recreational activities

The lake supplies a wealth of recreational activities with four excellent beaches providing access to warm waters. There is a boat launch, and fishing for large-mouth bass is a favourite pursuit. A self-guided 2.7-kilometre nature trail, which takes about an hour to complete, gives details of the flora and fauna of the area. The Lazy Lake Bike Loop is a 33-kilometre mountain-bike ride leading from Wasa Lake to Lazy Lake and back. There is also an adventure playground for children. Beyond the park, the historic town of Fort Steele is only 18 kilometres to the south; likewise, the "Bavarian" community of Kimberley, Canada's highest city, is within easy reach. Here visitors can marvel at the world's largest operating cuckoo clock, stop at gingerbread-fronted stores, or play a round of golf.

> Additional information

Each year on the Sunday of the August long weekend, a sand-sculpture contest is held at Camper's Beach, the main beach on the lake. The park contains a variety of vegetation, including an area of endangered grasslands. A few years ago, Wasa had a bad reputation for mosquitoes, which arrived the second week of July and stayed until the end of August (like most of the tourists), but when we stayed one August they were not an issue. The local population is keen to preserve Wasa as a family camping location. A few years ago they constructed the Wasa Lions Way—an 8-kilometre paved trail encircling the lake for walking, cycling, and rollerblading. A BC Parks representative informed me that two grandmothers in Wasa had recently purchased rollerblades, so keep an eye out for the rolling grannies.

WHITESWAN LAKE

> Location

Driving to Whiteswan Lake can be an adventure in itself. Huge logging trucks frequent the gravel road, and in places it narrows to one lane, necessitating excellent driving skills. The journey is well worth the effort. This provincial park is located on a plateau in the Kootenay Range of the Rocky Mountains, east of Canal Flats, which has a store and restaurant. Both Alces and Whiteswan lakes are contained in the 1,994-hectare park, which has some fantastic views of the surrounding mountains. The park is reached by turning off Highway 93/95 and travelling along Whiteswan Lake Road (gravel) for 18 kilometres. The nearest comprehensive services are at Invermere, 78 kilometres away.

> Facilities

The park has five campgrounds, providing 114 vehicle-accessible spaces. Alces Lake (28 spots) has a sani-station and is reached after travelling 21 kilometres from the main highway; Packrat Point (16 spots) is 24 kilometres from the highway; and Inlet Creek (16 spots) is a further 4 kilometres. Located near the northeastern entrance of the park, White River (17 spots) is off White River Forest Road while Home Basin (37 spots) is off Moscow Creek Forest Road; both are about 33 kilometres from the highway. Home Basin and Alces Lake have lakeside camping and are my personal preferences. All campgrounds offer the basic amenities (drinking water, fire pits, picnic tables, and pit toilets). Home Basin has a wheelchair-accessible campsite. No reservations are taken.

> Recreational activities

One of the main attractions of this location is the undeveloped Lussier Hot Springs, near the park's western boundary. The hot springs flow from the mountainside into a series of pools and, unlike the ones at Radium, Ainsworth, and Fairmont, are unspoiled by commercial development. Both Whiteswan and Alces Lakes provide plenty of swimming opportunities, with a beach at the north end of Whiteswan Lake. The two lakes have among the most productive fisheries in the East Kootenays, and in May and June rainbow trout can be seen spawning in Inlet and Outlet creeks. Boat launches are available at Packrat Point and Home Basin (electric motors only on Alces Lake). An 8-kilometre hiking trail takes walkers from Alces Lake to the Home Basin campground, and there are opportunities for viewing wildlife, such as golden and bald eagles, mountain goats, bighorn sheep, and moose.

> Additional information

Used by the Ktunaxa First Nation for more than 5,000 years, this is an area rich in history. In the 1800s and 1900s, trappers and prospectors worked the region, and today logging is the prime industry—a fact you will be well aware of if you encounter a logging truck on your journey to this beautiful away-from-it-all camping location. It's a huge park not oriented toward families but is great for anglers.

YAHK

> Location
This 11-hectare provincial park is found in a quiet, uncommercialized area of BC, on the banks of the Moyie River. It is close to the United States border and the state of Idaho. Situated on Highway 3/95 at Yahk, 39 kilometres east of Creston, it's very much an overnight camping or picnic spot. Services can be found in Moyie, Yahk, or Creston, or at the gas station just south of the campground.

> Facilities
There are 26 campsites here, able to accommodate every size of recreational vehicle and set amidst a forest of Douglas fir, lodgepole pine, and ponderosa pine. The basic amenities are offered (cooking pits, picnic tables, drinking water, and pit toilets), and the campground is wheelchair accessible. The campground is located close to both the railway line and road, so traffic noise may disturb some campers.

> Recreational activities
Yahk is primarily for one-night camping, or for brief rest stops, as there is not a great deal to do here besides canoeing, kayaking, or fishing in the Moyie River for trout. (We saw a man fly-fishing and he caught two small fish in the space of 30 minutes.) As you travel down Highway 3/95 following the Moyie River, moose and mule deer can be seen feeding, so keep your eyes peeled. The park's day-use area is an ideal picnic spot.

> Additional information
Yahk was once a major supplier of railway ties to the Canadian Pacific Railway, an industry that still exists but has been in steady decline since the 1940s. Today, Yahk has a population of about 350, but it seems to be growing. When we visited in 2008, a new bakery and coffee shop had opened just south of

the campground. Two Scoop Steve's ice cream bar is a must for kids. In 2020, I passed by again and am delighted to report "Two Scoop Steve" was still in business. Set on a hillside overlooking the lake, the pretty community of Moyie to the south has some interesting buildings. Moyie owes its development to silver-lead mining and at one time was the richest mine of this type in the province. This campground can be subject to flooding.

See maps on pages 148–49.

N 1911, CANADA introduced the world's first national parks service, numbering six parks. There are now forty-eight, with a combined area the size of Italy. This chapter lists the six national parks of the Rockies that offer developed, vehicle-accessible (not back-country-only) camping opportunities. Because of their high-altitude location, many campgrounds do not open until mid-June, and most close in early October. It is not unusual to have snow in August, something that needs to be considered by those planning to camp in a tent. Services and fees in these parks vary slightly from those of provincial or territorial parks. Excellent detailed information about all the national parks listed below, including their fees and reservation processes, can be found on the Parks Canada website (see the reservation information on page 7).

BANFF (NP)

> Location

Banff National Park receives over 4 million visitors each year, over half arriving in July and August. So, if there is one piece of advice I would offer to those wishing to visit this iconic and most famous of Canada's national parks, it would be to visit some time other than these busy months. As one of the seven parks in the UNESCO World Heritage site called the Canadian Rocky Mountain Parks, Banff includes snow-capped mountains, glacial lakes, and rich forests, in addition to the towns of Banff and Lake Louise. This national park encompasses 6,641 square kilometres as well as a large section of the Icefields Parkway, a route that runs along the backbone of the mountains and reveals

breathtaking scenery (as long as the weather and visibility is good). The park also features Lake Louise, Moraine Lake (splendid enough to be illustrated on the Canadian twenty-dollar bill for decades) and the slightly lesser known Peyto Lake, all easily accessible by car. Banff National Park runs northwest from Canmore, Alberta, to the Columbia Icefield. All services are provided at the communities of Banff and Lake Louise, which during the summer months can become very, very busy and parking nearly impossible. If you are camping at one of the large Banff campgrounds, consider taking the Roam bus to local places of interest including Lake Louise, and leave your RV at the campground where there is a bus stop.

> Facilities

There are almost 2,500 sites within the numerous campgrounds at this national park. Over 1,000 sites are adjacent to the town of Banff. While this number may suggest there is supply for all, this is not the case during the high season, when overflow campgrounds accept campers. The closest campground to the town of Banff is Tunnel Mountain, which is really three campgrounds rolled into one. It has showers and flush toilets but no hook-ups. One of the largest campgrounds in the province (1,249 spaces), it can become quite noisy and tends to be oriented more toward the RV crowd rather than tenters. For me, it does not offer that away-from-it-all camping experience. Slightly farther from Banff are Two Jack Lakeside Campground (74 sites) and Two Jack Main Campground (380 sites). These are more scenic and secluded. Along the Bow Valley Parkway, 26 kilometres west of Banff, Johnston Canyon Campground has 132 sites; some of the more desirable ones back directly onto Johnston Creek. This campground has showers. Castle Mountain Campground, also on the Bow Valley Parkway, has 43 sites but no showers. While this campground is more basic, it's a great location from which to explore the many trails. About 12 kilometres farther north you will find Protection Mountain Campground (72 sites), with flush toilets but no showers or sani-station. This campground was closed in 2011 and cleared due to destruction by pine beetles; it reopened in 2017 but there is no shade yet as the trees are still quite small. The Lake Louise Campground (395 spaces) has showers and flush toilets. All the campgrounds on the Bow Valley Parkway, including Lake Louise, are close to the railway track and there can be twenty-five to thirty trains a day rumbling through, so you may wish to consider packing earplugs. Reservations are strongly advised, and if you want a fire an additional fee is charged.

North from Lake Louise on the Icefields Parkway there are four campgrounds but these have no reservations. Mosquito Creek (32 sites) located near the Bow River is best suited to smaller RVs and has pit toilets. Silverhorn Campground (72 sites) is a bit of an oddity. It was originally an overflow campground but is now open for regular use. It has only pit toilets and no other facilities, not even water, but is useful if everywhere else is full. Waterfowl Campground (116 sites) is on the Mistaya River, and there are large well separated sites, flush toilets, and a sani-station. There are also good hikes from here, but keep a lookout for moose. About 20 kilometres north is Saskatchewan River Crossing where you will find a hotel, store, and gas station, which has a sani-station. The last campground in the north of Banff National Park is Rampart Creek (50 sites) situated in a lightly wooded area with good views of the mountains and the Saskatchewan River. It is best suited for smaller RVs and has basic facilities.

> Recreational activities

The primary activity in this park is hiking, with trails ranging in size from easy, flat one-hour strolls to overnight, multi-day hiking excursions. The classic Lake Agnes/Big Beehive hike takes walkers to a historic tea house above Lake Louise, while the trip to the turquoise Peyto Lake and Bow Summit is a brief 20-minute walk with amazing views and, at certain times of the year, a stunning amount of alpine flowers. The visitor centres in the communities of Banff and Lake Louise provide free information on the many hikes available. In addition, there are opportunities to bike, ride a horse, and go rafting and canoeing. If the weather is uncooperative, Banff Hot Springs offers a lovely location to hang out, and the town of Banff has numerous shopping and dining opportunities.

The village of Lake Louise, 56 kilometres northwest of Banff, is much smaller and quieter. From here you can access the iconic Moraine Lake. Lake Louise is also the start of the 278-kilometre stretch of the Icefields Parkway up to Jasper National Park. This jaw-dropping road winds through the Rockies, and although the route can be completed in 3 hours, there are dozens of turn-outs and stops for the explorer. I have taken this route on wonderful clear days and been in absolute awe of the vista, but have also suffered the misfortune of travelling the road in early September when heavy clouds obscured the views. There is an element of luck, even in the summer, to experiencing what National Geographic Magazine describes as one of the top ten roads in the world. Make time to stop at the Columbia Icefield Discovery Centre and maybe consider a trip to the Athabasca Glacier, which is rapidly receding.

> Additional information

Banff National Park celebrated its 135th birthday in 2020 and, as mentioned above, is Canada's oldest national park. Established in 1885 after railway workers discovered a cave in the area containing hot springs, it is probably the most famous national park in Canada. Consider a sojourn here when the weather may be more unpredictable, but the crowds are smaller (June or September). Forgo the hot showers (visit the hot springs in Banff instead), camp in the smaller campgrounds, and take time not within the commercial honeypot of Banff, but with a slow multi-day excursion up the Icefields Parkway. Accept that the weather may be uncooperative, but bask in the knowledge that you are not seeing Banff with the masses. That being said, even in peak season it is easy to escape the crowds just by taking one of the longer hikes, although it is advisable to reserve a camping spot. Probably the best way to explore Banff and the Canadian Rockies is to do it in conjunction with Jasper National Park (see page 185). But visit you must.

GLACIER (NP)

> Location

A region of spectacular high-
mountain scenery shaped by
avalanches and snow, Glacier
National Park is found in the
northern Selkirk range of the
Columbia Mountains, 49 kilometres
east of Revelstoke on Highway 1.
The Trans-Canada Highway bisects

this massive park, reaching 4,350 feet at Rogers Pass, where there is a visitor
centre with a theatre and exhibits describing the history of the area. The park
is aptly named: nearly 12 percent of its total 136,500-hectare area contains more
than 400 active glaciers and ice-fields. The towns of Golden to the west and
Revelstoke to the east have services.

> Facilities

Glacier has three campgrounds a short drive from the park's western entrance,
all fairly close together: Loop Brook (20 spots), Illecillewaet (60 spots), and
Mount Sir Donald (15 spots). They generally open around the end of June. The
first two campgrounds have flush toilets, kitchen shelters, and food lockers,
while Mount Sir Donald is more primitive and campfires are not permitted
within it. There are no showers or sani-stations. Only about 25 percent of
spaces are suitable for large RVs. Reservations are taken for Loop Brook, and
all other campsites are on a first come, first served basis.

> Recreational activities

Anyone visiting this national park should stop at the snowshed-shaped visitor centre, which has displays of natural and human history, as well as videos
illustrating various aspects of the park, its early relationship with the railroad, and subsequent development. Park staff are always willing to provide
advice on Glacier's numerous attractions and can gear suggestions to personal
preferences and timelines. Interpretive programs are offered in the summer
months. Twenty hiking trails zigzag across 140 kilometres of park and include

the Abandoned Rails Interpretive Trail, which starts at the Rogers Pass Summit picnic area, and the Hemlock Grove Boardwalk Trail, which provides a barrier-free experience of the rainforest. Unlike other national parks, none of the trails are open to cyclists. Renowned for climbing and mountaineering opportunities, the park also offers potential for canoeing, horseback riding, and fishing for whitefish, Dolly Varden, and trout in the Illecillewaet River. Fishing in national parks is governed by a number of regulations and requires purchasing a permit. Forty kilometres west, Canyon Hot Springs offers two hot pools, whose water is supplied by the adjacent hot springs (canyonhotsprings.com). A short drive away, Mount Revelstoke National Park does not offer camping but does grant access to a 26-kilometre switchback road, the Meadows in the Sky Parkway. At the right time of the year, the alpine flowers are abundant along this route.

> **Additional information**

Even if you do not intend to stay at Glacier National Park, stop and visit the information centre and learn about the history of Rogers Pass, named for the railway engineer Major A.B. Rogers. In 1882, he followed the Illecillewaet River and discovered the pass through which it was possible to construct the railroad. By 1885, railway construction had been completed. In 1956, the Trans-Canada Highway was surveyed through the area, and the road linking the Illecillewaet River to the Beaver River was completed in 1962. Videos and displays give testimony to how hazardous and challenging this construction process was. Today, experts constantly monitor the snow conditions, and there is an avalanche control program. Glacier National Park is very much the poorer relation to the national parks of Banff and Jasper, but it does offer quieter camping in addition to some good picnic spots and rest stops along a busy section of the Trans-Canada Highway. Further information is available on the park's website.

JASPER (NP)

> **Location**

Jasper National Park, created in 1907, is the largest and most northerly of the seven national and provincial parks that form part of the Rocky Mountain

Parks UNESCO World Heritage Site. Encompassing a massive 11,200 square kilometres, Jasper incorporates a section of the Yellowhead Highway, from Edmonton to Mount Robson and the Icefields Parkway (from Jasper to Lake Louise). Jasper was created to protect the upper watershed of the Athabasca River and the Columbia Icefield. It stretches down to meet Banff National Park, positioned on the Alberta side of the Canadian Rockies. With glaciers, mountains, rivers, lakes, and more trails than any other national park in Canada, it receives over 2 million visitors a year.

The town of Jasper is the main commercial outlet for these visitors, with a population of only 4,500.

I much prefer the town of Jasper to the community of Banff. Located where the Athabasca River meets the Miette River and overlooked by the magnificent Mount Edith Cavell (named after an English nurse executed by the Germans in the First World War after helping smuggle over two hundred Allied soldiers into neutral Holland), Jasper has an almost alpine feel. It can be easily explored within 3 hours. The town grew from a Grand Pacific Railway construction site set up in 1911. While the tourists and the tour buses do arrive in droves, it is far less commercial and touristy than Banff.

> Facilities

As with any of the national parks included in this chapter, bear in mind the campgrounds generally do not open until mid-June and they close by mid-October. The camping season, in comparison to other areas of British Columbia, is short. Jasper National Park accepts reservations at Whistlers, Wapiti, Wabasso (all on Highway 93), and Pocahontas (Yellowhead Highway) campgrounds. The Whistlers Campground is located just 3.5 kilometres from Jasper, and with 781 sites, it is the largest, and includes showers, flush toilets, and accommodation for every size of vehicle. It has a number of hook-up sites and comprehensive services, including interpretive programs in the summer and pre-erected tents for rent. Five kilometres from the town, Wapiti Campground has 363 sites, again with showers. Wabasso Campground has 231 sites and can be found 16.5 kilometres from Jasper (no showers). Pocahontas Campground is near Miette Hot Springs, 45 kilometres east of Jasper on the Yellowhead Highway, with 140 sites (no showers).

The remaining campgrounds do not take reservations. Snaring River is only 13 kilometres from Jasper on the same highway, with only 62 rustic spaces (pit toilets, no showers) but the best cheap alternative to accommodation in Jasper. Along the Icefields Parkway are an additional five campgrounds, all with only basic facilities (pit toilets, water, fire pits, picnic table). Wilcox (46 sites) and Icefield (33 tent-only sites with water and pit-toilets, and 100 RV sites, really just a paved parking lot with pit toilets) are close to each other and the Columbia Icefield Discovery Centre; Jonas (25 sites) has heavily treed sites with great privacy, while Honeymoon Lake (35 sites) has a few desirable sites on the water's edge. Kerkeslin (42 sites) has the best views of the mountains.

> Recreational activities

Anyone visiting Jasper National Park should make the visitor centre in the town of Jasper their first port of call. Here, depending on time constraints, the climatic conditions (both existing and expectant), and personal preferences and fitness levels, itineraries can be developed. An easy 8-kilometre trail, partly paved, rings the town and highlights the town's history, providing an introduction to the town. One of the most popular attractions is a tramway that ascends over 973 metres (to 2,277 metres above sea level) with rewarding views. This is Canada's longest and highest aerial tramway (jasperskytram. com). A number of flat, easy trails can be accessed from the town of Jasper alongside the Athabasca River, many open to horses and bikes. Bike rental agencies are in town.

Just driving the Icefields Parkway to Lake Louise or the Yellowhead Highway to Edmonton or Mount Robson Provincial Park will award the opportunity to explore numerous trails and lookouts and, hopefully, scenery. Off Highway 93, popular sites include Mount Edith Cavell and Athabasca Falls, where a bridge and platforms provide views of the thundering water. Driving to Maligne Canyon (about 15 minutes east of Jasper) and then walking the adjacent trails is one of the more popular easy excursions, with a footbridge over the canyon itself. The 22-kilometre-long Maligne Lake is the largest natural lake in the Rockies, and in the summer months, visitors can rent boats or hire a cruise on the lake.

Forty-two kilometres from Jasper, on the Yellowhead Highway, Miette Hot Springs is a little dated, but if the weather is inclement, it is a great excursion, allowing access to the hottest thermal waters in the Rockies surrounded by snow-capped mountains. Although it is possible to fish, the season is short, with the best fishing in Celestine, Princess, Maligne, and Pyramid lakes. As would be expected, opportunities to view wildlife abound. I think I have seen more wildlife in Jasper than any other provincial or national park, and have regularly caught sight of grizzlies, black bears, moose, wolves, mountain goats, and elks, which seem to be very easily spotted adjacent to the town. Finally, Jasper National Park was recently named a Dark Sky Preserve by the Royal Astronomical Society of Canada. One of the truly wonderful things camping offers are the limitless opportunities to stare at the heavens (see jasperdarksky.travel).

> Additional information

Without sounding too biased, I really do prefer the Jasper park to its more famous sister, Banff, to the south. The compact town, the quieter roads, the away-from-it-all hot springs, fewer commercial campgrounds, the vast expanse of trail systems, the wildlife, and the ease with which the visitor can escape other tourists and bond with the environment make it this gal's favourite national park. That being said, the route linking Banff and Jasper, the iconic Icefields Parkway, should not be missed.

KOOTENAY (NP)

> Location

Kootenay National Park is another destination offering mountain scenery and hot springs in the Rockies, appealing to both adults and children. While the adults may be most struck by the

spectacular scenery and wildlife, kids will love the hot springs and the various short walks. During my first visit to Kootenay National Park (not to be confused with Kootenay Lake Provincial Park), I met a park representative who told me that Kootenay was often overlooked in favour of its well-known neighbours, Banff and Jasper national parks. For anyone who has experienced the crowds at Lake Louise or Banff in August, this can only be good news.

Kootenay's 1,406 square kilometres are rich in variety. It is the only park to contain both glacial peaks and cacti within its boundaries, but these are not the only rewards. Radium Hot Springs, numerous gorges, waterfalls, mountains, and two major river systems (the Vermilion and the Kootenay) add to its glory, as do a host of interesting excursions for the tourist. In 1985, UNESCO designated Banff, Jasper, Yoho, and Kootenay national parks as part of a larger World Heritage Site, officially recognizing the beauty and significance of the Rocky Mountains and creating one of the largest protected mountainous areas in the world. The park encompasses land of the Continental Divide and the Columbia Valley. The west entrance is 1 kilometre north of Radium Hot Springs, and the park stretches along 90 kilometres of Highway 93 as it heads north. All services can be found at Radium Hot Springs, and there is also a restaurant, store, and information office at Vermilion Crossing, operated by Kootenay Park Lodge and located roughly in the centre of the park.

> Facilities

Three campgrounds operate within the park's boundaries. The largest and most popular is Redstreak, which is open from late April until the beginning of October and has 242 sites, including 50 with full hook-up and 38 with electricity. Flush toilets, showers, and a sani-station are available, as are

facilities for the disabled. Redstreak Campground is my personal preference, as not only does it have all amenities, but also it is within walking distance to the hot springs (about 15 minutes). This campground is not signposted very well; you enter it by exiting the park and taking a paved road beside the park information centre in Radium Hot Springs on Highway 93/95. Stay here if you want easy access to the hot waters. McLeod Meadows Campground is open from mid-June until mid-September and is 26 kilometres north of Radium Hot Springs between Meadow Creek and Kootenay River. It has 80 spaces, flush toilets, and a sani-station, but no showers. The spaces are large enough for every size of RV and are in a lightly forested area, with some of the best locations being close to the river. The third campground is Marble Canyon, open from mid-June until early September, 86 kilometres north of Radium. With 61 spaces set in a dense, subalpine forest, it is the quaintest of the campgrounds and has flush toilets and a sani-station, but no showers. Reservations are accepted.

> Recreational activities

Radium Hot Springs is probably the best known of BC's hot springs and is among the most developed. It is also the most radioactive in Canada, but don't worry—this radioactivity is too weak to be harmful. The pools are immensely popular; over 400,000 people use the facilities each year. There are two developed open-air pools: a hot soaking pool with temperatures up to 47.7°C, and a swimming pool, 24 metres long, cooled by creek water to 27°C. The smaller, hotter pool nestles within cliff walls, and it is possible to look up to see bighorn sheep on the ledges above the pool. You can access the pools via a trail from Redstreak Campground or by vehicle. For those who arrive unprepared, locker rooms, showers, and swimsuit and towel rentals are all available. This is a great place for kids of every age and is fully accessible for those with disabilities.

One of the joys of Kootenay National Park is the number of short, easy, yet fascinating trails that can be undertaken by any age group. Among the most popular are the following: Olive Lake, a boardwalk trail with interpretative signboards and a fish-viewing platform, 13 kilometres from Radium; Paint Pots (85 kilometres north of Radium Hot Springs), a 2-kilometre trail leading to cold, iron-laced mineral springs that bubble up through the earth and stain it a deep ochre colour; and Marble Canyon, a 1.6-kilometre interpretative trail, easily completed with young children, through an impressive narrow canyon of grey limestone that leads to a pounding waterfall. There are over 200 kilometres of trails in the park, so numerous day hikes are possible in addition to overnight excursions. One of the most popular day hikes is a 10-kilometre,

3-hour return trek to Stanley Glacier through a dramatic landscape of fire and ice. Details of all these routes can be obtained from the park information centre, in the centre of Radium Hot Springs, or at the Vermilion Crossing visitor centre, 63 kilometres north of Radium Hot Springs.

While it is possible to fish for brook and rainbow trout, whitefish, and Dolly Varden, most of the streams and rivers are fed by glaciers, so the water is too cold to yield high fish populations. Only non-motorized craft are permitted on the lakes and rivers in the park. In addition to 179 species of birds found in the park, Kootenay is home to grizzly bears, black bears, wolves, elk, moose, bighorn sheep, and mountain goats. The best time to see these creatures is in the early morning and at dusk. With no developed beach or natural waterfront, Kootenay is not a prime family location if your children are very young.

> Additional information

Interpretative boards at Marble Canyon detail the area's 500-million-year-old geological development. Human habitation is a little more contemporary, but it still goes back a long way. Indigenous Peoples have travelled, hunted, and camped in the region for over 11,000 years. They recognize the magic of the hot springs and regard them as sacred waters, a place to cure illness and to gain spiritual peace. The first registered owner of the hot springs was Roland Stuart, an Englishman who purchased 65 hectares of land, including the hot springs, for $160.00 in the first decade of the 1900s. The government of Canada expropriated the land and springs from Stuart in 1923 and has been responsible for them ever since. Kootenay National Park opened in 1920 and owes its birth to Highway 93, the first road to cross the central Canadian Rockies, which in turn led to the development of motorized tourism. The province of BC gave the park to the government of Canada in return for the road.

For me there are two sides to Kootenay National Park. The southern portion near Radium Hot Springs is busy and somewhat commercialized. It is particularly crowded during the summer, when tourists congregate around the therapeutic waters of the hot springs. The other side of Kootenay is its vast expanse away from the hot waters, which provides a cornucopia of things to see and do. It is easy to spend two to three days travelling slowly through the park, exploring its natural wonders, walking the trails, and camping at the different locations.

MOUNT REVELSTOKE (NP)

> ## Location

This 260-square-kilometre park is relatively small for a national park, but it certainly packs a punch. Established in 1914, it is renowned for its wonderful subalpine wildflowers, rugged peaks, and the Meadows in the Sky Parkway. Mount Revelstoke stands at 480 metres and is situated in the world's only temperate rainforest. Located in the Selkirk Mountains, it is part of the string of national parks (namely Banff, Yoho, and Glacier) that owe their creation to the Canadian Pacific Railway, and although not as popular as its siblings, it receives over 600,000 visitors a year. The town of Revelstoke has all services and is adjacent to the park.

> ## Facilities

There is only one frontcountry campground here, Snowforest, situated in a lightly forested area a 5-kilometre drive from Revelstoke (or 2 kilometres from the town by bike or on foot). Sixty-three camping spots are on offer, a small number only suitable for tents. While there is no sani-station, there are flush toilets, showers, electrical hook-ups, and food lockers. Snowforest accepts reservations for 43 sites, which is advisable. If you are not lucky, though, Glacier is an alternative and there are also a number of backcountry camping options.

> Recreational Activities

There are a number of hikes through the spectacular Columbia Mountains on offer at Mount Revelstoke, from relaxing valley strolls, such as the popular Giant Cedars Boardwalk (500 metres) and the Skunk Cabbage Boardwalk (1.2 kilometres), to arduous, long day hikes. Many of these feature old growth forests, subalpine meadows, and wonderful views. A very informative map with all trail information can be downloaded from the park website. For those who do not want to climb a mountain to experience the summit, a 26-kilometre paved road, which was conceived in 1911 and completed in 1927, leads from the Trans-Canada Highway to Balsam Lake, easily taking the tourist from an elevation of 470 metres to 1,835 metres. The road, known as the Meadows in the Sky Parkway, features numerous look-out opportunities and should not be completed in haste—cameras should be at the ready. Upon arriving at Balsam Lake, strolls and longer hikes await. Be advised that the snow may linger into August, so access to some of these walks may be denied. In addition to hiking, biking is also popular in the summer. Experiencing the wonderful carpet of wildflowers for which the park is known is one of the primary activities here, and bird watching is also popular.

> Additional Information

Over the recent past, the town of Revelstoke has been successful in promoting itself as a key destination for skiing. This is no surprise as Revelstoke promotes itself as the birthplace of alpine skiing in Canada. Here, there are funky restaurants, coffee shops, local breweries, and a delightful shopping centre with various artisans. In addition, museums detailing the history of the railways, the forestry industry, and the town itself can be explored. There is something for everyone. A short drive away, the Revelstoke Dam Visitor Centre offers tours. The Rogers Pass Discovery Centre (in Glacier National Park) should also not be missed. Between October and June, this park is snowbound, restricting camping opportunities to just a few months.

WATERTON LAKES (NP)

> Location

The first time I visited Waterton Lakes National Park, the weather was not brilliant, but as we arrived and took our first steps to the visitor centre, a red fox casually meandered up the adjacent path toward the women's washrooms, just as two women emerged. They were as surprised by the four-footed visitor as we were. From this initial encounter, I knew Waterton was special, and it is. In comparison to other national parks, Waterton is not large and is somewhat out of the way, so it is much quieter, but just as spectacular. This is a national park for every age group, with the majestic Prince of Wales Hotel dominating the skyline. It is located in the southwestern corner of Alberta, 264 kilometres from Calgary and 130 kilometres from Lethbridge. It is a relatively small park, at 500 square kilometres, but that space contains more plant and animal life than the Banff and Jasper parks combined (960 species of plants, 250 species of birds, and over 60 species of mammals). All services can be found within the community of Waterton, which is much less crowded than the towns of Banff, Jasper, or Lake Louise and is consequently a far more pleasant environment in which to spend time.

> Facilities

There are primarily three campgrounds at Waterton Lakes National Park. The main Waterton Townsite Campground, open May to September, is the only one with showers and is located in the town. It is very exposed and can get somewhat windy. While it accommodates tents and all sizes of RV (237 spaces), the openness offers little privacy, and there are no individual fire pits. If you want to be near the cappuccino bars and restaurants, though, it is the place to be. I stayed at Crandell Mountain Campground, which was fantastic, with large sites and excellent views; no showers, but well-kept bathrooms with flush toilets and sinks. There are 129 spaces here, and it's ideal for kids of any age as there is so much to explore just in the surrounding undergrowth or by cycling on the gravel roads. Since 2017, this campground has been closed due to wildfire damage, a situation which will no doubt change. Similarly, Belly River Campground offers the same type of camping experience but is much smaller (24 spaces) and pretty rustic. Reservations are accepted for the Townsite Campground.

> Recreational activities

This national park boasts over 200 kilometres of trails, and what we really appreciated was the number of trails that were easily accessible, not lengthy but nevertheless interesting. From the visitor centre, try the 1.2-kilometre climb up Bear's Hump Trail—well worth it for the views of the lakes. The Linnet Lake loop is wheelchair accessible, so it's ideal if your offspring are in a stroller or want a really easy, short walk. This trail offers lots of interpretive information along the way. There are also a number of far more strenuous hikes. Free trail information is given at the visitor centre, which also offers guided hikes. Canoes, kayaks, paddleboats, and rowboats can be rented at Cameron Lake from a funky little outlet that also sells candy bars, coffee, and fishing supplies.

Boating, water-skiing, and scuba diving are popular on Upper and Middle Waterton lakes, but be warned—the water is cold so wetsuits are advised. Interpretive boat cruises, which have been in operation since 1927 and which take about two and a half hours, seem popular with visitors to Waterton, though they can work out to be quite costly for a family. Bikes are available for rent in the town of Waterton. Mountain biking in the park is limited to five trails. Waterton has a fantastic golf course and a playground, ideally situated opposite an ice cream store, with a water spray park. Park staff offer interpretive programs in the summer at the two main campgrounds, and during the peak summer months, a number of children's programs are offered; check out the visitor centre when you arrive to learn what is available. For the angler, cutthroat trout, rainbow trout, Arctic grayling, northern pike, and whitefish can all be caught. The town itself is flat and a great place to wander and window shop, and the Lakeshore Trail from Waterton itself is a nice stroll. It is possible to swim in Upper Waterton Lake, but the lake is cold and subject to strong winds, and consequently swimming is not a key activity here. Waterton is reputed to have Alberta's highest average annual precipitation (1,072 millimetres); April, May, and June are the wettest months. As mentioned above, the Prince of Wales Hotel is well worth a visit and serves a wonderful "high tea" from June to September, with great views of the lake from the dining room.

> Additional information

Waterton is renowned as the place "where the mountains meet the prairies." It became Canada's fourth national park in 1895, ten years after the first was established at Banff. It meets Montana's Glacier National Park at the border of United States and Canada, and in 1932 both were together designated the world's
first International Peace Park, acknowledging the bonds of peace and friendship between the two countries. In 1995, they were given World Heritage Site designation because of the area's fantastic glacier-carved landscapes and rich biological diversity, with over 1,200 species of plants and animals. The elegant Prince of Wales Hotel, reputed to be one of the most photographed hotels in Canada, was built in 1926 by the Great Northern Railway's president, Louis Hill, and it retains much of its 1920s charm. The downside of Waterton Lakes National Park is the lack of beach or warm waters, and if you stay for more than three days, you'll probably need to wear weather-proof clothing at some time. The upside, though, is far greater: spectacular scenery, brilliant wildlife, and gorgeous wildflowers that seem to dominate every hillside not covered with forest; a number of easy walks; and a lovely camping experience. The four

main lakes—Lower, Middle, and Upper Waterton, and Cameron—can easily
be accessed by car, and the roads provide ample opportunities for picnicking
and exploring. It is a great alternative to Banff and Jasper for those wanting
comparable beauty from a quieter vantage point (mywaterton.ca). In 2017,
Waterton Lakes suffered severe wildfire damage and is consequently rebuild-
ing. For current information go to the Parks Canada website (page 303).

YOHO (NP)

> Location

"Yoho" is a Cree word to express awe, which visitors will certainly experience
in Yoho National Park, Canada's second-oldest national park. One of the group
of national parks designated by UNESCO as a World Heritage Site, and often
compared to the Swiss Alps, Yoho has over twenty-eight mountain peaks
over 3,000 metres in height and spectacular lakes, icefields, alpine meadows,
glaciers, and waterfalls. The park is found on the Trans-Canada Highway
(Highway 1) between Golden and Lake Louise. The small community of Field,
which is inside the park, offers services. A lovely restaurant/coffeehouse that
also sells camping supplies is located near the Kicking Horse Campground.

> Facilities

Almost 200 vehicle-accessible camping spots
are available to campers wanting to access the
delights of Yoho, spread among the following
campgrounds: Hoodoo Creek (30 sites); Kicking
Horse (88 sites); Monarch (44 sites); and Takakkaw Falls (35 sites). Hoodoo Creek is densely
wooded and peaceful. The park's only sani-
station is located here. Kicking Horse is located
in a lightly forested area 5 kilometres east of Field.
While this is the largest campground, arrive early
to avoid disappointment. This campground also
has the most amenities; in addition to the basics,
there are showers, flush toilets (wheelchair-
accessible), food storage, an outdoor interpretive theatre, and a play area for children. Closer
to Field, and within walking distance of Kicking
Horse, Monarch's sites are set in a large meadow.
Facilities include wheelchair-accessible washrooms with flush toilets, food storage, a kitchen
shelter with a wood-burning stove, and recycling.
Takakkaw Falls is the campground farthest from
Field, 17 kilometres east of the village, on Takakkaw Falls Road, off Yoho Valley Road (which has
switchbacks that should not be attempted if you

have a long RV or are towing a trailer). You have to walk a short distance from
the parking lot to access the tenting-only campsites here, but a cart is available
for wheeling in supplies. The walk is worth it for the views. This campground
also has the basics plus food storage, a kitchen shelter with a stove, and recycling. Reservations are possible at Kicking Horse Campground.

> Recreational activities

Like all visitors to national parks, visitors to Yoho should make their first
stop at the visitor centre located at the junction of Highway 1 and the access
road into Field. Detailed maps of the vicinity can be obtained here. In a park

of this size (1,313 square kilometres), there are multitudes of things to do. Water-focused activities include rafting, fishing, canoeing, and kayaking. Canoes can be rented on Emerald Lake, a lake that should be on everyone's "to do" list and whose beauty rivals Moraine Lake and Lake Louise. Power-boats are not permitted in the park, and fishing in national parks is governed by a number of regulations and requires purchasing a permit.

Other ways to pass your time include mountain biking on designated trails and fire roads, mountaineering, and of course, hiking. As there are over 400 kilometres of trails, fantastic hiking opportunities abound; choose between short interpretive trails or hikes that last for days (some of the shorter ones are wheelchair-accessible). When I stayed, I hiked the Iceline Trail, a day hike that takes you to glaciers, alpine meadows, forests, mountains, and some of the best scenery in the world. It is impossible to recommend this trail too highly. This trail and others have views of Takakkaw Falls, which is one of the highest waterfalls in North America, at 254 metres. "Takakkaw" is a Cree word meaning "magnificent." The short, 10-minute walk to these falls, where the noise of the thundering water is almost deafening, is also well worth under-taking and is easily accessible by vehicle. Keep an eye out for wildlife in Yoho: while driving to the start of the Iceline Trail, we saw a grizzly bear, and there are also elk, moose, coyotes, and wolves in the park.

> **Additional information**

Yoho National Park was established in 1901. Yoho owes its development to the Canadian National Railway workers who pushed the tracks through Kick-ing Horse Pass and built the first company hotel in Field. Climbers, tourists, and artists came to the hotel and recognized the overpowering beauty of the area. In 1886, the Mount Stephen Reserve was created, and fifteen years later this area was renamed Yoho. Be aware of where to find the weekly reports of bear sightings, such as the Parks Canada website, where you will also find lots of useful information for planning a trip to this awesome recreational area. While Yoho may not be as large or as well-known as Banff and Jasper, it shares much of their beauty, and is far quieter.

CARIBOO-CHILCOTIN COAST

STEEPED IN THE history of the gold rush and covering an area of over 100,000 square kilometres, the Cariboo–Chilcotin region has campgrounds situated off Highway 97 north of Cache Creek to Prince George. This section of road is known as the Gold Rush Trail, after the pioneers who travelled it in search of the precious metal. Today, many buildings and historical markers recount the days of this original wagon road built in the 1860s. Campgrounds are also found on minor roads off this major route. The Cariboo is characterized by rolling hills, grasslands, over 8,000 lakes, and numerous rivers stretching from the foothills of the Rockies to the Pacific coast. Recently the area has become known for its many guest ranches and for being "cowboy country," so go and ride 'em, cowboy!

Bull Canyon Provincial Park is between Williams Lake and Bella Coola.

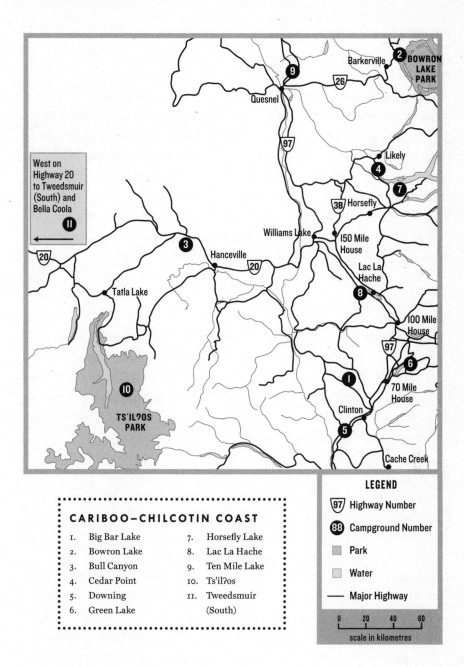

West on Highway 20 to Tweedsmuir (South) and Bella Coola **11**

BOWRON LAKE PARK

Barkerville

2

9 Quesnel

26

97

Likely

4

7

3B Horsefly

Williams Lake

150 Mile House

3 Hanceville

20

20

Tatla Lake

Lac La Hache

8

100 Mile House

97

6

70 Mile House

10

TS'IL?OS PARK

1

Clinton

5

Cache Creek

LEGEND

97 Highway Number

88 Campground Number

Park

Water

— Major Highway

0   20   40   60
scale in kilometres

CARIBOO–CHILCOTIN COAST

1. Big Bar Lake
2. Bowron Lake
3. Bull Canyon
4. Cedar Point
5. Downing
6. Green Lake
7. Horsefly Lake
8. Lac La Hache
9. Ten Mile Lake
10. Ts'il?os
11. Tweedsmuir (South)

BIG BAR LAKE

> Location

The people who once walked the land around Big Bar Lake were Indigenous
hunters, cowboys, cattle rustlers, and gold prospectors. According to local legends, their ghosts can often be seen and heard, so be attentive when you stay
here. Big Bar Lake is on the southern edge of the Fraser Plateau, a landscape
formed millions of years ago by debris left by glaciers. Evidence of the ice age
can be seen west of the lake, where gravel eskers remain; much of the topography owes its development to this geological period. To reach Big Bar Lake,
drive 8 kilometres north of Clinton on Highway 97 and then take a gravel road
west for 34 kilometres to the park itself. The nearest services can be found at
70 Mile House.

> Facilities

The 332-hectare park has two campgrounds with a total of 46 spots accommodating every size of recreational vehicle. The Lakeside Campground's 27 sites
overlook the lake, and 15 are right on the lakeshore, while the Upper Campground's larger sites are located in the forest above the lake and are mostly
used for overflow camping. The facilities are basic (fire pits, picnic tables,
drinking water, pit toilets). Reservations are accepted at 20 sites.

> Recreational activities

A naturalist's delight, this area is characterized by forests of lodgepole pine
and spruce, providing an excellent habitat for wildlife, including mule deer,
black bears (which we saw while travelling here), cougars, lynx, marmots, and
snowshoe hares. Easy access to the lake and a boat launch means boating and
fishing are possible. The lake is stocked annually with rainbow trout, some
rumoured to be as heavy as 3 kilograms. Big Bar Lake is a gorgeous body of
water that is also ideal for swimming: crystal-clear water, quite warm, and no
reeds. Water-skiing is not permitted and there is a speed limit for boats. The
3.5-kilometre Otter Marsh Interpretive Trail provides excellent waterfowl and
birdwatching, which is facilitated by a water-control structure built by Ducks
Unlimited to encourage nesting. Longer hikes are also possible. There is a children's playground in the day-use area.

> Additional information

Big Bar Lake Provincial Park is in an area of rolling hills originally settled by the people of the Tŝilhqot'in, Dakelh (Carrier), and Secwépemc Nations. Today, it's known as ranch country, and trail rides can be arranged through the numerous guest ranches located in the area. These ranches operate year round and also offer riding lessons, pack trips, gold-panning excursions, and skiing. The fact that snowshoe hares are found around Big Bar Lake should forewarn you that even early in the season, beautiful warm days can turn into clear, cold nights. So, act like a cowboy and remember the long johns if you'll be camping under canvas. We stayed here in 2006 and I swam at 8:00 PM, when the entire lake was mine. Bliss. Be warned, though, that mosquitoes affect certain areas of the park, but that problem can be avoided by changing locations.

BOWRON LAKE

> Location

Bowron Lake Provincial Park is famous for its wilderness canoe circuit, which covers over 116 kilometres around eleven different lakes, but there's also a vehicle-accessible campground anyone can use. The park is located 120 kilometres east of Quesnel and 30 kilometres beyond Wells, reached by taking a 27-kilometre dirt road found at the end of Highway 26. Two resorts and some stores on Bowron Lake offer a selection of services, including food and camping supplies, while a full range can be found in Wells.

> Facilities

Twenty-five wooded, secluded campsites suitable for vehicles and tents are located near the park entrance and start of the canoe circuit. Facilities are basic (picnic tables, fire pits, drinking water, and pit toilets) and reservations are accepted for 9 of these sites. There are 54 wilderness sites located elsewhere in the 139,700-hectare park for those undertaking the canoe circuit.

> Recreational activities

Near the campground, which is on the eastern shore of Bowron Lake, is a canoe-landing dock, and it is possible to swim, canoe, and fish for Dolly Varden, rainbow trout, and lake char. Boat and canoe rentals are available nearby, as is a public boat launch (though powerboats are only permitted on Bowron Lake). Wildlife includes moose, deer, caribou, black bears, grizzly bears, and coyotes. There are bald and golden eagles, ospreys, and hawks, as well as a wealth of waterfowl and songbirds. The visitor centre has an informative video about the park that is well worth watching.

> Additional information
To be able to fully appreciate the beauty of Bowron Lake Provincial Park, you should spend a week or more here. The park's reputation grows annually, both within North America and Europe; consequently, it is becoming increasingly difficult to get a canoe-circuit reservation and only a few first-come, first-served spots are offered each day. Advance planning is required if you want to canoe the circuit (in its entirety, or just the west side); reservations are accepted. Dogs are not permitted on the canoe circuit. This campground is a delightful place to stay even if you're not a canoeing enthusiast, but for those who just want to visit the area, it may be easier to stay at Barkerville, which has two private campgrounds. Wells is a neat little community where canoe-rental companies also operate, delivering canoes and kayaks to Bowron Lake for those interested in paddling the circuit or just spending a day on the water enjoying the beauty of the area.

BULL CANYON

> Location
Bull Canyon Provincial Park has a particularly beautiful setting on the Fraser Plateau by the Chilcotin River. It is an excellent overnight stop for those travelling between Williams Lake and Bella Coola along Highway 20, as it has the only provincial campground between Williams Lake and Tweedsmuir Provincial Park. This pleasantly treed 343-hectare park is found 6 kilometres west of Alexis Creek. The nearest full range of services is at Williams Lake, 122 kilometres away, but gas and basic food items can be purchased at Alexis Creek.

> Facilities
Bull Canyon was given provincial-park status in 1993 and has 20 basic campsites in an open camping area overlooking the azure Chilcotin River. Facilities

are rudimentary (drinking water, fire pits, picnic tables, pit toilets). There is one wheelchair-accessible pit toilet but no sani-station, and water is obtained from a pump. The campground is really quiet with only the sound of the river lulling you to sleep; the road isn't busy and is a little ways away from the campground.

> Recreational activities

The fast-flowing Chilcotin River is suitable for fishing, canoeing, and kayaking (as are the lakes in the area), but special fishing restrictions apply. Archaeological sites apparently exist in the park, but when we stayed here in 2006, we couldn't find them. Although insects often plague this area of the province, the pleasant breeze we had while camping here meant we didn't have any problems. There is good birdwatching and wildlife viewing, and a wonderful array of wildflowers can be found here at certain times of the year. There is a small, 2-kilometre interpretive trail in the park. This is a good picnic spot even if you don't want to camp. In the winter, this region experiences very cold temperatures, sometimes as low as –50°C.

> Additional information

While staying at another provincial park, I met a retired gentleman from Germany who had been holidaying by RV in BC for the past ten years and claimed to have travelled on every road other than Highway 20. The year I talked with him, he was about to undertake that journey. One of the more pleasant aspects of staying in BC provincial parks is having the opportunity to meet people from all over the world, who often give advice on travelling in the province, including which campgrounds are their favourites.

CEDAR POINT

> Location

This is one of BC's newest provincial parks and labelled Class C, which means it is jointly administered with a board from the local community of Likely. As it is co-operated, the facilities it offers and the general "feel" is different from other BC provincial parks. The 8-hectare park is located on Quesnel Lake, 6 kilometres from Likely, which is 120 kilometres on a paved road northeast of

150 Mile House. Services are found in Likely. The campground administrator's house is in the park.

> Facilities
Camping exists for 29 parties, with sites varying in size. Besides the basics you'd expect (drinking water, picnic tables, fire pits, pit toilets), there is a sani-station but no showers.

> Recreational activities
One of the major attractions here is Quesnel Lake, which is huge, and there is a boat launch in the park. Be prepared: because of the size, the lake can get quite windy. The campground provides access to short and multi-day canoe and kayaking trips. Whitewater kayaking on the adjacent Cariboo and Quesnel Rivers is also an option. A good sandy beach is accessible just outside the park on Quesnel Lake, and a public dock provides swimming opportunities. Fishing for rainbow trout, char, and kokanee is good in the park. Some small trails can be taken along the creek and beach, but these may be inaccessible if the water is too high. There is also a playground, a baseball diamond, and grassy playing areas.

> Additional information
I have not visited this campground, which is more than a little out of the way, but in researching it I found that the area was once a rendezvous point for trappers and fur traders, first included on Hudson's Bay Company maps in 1832. Gold was discovered in 1858 in Cedar Creek, which runs through the park, and there is a small outdoor mining museum with old mining machinery and mock mine shafts. If you are looking for an out-of-the-way location for a while, this could be just the spot.

DOWNING

> Location
In June 2013, this campground was closed for the season due to flooding. In 2015, it was rebuilt and reopened in 2016. The scenery at this 139-hectare

park is quite lovely. Mount Bowman, which can be seen to the north, is, at 2,245 metres, the highest mountain in the Marble Range. Downing Provincial Park almost completely encircles Kelly Lake and is located 18 kilometres southwest of Clinton off Highway 97 on a paved road. Services are available in the quaint town of Clinton and include restaurants, a post office, grocery store, pub, bakery, gas station, and ice cream store.

> Facilities

There are 18 reconstructed gravel campsites near to the lake, with limited space for RVs. Facilities are restricted to the basics (drinking water, picnic tables, fire pits, pit toilets), and there's a 20-metre walk from the parking lot to the camping area. There is no sani-station and only limited wheelchair accessibility.

> Recreational activities

Things to do here include fishing for rainbow trout, hiking, swimming, and sunbathing on the small beach. There is a boat launch at Kelly Lake and canoeing and kayaking are possible. The nearby community of Clinton has a small museum and excellent ice cream shop, and is a pleasant place to while away a few hours. The town also boasts the largest log building in BC, which is a combination hotel, pub, and restaurant. It offers a really good breakfast and is a pleasant place to play pool in the evening should you decide to escape from your tent for a while.

> Additional information

Located on Secwépemc Nation land, Downing Park was donated to the province by C.S. Downing in 1970, and his family still owns the adjoining property. BC Rail runs along one side of the lake, so you may be lulled to sleep by the sound of trains. If you don't have time to stay here, this site is an ideal spot to rest, picnic, and bathe, and is particularly inviting to travellers who have taken the unpaved road between Pavilion, north of Lillooet, to Clinton. Drivers should be warned that the unpaved road between Downing Park and Pavilion is at times very steep and has hairpin bends that can be nerve-racking, but Pavilion has a beautiful little church well worth a photograph.

GREEN LAKE

> Location

The Green Lake area was recognized as bountiful by Canada's Indigenous population many years ago; today, campers of every age continue to appreciate its bounty. Green Lake Provincial Park is situated among groves of aspen and lodgepole pine, 15 kilometres northeast of 70 Mile House off a paved road and adjacent to the 14-kilometre lake from which it takes its name. Three campgrounds are available on both sides of the lake. Information about the exact location of the campgrounds is available at the road junction 10 kilometres east of 70 Mile House. Services are available at 70 Mile House, and a store and restaurant are located at Emerald Bay.

> Facilities

Each of Green Lake's three campgrounds has something different to offer. The most popular, Arrowhead, is fairly open and relatively small, with just 16 spots, all situated on the beachfront. (Probably the best family swimming is to be found here.) The second camping area is Emerald Bay. Like Arrowhead, Emerald Bay is situated on North Green Lake Road, but it has 51 sites, several of them on the water's edge. Sunset View, on South Green Lake Road, has 54 sites and is usually the last campground to fill up. All campsites are relatively private and situated among aspen trees. There is a nearby sani-station (with adjacent flush toilets) and the pit toilets at Emerald Bay and Sunset View campgrounds are wheelchair accessible. Reservations are accepted at all sites.

> Recreational activities

Boredom should not be a problem here, as there are numerous activities to entertain every age group. The lake has moderately good fishing for rainbow trout and is restocked annually. There are two boat launches (one at Sunset View, the other at the Little Arrowhead picnic site) and water-skiing is allowed, but boats and skiers should keep well away from the swimming areas. The winds here can be quite strong, and the use of powerboats means canoeing and kayaking is not popular. There are children's playgrounds at both Emerald Bay and Sunset View, and hiking trails leading from the park. The shallow west area of the lake attracts numerous waterfowl and migratory birds and is a magnet for ornithologists. Horseshoe pits are located at each campground, but you have to bring your own horseshoes.

> Additional information

Green Lake is 14 kilometres long and averages 1.5 kilometres in width. It has minimum outflow, which enables a high buildup of algae and other micro-organisms. This, along with the composition of the water, gives the lake its greenish tinge. BC Parks suggests using the park in the spring, when large rainbow trout spawning in the creeks attract large numbers of bald eagles, and in the fall, when the aspens turn fantastic shades of red and orange, each occurrence being quite beautiful for those with an appreciative eye.

HORSEFLY LAKE

> Location

Horsefly Lake is a delightful 186-hectare provincial park set among an assort-ment of trees including western hemlock, redcedar, various types of spruce and subalpine fir, as well as old-growth forest and Douglas fir. It is accessed by turning off Highway 97 at 150 Mile House and travelling 52 kilometres on a paved road to Horsefly, then 13 kilometres along a good gravel road. Services at Horsefly include a cafe, grocery store, and gas station.

> Facilities

Horsefly Lake has 23 private vehicle-accessible sites in a coniferous forest, and 7 walk-in tenting sites along the lakeshore. Until recently, there were just the basic facilities (pit toilets, drinking water, picnic tables, fire pits), but coin-operated showers and laundry facilities have now been installed. One of the pit toilets is wheelchair accessible. Reservations are accepted at 12 sites.

> Recreational activities

There is a short hike up to a lookout above the lake, and other park trails lead to Viewland Mountain and Eureka Park; details are available at the information board at the park entrance. Anglers visit the park to fish for rainbow trout in Horsefly Lake and in the smaller adjacent lakes. There's a boat launch so canoeing and boating are also possible, and the beach has a change room and roped-off area for swimmers. Just outside the community of Horsefly there are spawning channels for salmon, with a system of dikes for walking and viewing. The best viewing is in mid-September when the salmon are spawning, and there are often festivals that month to celebrate the return of the sockeye. There is also a horseshoe pit and basketball hoop in the day-use area.

> Additional information

This area was once a centre for gold mining. Some of the first gold in the Cariboo was discovered here in 1859, and even today some people are drawn to the area in search of gold. Horsefly was originally called Harper's Camp after one of the early settlers, but was renamed by later pioneers when they discovered one of the area's drawbacks. Seriously, don't be put off by the name. Recent information supplied by the park's administration notes that there are few biting flies in the park, and when I visited one June there were none (there were also no other campers). The park covers a considerable area, most of which is semi-wilderness and inaccessible to the visitor. More recent visits have shown this provincial park and the area to be loved by fishers.

LAC LA HACHE

> Location

Lac La Hache means "axe lake," and numerous stories have been advanced to explain how this name came to be. According to one, the name is based on the shape of the lake; another story holds that it gained its name when a trapper lost his axe through the frozen lake when trying to reach into the water. To the Tŝilhqot'in People, the lake is known as Kumatakwa Lake, which means "Chief or Queen of the waters." Whichever name you prefer, this is a wonderful provincial park. It's situated 13 kilometres north of the community of Lac La Hache on

Highway 97. Services can be found in Lac La Hache, and there is a small store opposite the campground, which has been open whenever I have visited or driven past.

> Facilities

There are 83 campsites here and good facilities, including wheelchair-accessible flush toilets, tap water, and a sani-station. All sites are large, relatively private, and set in open Douglas fir and aspen woodlands. Some sites are close to the road, however, and it is possible to hear the traffic from busy Highway 97. Thirty campsites can be reserved.

> Recreational activities

Small trails lead around the park, which allow you to see and walk remnants of the historic Cariboo Wagon Road. There is an adventure playground and a self-guided interpretive trail. There is a boat launch, and the lake is popular for water-skiing, boating, and fishing. Rainbow trout, kokanee, and burbot can be caught here. There is a pebbly beach and excellent swimming to be had in fairly weed-free water. A change house and showers are located near the beach, which is on the other side of the highway from the campground but connected to it by a tunnel since 2004. Three kilometres north of the campground is the Cariboo Nature Provincial Park, which is an excellent location for birdwatching. Lac La Hache also claims to be BC's longest town. Unfortunately, with the exception of some small cafes and restaurants, I find there is little in the town to attract visitors.

> Additional information

I am sentimentally attached to this park, as it was the first BC provincial park I ever stayed in over thirty years ago. That time, and on the rare occasions I have had the opportunity to visit again, I have been impressed by the friendly and informative camp hosts. The lack of other provincial parks on Highway 97 coupled with this one's good family facilities make it a popular location. The small store is a magnet for children walking to and from the lake, and during the early evening pop and candy seem to be the store's most popular wares. Swimmer's itch can be a problem here in July and August, and the dreaded mosquito is often around in the evenings.

TEN MILE LAKE

> Location

Looking for somewhere to camp with children? Then look no further than Ten Mile Lake Provincial Park. Situated in a pine and aspen forest 11 kilometres north of Quesnel on Highway 97, the park's large campground is popular with both RVers and tenters, and it is particularly appealing for those with little ones to entertain. Services are available in Quesnel, and a small store in the park sells chips, pop, ice cream, bread, milk, and other supplies.

> Facilities

Ten Mile Lake has two campgrounds with a total of 106 campsites offering excellent facilities: Lakeside (60 spots) is near the lakeshore and Touring (46 slightly larger spots) is set among pine trees. Both campgrounds offer flush toilets and a pressurized water system, but Lakeside also has pay-to-use showers (coin-operated: $1.00 for 4 minutes) and wheelchair-accessible flush toilets. There are a number of pull-through sites and a sani-station near the park's entrance. Reservations are accepted at the Lakeside Campground.

> Recreational activities

As is common among the larger provincial parks, a variety of leisure pursuits for both old and young are available, but 343-hectare Ten Mile Lake is particularly attractive for those with children. There is a playground and horseshoe pits, and a gently sloping beach gives swimmers easy access to the lake. There is a boat launch, and fishers can cast their lines for rainbow trout. An extensive 10-kilometre network of trails leads explorers through mixed forest; the trail to a huge beaver dam and lodge is only half a kilometre long and well worth the effort. Mountain bikes can be ridden on a number of other trails. Ducks Unlimited has placed nesting boxes in the area to encourage avian wildlife. When I visited the park, I discovered musical jam sessions taking place in the pavilion. Ten Mile Lake also has park hosts, who welcome campers, answer questions, and give advice.

> Additional information

At the start of the 1900s, Ten Mile Lake was a milepost for the Pacific Great Eastern Railway, evidence of which can still be seen in the day-use area. This campground is a delight, as there are numerous activities within the park itself, as well as in the immediate vicinity. The town of Quesnel, named after Jules-Maurice Quesnel, a member of Simon Fraser's exploration party, is only a short distance away. It is rich in pioneer gold-rush history and has a museum, historical markers, and, for those less interested in the past, a couple of golf courses. When we stayed here in 2004, we met Gord, the wonderful park administrator, who told me that in the summertime, he works from 5:30 AM to 11:00 PM. When we returned two years later, he was still there offering his brilliant service. I visited a few years ago and could not find Gord, but it was late in the season.

TS'IL?OS

> ### Location

Do not expect to explore much of Ts'il?os (pronounced "sigh-loss") when you visit, as this provincial park, approximately 200 kilometres from Williams Lake, is roughly the size of Prince Edward Island (233,240 hectares) and, for the most part, is a vast undeveloped wilderness. There are huge mountains, glaciers, clear blue lakes, waterfalls, and meadows, many of which are inaccessible to the common camper. Ts'il?os is accessed either from Highway 20 at Hanceville by driving 150 kilometres of rough gravel road, or from Tatla Lake via a 60-kilometre slightly better rough gravel road (which is the only option for those without a four-wheel-drive vehicle). Both routes take 4 to 6 hours from Williams Lake, and BC Parks actually recommends using four-wheel-drive vehicles in the park. Limited services are available at Tatla Lake.

> ### Facilities

There are 16 campsites at the Nu Chugh Beniz site on the east side of Chilko Lake, reached by driving in from Hanceville. At the north end of the lake, the Gwe Da Ts'ih Campground (reached by driving in from Tatla Lake) has 8 "rustic" sites. Campers staying at Nu Chugh Beniz have access to gas, propane, laundry, and internet at the Nemiah Valley Tl'ebayi Community Centre, while those staying at Gwe Da Ts'ih are close to commercial lodges, where they may find meals and basic supplies. BC Parks informed me that Gwe Da Ts'ih may be closed during the salmon season because of the threat of bears (mid-August to

October). Reservations aren't accepted, and despite its away-from-it-all location, the campgrounds do get full.

> Recreational activities

The most popular recreational activity here is fishing. At 50 kilometres long, Chilko Lake is the largest natural high-elevation freshwater lake in North America and has lake and rainbow trout and Dolly Varden. Other activities include hiking and wildlife viewing. BC Parks does not recommend canoeing, as the lake is frequently prone to rough conditions. For those who really want to get a feel of the place, a five-day hiking trail leads through the Yohetta Valley, Spectrum Pass, and Tchaikazan Valley. To make arrangements to undertake this route, contact the Ts'ylos Park Lodge (tsylos.com). The lodge offers a number of excursions including horseback riding, flyfishing, and hunting trips.

> Additional information

The park takes its name from the mountain Ts'il?os (Mount Tatlow), which stands over 3,000 metres high. Legend tells how a man, his wife, and six children watch over the people of the Tsilhqot'in First Nation and intervene when necessary. A number of private lodges operate in the area for those who want to experience the park in relative luxury. BC Parks advises anyone wanting access to the Declared Title Area (see the BC Parks site for what that entails) should get in touch with the Tsilhqot'in National Government (tsilhqotin.ca).

TWEEDSMUIR (SOUTH)

> Location

It is not just people who are attracted to this area. In salmon-spawning season, grizzly bears can often be seen fishing in the numerous streams that flow through Tweedsmuir, so be careful. When we visited, there were numerous "Beware of Bears" signs and posters with instructions for safe camping. Sometimes the campground is closed as a result of bear activity. Tweedsmuir, one of the largest parks in the province at 989,616 hectares, is named after the fifteenth Governor General of Canada, John Buchan, Baron Tweedsmuir of Elsfield, who travelled in the area in 1937 and was impressed by its beauty. The park is divided into north and south regions, but only the south is accessible by road. The southern section is located on Highway 20, approximately 400 kilometres west of Williams Lake and 50 kilometres east of Bella Coola (which can be reached from Vancouver Island by taking the ferry from Port Hardy). Services are found in Bella Coola. There is also a small lodge in the park.

> Facilities
There are two campgrounds accessible from Highway 20: Atnarko is 28 kilometres from the eastern entrance of the park and has 15 sites set amidst a grove of old-growth Douglas fir, while the Fisheries Pool Campground is located near Stuie, 44 kilometres from the park's eastern entrance, and has 9 high-density open sites. Facilities at both sites are basic (picnic tables, fire pits, pit toilets, pump water). There is a sani-station near Atnarko.

> Recreational activities
As one would expect in a provincial park of this size, there is a wealth of things to see and do. The park is home to a wide variety of wildlife, including deer, moose, caribou, black and grizzly bears, wolves, and cougars. Rainbow trout, cutthroat trout, and Dolly Varden are found in the park's many lakes and streams, while the Atnarko and Dean Rivers are spawning grounds for trout and salmon. Water sports include swimming (although the water is very cold), canoeing, and kayaking. There are a number of canoe circuit trips ranging in length from one to five days. The area is known as one of BC's most outstanding for alpine hiking, and numerous trails take backpacking enthusiasts into the spectacular mountain scenery. Rustic wilderness campsites exist along these trails. For the less energetic, a number of less arduous day hikes are also available. The park is also popular for horseback riding.

> Additional information
With some superb scenery and varied terrain, the South Tweedsmuir area definitely is worthy of more than an overnight stop. The area is a real delight for those who enjoy backcountry exploration. Details of all the facilities and activities available can be obtained from the park's headquarters near the Atnarko River Campground. Tweedsmuir's two vehicle-accessible campgrounds are very much adult-oriented and ideal if you're a serious outdoorsperson.

Naikoon Provincial Park on Haida Gwaii is a photographer's paradise.

Tyhee Lake's campsites are suitable for RVs of all sizes.

NORTHERN BC

FAMOUS FOR EXCELLENT fishing and big game, the northern BC region stretches from the Canadian Rockies to the Pacific Ocean and incorporates mountain ranges, deep valleys, majestic fjords, glaciers, dense forests, lakes, and rivers. In addition to its natural beauty, it is an area rich in Indigenous history and culture. Although there are not a lot of large settlements, excellent wildlife viewing opportunities compensate for the lack of people, and travellers are usually blessed with an open road. Even at the peak of summer, it is not unusual to drive for 30 minutes without seeing another vehicle. This region includes campgrounds accessible from the minor roads leading off the Trans-Canada/Yellowhead Highway (Highway 16) and from the highway itself west of McBride, all the way to and including Haida Gwaii. This region also encompasses Highway 37, which stretches from Kitimat to the road's junction with the Alaska Highway, and Highway 97 north of Prince George, which leads all the way to Dawson Creek and beyond, following the Alaska Highway up to the Yukon border. Finally, it includes Highway 29 from Fort St. John to Tumbler Ridge and Highway 2. So hop in your car or RV and go enjoy a region of BC that feels like it has been created with only you in mind.

BABINE LAKE MARINE

> Location

Campers who choose to stay on the banks of the longest natural lake in BC have the choice of three campgrounds: two are in Babine Lake Marine Provincial Park, while the third is in Red Bluff Provincial Park (described separately). Babine Lake's two campgrounds are Pendleton Bay at the southern end of the lake and Smithers Landing to the north. To reach Pendleton Bay, turn off

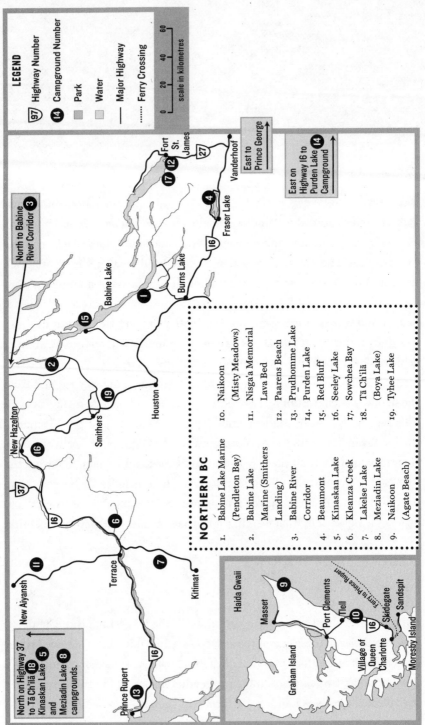

LEGEND

97 Highway Number
14 Campground Number
Park
Water
— Major Highway
···· Ferry Crossing

scale in kilometres
0 20 40 60

North to Babine River Corridor 3

East to Prince George

Vanderhoof

East on Highway 16 to Purden Lake 14 Campground

Fort St. James

27

12
17

4

Fraser Lake

16

Burns Lake

1

Babine Lake

15

2

New Hazelton

16

19

Smithers

Houston

37

16

6

11

New Aiyansh

North on Highway 37 to Tā Ch'ilà 18 Kinaskan Lake 5 and Meziadin Lake 8 campgrounds.

Terrace

7

Kitimat

16

13

Prince Rupert

NORTHERN BC

1. Babine Lake Marine (Pendleton Bay)
2. Babine Lake Marine (Smithers Landing)
3. Babine River Corridor
4. Beaumont
5. Kinaskan Lake
6. Kleanza Creek
7. Lakelse Lake
8. Meziadin Lake
9. Naikoon (Agate Beach)
10. Naikoon (Misty Meadows)
11. Nisga'a Memorial Lava Bed
12. Paarens Beach
13. Prudhomme Lake
14. Purden Lake
15. Red Bluff
16. Seeley Lake
17. Sowchea Bay
18. Tā Ch'ilà (Boya Lake)
19. Tyhee Lake

Haida Gwaii

Masset

9

Graham Island

Port Clements

Tlell

10

16

Village of Queen Charlotte

Skidegate

Sandspit

Ferry to Prince Rupert

Moresby Island

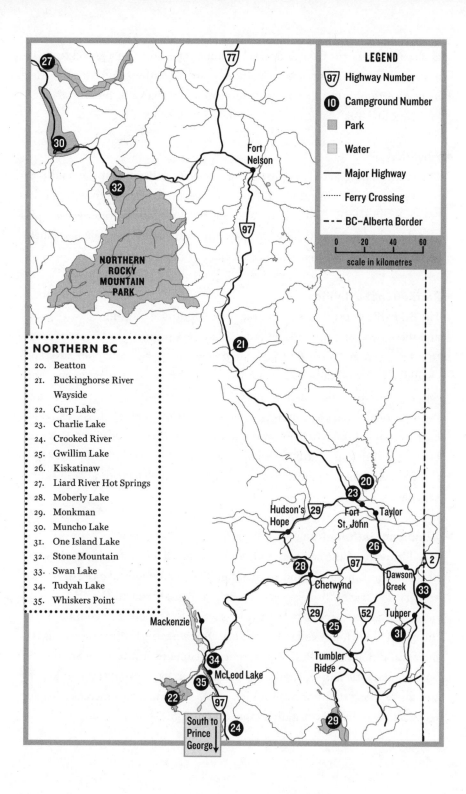

LEGEND

[97] Highway Number

🔟 Campground Number

Park

Water

—— Major Highway

········ Ferry Crossing

–·–· BC–Alberta Border

0   20   40   60
scale in kilometres

NORTHERN
ROCKY
MOUNTAIN
PARK

NORTHERN BC

20. Beatton
21. Buckinghorse River
    Wayside
22. Carp Lake
23. Charlie Lake
24. Crooked River
25. Gwillim Lake
26. Kiskatinaw
27. Liard River Hot Springs
28. Moberly Lake
29. Monkman
30. Muncho Lake
31. One Island Lake
32. Stone Mountain
33. Swan Lake
34. Tudyah Lake
35. Whiskers Point

Fort
Nelson

Hudson's
Hope

Fort
St. John

Taylor

Mackenzie

Chetwynd

Dawson
Creek

Tupper

McLeod Lake

Tumbler
Ridge

South to
Prince
George

Highway 16 at Burns Lake and travel 35 kilometres north on a gravel road. To reach Smithers Landing, turn off Highway 16 at Smithers and travel 35 kilometres northeast on a gravel road. Services are available in Burns Lake and Smithers, and Tukii Lodge has a store near Smithers Landing.

> Facilities

The two camping locations provide 24 sites: 16 at Pendleton Bay and 8 at Smithers Landing, some under the cover of trees and others at the edge of the beach. Facilities are rudimentary and consist of pit toilets, water access, picnic tables, and fire pits. (There are a few other sites in the park, but as vehicle access is difficult, they have not been included in this text.)

> Recreational activities

The BC Parks website says this park is "ideal for those wanting a slower pace," and these two campgrounds on Babine Lake are perfect for those who want to get away from it all and fish. If you prefer other recreational pursuits, you should stay somewhere else. Both campgrounds have boat launches, and Babine Lake provides angling opportunities for rainbow trout and char. Because of the park's somewhat remote location, Babine Lake campers have an opportunity to see a wide array of wildlife, including moose and bear. Swimming and sailing can also be enjoyed here. Numerous commercial resorts in the area offer fishing, canoeing, horseback riding, and skiing excursions.

> Additional information

The distance to these campgrounds and their limited facilities dissuade some people from coming to Babine Lake. But if you can undertake the drive, the scenery and tranquility are very rewarding. Bears frequent the area, so you must take all the necessary precautions for storing food. The community of Burns Lake, originally called Burnt Lake after a nearby fire, now serves as the major retail source of fishing equipment and supplies. The town of Smithers is larger and a little more geared toward tourists. It has a delightful main street to wander along that has restaurants, stores specializing in merchandise for enjoying the outdoors (including rainwear), and gift shops.

BABINE RIVER CORRIDOR

> Location

This park must win an award for being one of the most remote provincial parks in the province with vehicle-accessible camping facilities; however, if your passion is fishing or wildlife, particularly bears, this is the place for you! The nearest town is Smithers, 130 kilometres away. Access the park from Smithers by taking Babine Lake Road east, then taking a gravel Nilkitkwa Forest Service Road for 58 kilometres.

> Facilities

Four kilometres from the 15,359-hectare park's entrance is a small vehicle-accessible campground with 10 spots and basic facilities (picnic tables, fire pits, drinking water, and pit toilets). Because of the prevalence of bears in the area, all food and garbage must be stored in a vehicle, dogs must be kept on a leash, and children should be with adults at all times. Wilderness camping is permitted, if you are brave enough.

> Recreational activities

The primary pastime here is fishing. There is a boat launch in the park and BC Parks describes "world-class angling opportunities" for steelhead and sockeye salmon, which attract visitors from all over the world. Rafting and kayaking are possible, and there are commercial operators offering guided trips in the park. Be warned: the river can be quite challenging. Hiking is also possible.

> Additional information

While this provincial park has all the facilities required to be included in this guide, it is very remote and I have not camped here or even visited. However, in undertaking the research for this guide, it seems the area is spectacular for fishing and apparently attracts not only national but international visitors. It is not only anglers who seek fish: numerous grizzly bears inhabit the area and are frequent visitors to the park; indeed, the park is closed for fishing for one hour after sunrise and one hour before sunset as BC Parks claims this "gives the bears some time to fish during daylight hours without the disturbance of humans." Anyone with a bear phobia may want to go elsewhere.

BEATTON

> Location

For the angler, Beatton Provincial Park boasts the best fishing for walleye in BC. For those who do not fish, it is a lovely camping retreat that has been enjoyed by campers for decades. Established on September 14, 1934, this is one of BC's oldest provincial parks. Beatton is located 13 kilometres northwest of Fort St. John off Highway 97 on a paved access road. Limited services can be found along Highway 97, but a more comprehensive range is available at Fort St. John.

> Facilities

Thirty-nine campsites are found here on the eastern side of Charlie Lake, set among poplar and spruce trees. Some spots are on the lakeside; all are large and very private. There is no sani-station and facilities are restricted to the basics (fire pits, drinking water, pit toilets, and picnic tables). Some park facilities are wheelchair accessible, and reservations are accepted for 27 of the camping spots.

> Recreational activities

Aspen-lined trails lead from the campground to a 300-metre beach on the banks of Charlie Lake, which is suitable for water-skiing, windsurfing, and paddling. Although it is possible to swim, the high algae content of the lake at times may make it unappealing. A boat launch is available, and there is excellent fishing for northern pike and walleye. In addition to over 40 species of birds and waterfowl, moose, mule, and white-tailed deer can be seen in the park. Hikers will enjoy the 12 kilometres of trails and mountain bikers have 12 kilometres of cross-country ski trails available to them in the summer. Beatton Provincial Park also has an adventure playground in the day-use area, a horseshoe pit, and a baseball field.

> Additional information

Nearby Charlie Lake Provincial Park has similar facilities, but I prefer Beatton. This 330-hectare park is not just popular in summer: during the colder months, visitors can go tobogganing, cross-country skiing, ice fishing for walleye and northern pike, and snowshoeing. Both moose and deer frequent the park during winter months. The park provides "warm-up huts" (which, for someone from the south of the province, conjures wonderful images).

BEAUMONT

> Location

This 178-hectare provincial park is located on Fraser Lake, west of Vanderhoof and 134 kilometres from Prince George on Highway 16. Ancestors of the Dakelh People named the area "Nadleh Whut'en" and used nearby trails to trade with the people of neighbouring settlements. During the nineteenth century, fur traders used the same trails. The remains of Fort Fraser, which was established by Simon Fraser in 1806, are situated within the park. Food, gas, and accommodation are available just a few kilometres away at Fort Fraser to the west of the park, or at Fraser Lake to the east.

> Facilities

There are 49 large campsites at this location. Some are quite open and exposed and others are situated among trees. The park has a sani-station, flush toilets, and facilities for those in wheelchairs (including accessible flush toilets). Reservations are accepted at 16 spaces.

> Recreational activities

A range of recreational activities is available, including swimming in a designated swimming area from a lovely sandy beach (a change house is located close to the beach), sunbathing, windsurfing, boating, and fishing for kokanee, char, burbot, rainbow trout, and sturgeon. There is a boat launch in the park, but boaters should be aware that strong winds can easily transform the generally calm waters of Fraser Lake and cause a serious hazard. In addition, there are hiking trails, a children's play area, a volleyball net, and horseshoe pits. Information on the park's noticeboard informs campers that bears, wolves, beavers, and moose inhabit the area. The park is also attractive to ornithologists who can spot warblers, Canada geese, loons, and red-winged blackbirds.

> Additional information

Beaumont Provincial Park was a gift from Captain E.G. Beaumont, who also gave two other parks to the province. The campground is surrounded by the Hazelton, Skeena, and Omineca Mountains and is set amidst an abundance of willow, poplar, birch, spruce, and aspen trees. The site was originally chosen by early pioneers for its commanding view and because of the breezes that kept mosquitoes at bay. When I visited in late August, there were no signs of the dreaded bug; other campers, however, may tell a different story. Beaumont is an ideal location to stop for a picnic or take a stroll. The play area and beach make it particularly attractive for parents who have young children to entertain, with sandy shores and clear waters adjacent to a grassy picnic area. This campground never feels busy or crowded—an ideal place for every age group.

BUCKINGHORSE RIVER WAYSIDE

> Location

Buckinghorse River Wayside Provincial Park's campground is oriented very much toward overnighters travelling the Alaska Highway. When I stayed in 2004, I recognized a number of vehicles that I had passed or that had passed me during the course of the day, and I found the campground a pleasant place for a one-night stay. When I returned a few years later, the site had been taken over by construction workers working on an adjacent project. It was ill kept and noisy, so I had to move on. The campground is located 200 kilometres northwest of Fort St. John, at kilometre 278 of the highway. A restaurant and gas station are conveniently situated near the campground. In 2016, it was administered by BC Parks and a "community partner," so the services may not be the same as those found in other provincial parks.

> Facilities

One of the better roadside campgrounds, Buckinghorse River Wayside has a different "feel," as the local community manages it cooperatively with BC Parks. There are 17 spots here, all with a view of the river. They are quite closely positioned, with no interspersed vegetation and little privacy; the better ones are toward the end of the campground. Because the campsite is set a short distance away from the highway, noise is not a problem. All the basic amenities are provided (fire pits, drinking water, pit toilets, picnic tables), and some park facilities are wheelchair accessible.

> Recreational activities

This campground is primarily for travellers en route to other destinations, so there are limited recreational activities. There is a boat launch and the river provides an opportunity to fish for Arctic grayling, and if you take a short walk downstream, you can find areas in which to swim. As is the case in many provincial parks in the north, it is possible to spend hours stargazing. The sky seems bigger in this area of the world. Peaceful evenings with only the noise of flowing waters and a crackling fire provide the ideal setting for this astronomical pursuit.

> Additional information

BC Parks warns that both black bears and grizzly bears inhabit the area, so caution must be exercised. During the winter months, moose graze here. For those who do not wish to cook their own breakfast or dinner, there is a restaurant conveniently located across the road from the campground. Although the camping spots are close to each other, when I originally stayed here (almost two decades ago), only 10 spots were taken, so it did not feel crowded. During my visit in 2013, every spot was taken and it felt like a construction camp. Hopefully this was only a short-term event as the only provincial park alternatives (Charlie Lake, if you are heading south, and Stone Mountain, if driving north) are considerable distances away.

CARP LAKE

> Location

Why not camp on top of the world? At an elevation of 841 metres, Carp Lake is a picturesque, island-dotted lake covering over 38,000 hectares of the Nechako Plateau located almost in the middle of the province. Two hours' drive north of Prince George, the park is accessed by turning off Highway 97 at McLeod Lake and then travelling along a gravel road for 32 kilometres. This gravel road is single lane and not particularly good in places. There are a number of tight corners, and the route is not suitable for cars or trailers during the spring breakup period. Services can be found at Prince George and McLeod Lake.

> Facilities

This provincial park has two campgrounds from which to choose. Carp Lake, the main one, is situated at Kettle Bay and has a sani-station and 90 large sites that can accommodate most recreational vehicles. At the east end of War Lake, there are 12 smaller sites, which are not suitable for larger vehicles. If you have a boat, wilderness camping is possible on three of the islands in Carp Lake. There is no wheelchair access, and the facilities are the basic ones found in parks of this type (fire pits, drinking water, pit toilets, picnic tables). There are also three campgrounds and a cabin accessible only by boat and these accept reservations.

> Recreational activities

Visitors do not lack for something to do here. Two sandy beaches are located along the beach trail, one a 20-walk from the main campground and the other a 40-minute walk. Boat launches are available at both campgrounds, and power-boating and canoeing can be enjoyed on the lake. Fishing is good, as rainbow trout, burbot, and northern pikeminnow are plentiful in the lake. There's also a short trail to McLeod River that leads anglers to an ideal fly-fishing spot. In addition, there are numerous trails for those who wish to hike or mountain bike. One of these trails follows a 3-kilometre section of a route originally used by the Dakelh People between Fort McLeod and Fort Stewart. Wildlife viewing is good, and moose are often seen at the lake, especially at dawn and dusk. The main campground has a playground and horseshoe pit.

> Additional information

In his journal of 1806, Simon Fraser wrote of the Dakelh People who visited the area to catch large quantities of fish similar to carp. The park is still a magnet for those who enjoy fishing. The lake can experience high winds and rough waters, but it's a good place to catch rainbow trout. The summertime temperature at Carp Lake can be cool—averaging 12 to 18 °C in July—and can drop considerably at night, so be sure to bring enough warm clothing. Unlike many other campgrounds, this one is rarely full.

CHARLIE LAKE

> Location

Naturalists love this area for the chance of seeing a wide variety of wildlife, including white-tailed and mule deer, black bears, beavers, moose, and an array of waterfowl. It is easy to see why this provincial park, situated on the southwestern shore of Charlie Lake in the broad valley of the Peace River, is popular with both locals and visitors. It is conveniently located 11 kilometres north of Fort St. John on the Alaska Highway at its junction with Highway 29. All services can be found at Fort St. John, while more limited facilities are available closer to the campground on Highway 97.

> Facilities

The 57-site campground is set among a heavily treed deciduous forest of aspen, birch, alder, lodgepole pine, and spruce on the southwestern shore of the 13-kilometre Charlie Lake. The sound of traffic is constant, even though most of the sites are not close to the road. The well-appointed sites are large and suitable for every type of recreational vehicle; some have grassy areas for tents. There is also a sani-station and a wheelchair-accessible pit toilet, but no showers or flush toilets. Reservations are accepted at 40 sites.

> Recreational activities

Fishing in summer and winter is popular here; northern pike and walleye inhabit the lake. BC Parks calls Charlie Lake the walleye "hot spot" of the province (what a claim to fame!). A 2-kilometre trail leads from the campground to the lakeside day-use area, where there is a boat launch. You can swim in the lake, although the high algae content of the water may put you off. The campground has a fantastic play area for children and a horseshoe pit in a large grassy field is ideal for picnics. For those who choose activities away from the campground, an eighteen-hole golf course and country club can be found nearby on the Alaska Highway.

> Additional information

Archaeological research in the area has revealed Indigenous habitation dating back 10,000 years. If you succeed in obtaining a campsite away from the road,

Charlie Lake is a delightful place to camp. A variety of berries grow in the vicinity, but remember that picking the vegetation in BC parks is prohibited. When we stayed, it seemed that every site housed a huge dirty truck and a boat. Fishing was obviously a key activity, so the campground was silent at 10:00 PM as all the campers needed to leave at daybreak to go fishing.

CROOKED RIVER

> Location

There are two kinds of campgrounds: those geared for overnight camping and those where you want to spend time relaxing and overdosing on BC's wonderful scenery. Crooked River falls into the second category. This delightful spot is found in the Fraser Basin amid a forest of lodgepole pine interspersed with alder, birch, aspen, and spruce. Recently, the area has been ravaged by the mountain pine beetle, which can be easily evidenced by the numerous brown trees. Crooked River is situated 70 kilometres north of Prince George on Highway 97. The nearby community of Bear Lake provides accommodation, gas, and food (try the Grizzly Inn for a good breakfast).

> Facilities

There are 65 spots of various sizes in this 963-hectare park. As with all provincial park campgrounds in BC, a map at the entrance to the park illustrates where the largest sites are and where the pull-throughs are located. Some sites overlook the lake, and trees provide privacy and shade. There is a sani-station, as well as flush and pit toilets and showers. Some park facilities, including the washrooms, are wheelchair accessible. During the peak summer months, campers register at a booth upon entering the park. Reservations are accepted at 29 sites, and long-stay camping is also offered.

> Recreational activities

The park is on Bear Lake, which has two good sandy beaches ideal for children. It is possible to canoe and kayak. With powerboats prohibited, paddlers are assured of a tranquil visit, as are windsurfers. Fishing is good and not just confined to Bear Lake: nearby Square and Hart lakes and Crooked River have rainbow and brook trout, Dolly Varden, Arctic grayling, and whitefish. There are a number of trails that take about an hour to complete, as well as longer hikes. The trail around Square Lake is great for viewing wildlife and birds (amateur ornithologists may be rewarded with sightings of bald eagles and ospreys), while the Crooked River Trail follows the same route that early Canadian explorers, such as Simon Fraser and Alexander Mackenzie, took in the nineteenth century. Youngsters will enjoy the park's adventure playground, volleyball court, and horseshoe pits.

> Additional information

BC Parks literature states that Crooked River Provincial Park was originally established to protect the area's attractive lakes and surrounding landscape. I stayed at this location in June one year and got completely bitten from head to toe by mosquitoes, despite dressing in layers of clothing and standing over the fire pit. This experience tainted my opinion of the park, but I have not had the same problem on subsequent visits.

GWILLIM LAKE

> Location

With its stunning location, 32,326-hectare Gwillim Lake Provincial Park is definitely a place to include on your camping itinerary. Set in the Rocky Mountain foothills, at an elevation of 765 metres, the park offers breathtaking mountain views and 25 kilometres of shoreline. It is found on Highway 29, a 40-minute drive from Chetwynd to the north and Tumbler Ridge to the south. Services are available in both these centres.

> Facilities

Gwillim Lake's 50 campsites are located in an area lightly forested with pines; many have commanding views of the lake and the Rocky Mountains. There are also numerous walk-in camping spots. All the basic facilities found within BC parks are available (fire pits, drinking water, pit toilets, picnic tables), and some park facilities are wheelchair accessible. No sani-station is provided.

> Recreational activities

A perfectly wonderful time can be had here just reading, relaxing, and enjoying the beauty of BC, but Gwillim Lake also has a designated swimming area and a boat launch. Arctic grayling, northern pike, Dolly Varden, burbot, and mountain whitefish can all be caught, although anglers should be warned that the deep blue waters of the lake do not yield fantastic fish populations. The park has hiking trails, too, and the area is very good for observing wildlife, particularly deer and moose, which are most often spotted in the early morning. For children, there is an adventure playground in the middle of the campground. Rock climbing activities also exist.

> Additional information

This park provides some panoramic views of the Rocky Mountains. Above the northwestern shore, an open meadow creates a viewpoint of the western part of the lake. The park is beautiful to visit in the fall when the colours are spectacular, but it really is a gem of a location any time of the year. The town of Chetwynd is basically a forestry community with a relatively small population (under 3,000), yet it boasts a pioneer and railway museum and a trapper's cabin—all open to the public. The town also displays a number of interesting chainsaw sculptures by BC artists. This campground is maintained by a local organization, so the services may be slightly different from those found in other provincial parks.

KINASKAN LAKE

> Location

This remote lakeside campground is a gift from the gods. Set in the south Stikine Plateau and Iskut River Valley between the Skeena and Coast Mountains, this park is found 100 kilometres south of Dease Lake—the "jade capital of the world"—which offers amenities such as gas, propane, food, lodging, and a huge grocery store that has everything the camper needs. More limited amenities are available at Iskut, approximately 40 minutes north of Kinaskan Lake.

> Facilities

The campground is situated in a desirable location on the lake itself, and a large number of the 50 campsites are on the water's edge where the views are wonderful. The sites, which are quite large and surrounded by trees, afford more privacy than those of Kinaskan Lake's nearest competitor, Meziadin Lake, which is a 3-hour drive away. There is no sani-station and only the basic facilities exist (picnic tables, pit toilets, drinking water, fire pits).

> ## Recreational activities
Lake fishing for rainbow trout in Kinaskan and Natadesleen lakes is reputed to be excellent. For boaters, there is a floating wharf and a boat launch, and swimming is possible, although the lake is prone to high winds and waves that can develop quite suddenly. This is the provincial park closest to Mount Edziza Provincial Park, a 230,000-hectare area established to conserve spectacular volcanic landscapes that include lava flows, cinder fields, and basalt plateaus. The Mowdade Trail leads from Kinaskan Lake to the Coffee Crater area of this park.

> ## Additional information
This area also offers beautiful scenery and is a welcome rest for those who have endured the long Highway 37 where there are few services. It was established in 1987, and its remote location makes it a magnet for fishermen, moose, black and grizzly bears, wolves, coyotes, minks, goats, and stone sheep. Staying here lets campers see the BC advertised in tourist media. I have only stopped to picnic here, which is a great pity, because it is a stunning location. When we last stopped here (August 2013), we had the place to ourselves. We all had a picnic and swam in the fantastic clear waters of the cool lake. It is well worth travelling Highway 37 just to visit the three awesome campgrounds along this stretch of road: Meziadin, Tā Ch'ilā (formerly Boya Lake), and Kinaskan.

KISKATINAW

> ## Location
Kiskatinaw Provincial Park is located on the old Alaska Highway. Nearby, aromatic cottonwood trees on the edge of the river exude a delicate perfume in the summer (a delight for most people except those with allergies). Primarily used as an overnight camping spot, this 58-hectare provincial park is located on the northern Great Plains, 28 kilometres north of Dawson Creek. A 5-kilometre

paved access road leads to the campground. Services can be found at Dawson Creek to the south or Taylor to the north. In 2021, the park was fully closed due to a high landslide risk and public safety concerns. Check the BC Parks website for the latest updates.

> Facilities

Kiskatinaw offers 28 spots, secluded in groves of poplar and spruce. Camping facilities are basic and include pit toilets, drinking water, fire pits, and picnic tables, but no sani-station or wheelchair access.

> Recreational activities

There are limited swimming possibilities, but the water is warm so tubing and wading are popular, and the campground has swings, a sandbox, and a horseshoe pit. An archaeological site is also located in the park. From the campground you can walk to the scenic deep-walled canyon of the Kiskatinaw River and view the historic curved wooden bridge that was developed for the original Alaska Highway in 1942. The bridge was built in just nine months by a Canadian construction company and was the first curved wooden bridge built in Canada. It is 58 metres long with a banked nine-degree curve to conform to the bend of the highway, and the only curved, banked trestle bridge remaining in western Canada.

> Additional information

The town of Dawson Creek was established in 1931 when the Northern Alberta Railways line was extended, and it flourished in 1942 when American soldiers and engineers arrived to build the Alaska Highway. Dawson Creek is now home to the Mile Zero Post, a 3-metre-high marker that identifies the beginning of the Alaska Highway, and the Dawson Creek Station Museum gives information on the construction of this famous road. Many tourists visit Dawson Creek to have their photographs taken at Mile Zero before heading north to the Yukon and Alaska. When I tried to visit this park, which is maintained by the local community, the access road was under construction. It is a great picnic spot even if you decide not to camp.

KLEANZA CREEK

> Location

At the beginning of the twentieth cen-
tury, the area around Kleanza Creek was
inhabited by gold seekers. Some years
later, in 1934, a 180-gram gold nugget
was taken from the creek, and there may
still be gold left. This wonderful, peaceful campground is situated 15 kilometres
east of Terrace on Highway 16, where all
amenities can be found.

> Facilities

Tall fir trees provide shade and privacy to the 34 large campsites of Kleanza
Creek Provincial Park. Many sites overlook the clear bubbling waters of the
creek itself—a calming sound that will lull you to sleep. Facilities are basic
(pit toilets, drinking water, picnic tables, fire pits); there is limited wheelchair
access and no sani-station. Reservations are accepted for 10 sites.

> Recreational activities

There is a relaxing ambience here. Leisure pursuits include a 1-kilometre
trail leading up to a viewpoint above the creek, and there is also a smaller
trail running alongside the creek. If you look hard, the remains of the Cassiar
Hydraulic Mining Company's operations can be seen above the canyon. Pink
salmon are often observed in the creek during the fall, but there is limited
fishing potential. Swimming is possible in cool pools. The campground has a
basketball hoop, horseshoe pit, and checkerboards. If it happens to be raining,
visit Mount Layton Hot Springs or the Heritage Park Museum in Terrace.

> Additional information

Kleanza means "gold" in the Gitxsan language. Maybe because I've only visited
this park during good weather, the campground lives in my memory as serene
and quite beautiful. I have never camped here, but I have visited on at least five
occasions. A few years ago, my teenage sons spent a couple of hours frolicking

in the water, while my spouse decided to skinny-dip farther upstream. Even if you don't stay the night, the park is great for a picnic, and BC Parks has conveniently placed benches to face the tumbling creek. The only note of caution is that bears occasionally pass through the area. Otherwise, a highly recommended and exquisite place to camp.

LAKELSE LAKE

> Location
Set amidst majestic old-growth forest and located 20 kilometres south of Terrace on Highway 37, Lakelse Lake is surrounded by the mountains of the Kitimat Range and provides a beautiful haven for travellers. Services are available either in Terrace or in Kitimat, 40 kilometres to the south.

> Facilities
Within a forest of cedar, hemlock, and Sitka spruce, the Furlong Bay Campground offers 156 large, well-organized, and well-maintained campsites catering to every type of recreational vehicle. A full range of facilities is provided, including a sani-station, flush toilets, and showers. As well, the toilets, shower buildings, and the Furlong Beach day-use area are wheelchair accessible. Reservations are accepted at all sites. Electrical hook-ups are also available at 50 sites. Recently, a visitors centre was built selling ice, snacks, and other items.

> Recreational activities
The lake offers excellent canoeing, sailing, and water-skiing, and there is a paved boat launch. There are wonderful golden, sandy beaches, picnic shelters, and a children's playground. A 45-minute educational trail that leads through the park allows closer exploration of the old-growth forest, and there are also interpretive programs offered in the summer. In the lake, and in the nearby Skeena and Kitimat Rivers, anglers can catch steelhead, rainbow trout, Dolly Varden, and all five species of Pacific salmon. In August, hundreds of sockeye salmon can be seen in Williams Creek at the end of the park. According to BC Parks, over one hundred bird species frequent the area. A 30-minute drive away, Kitimat offers a variety of activities, including tours of a salmon hatchery.

> Additional information

Lakelse really is a delight to visit for the wide array of activities it provides, both within the confines of the park's boundaries and in the larger vicinity. Should the weather turn, the town of Terrace has an excellent leisure centre with a pool and hot tub, as well as a Heritage Park Museum located on almost two acres with log buildings and an array of artifacts from the community's logging, mining, trapping, and farming past. To the south of the campground, the town of Kitimat has wonderful hiking trails.

LIARD RIVER
HOT SPRINGS

> Location

For any BC parks enthusiast, Liard River Hot Springs must be one of the biggest jewels in the crown. It certainly ranks as one of the top provincial parks for me. The only disadvantage to this beautiful park is that it is the most northerly in BC and therefore not easily accessible for most people. However, those who do travel as far as kilometre 765 on the Alaska Highway will be rewarded amply for their efforts. Liard River Hot Springs is situated 60 kilometres north of Muncho Lake and is the second-largest hot springs in Canada (after Banff). A restaurant and small shop are located across the road from the park itself, while more comprehensive services can be found at Muncho Lake.

> Facilities

At Liard River Hot Springs there are 53 large, well-appointed, and totally private campsites set among trees and suitable for every type of recreational vehicle. The park is wheelchair accessible, but facilities are restricted to the basic ones (fire pits, drinking water, pit toilets, picnic tables) and there is no sani-station. There are also no showers ... but here they aren't needed! Reservations are accepted and very strongly advised as this park operates at capacity from May until September.

> Recreational activities

The park's biggest attraction is, of course, the hot springs, which have been beautifully maintained in their natural setting. A boardwalk takes campers from the campground to the bathing pools, an 8-minute walk from the campground where changing rooms are located. Here bathers can choose which area of the water to sit in and which temperature to endure (from an almost unbearable 52°C, where the waters emerge, to a far more comfortable 42°C). It is possible to swim here. In addition to the mineral pools, a variety of fauna and flora unique to the region can be seen. More than 100 bird species visit the park. Moose and black bear also live here, and BC Parks literature states that over 28 species of mammals and 250 species of boreal forest plants are found here. A hanging garden displays this vegetation at certain times of the year, which is loved by photographers. For children, there is a play area, a horseshoe pit, and interpretive programs in the summer.

> Additional information

Travellers have enjoyed the hot springs here for centuries: for many hundreds of years, Indigenous Peoples, including the Kaska Dena, Dane-zaa, Tse'khene, Nahʔą Dehé Dene, and Tłı̨chǫ communities, bathed here. In 1835, the waters were charted by Robert Campbell, a Hudson's Bay Company factor. In 1942, the American army stationed in the area to build the Alaska Highway constructed the first boardwalk to the pools. I have extremely affectionate memories of the first time I was lucky enough to stay here. We went to the hot pools at 7:00 AM, before most people were up. A thunderstorm was passing, and we sat in the hot waters watching the lightning as the cold rain fell into the warm pools. After this therapeutic experience, we took our clean, glowing bodies for breakfast in the funky little restaurant across the road from the campground—a perfect start to the day. Our subsequent visit in 2013 reaffirmed my impression of Laird Hot Springs as one of BC's best provincial parks and one of my favourites; they are well worth a visit, and unlike many of the commercially developed hot springs in the south of the province, they remain in a totally natural environment. However, in 1997, two people were killed here in a bear attack and the park received some negative publicity. Such incidents are rare, but they remind us of the potential hazards of camping outdoors. In 2021, Laird became the first provincial park to have an electric fence installed to keep wildlife and visitors separate. Liard River's hot springs are ranked among the top five in North America, but if you don't camp here, you'll have to pay the day-use fee to access them. Finally, on the road to and from Laird, watch for herds of bison—they are quite stunning.

MEZIADIN LAKE

> Location

Ever seen a live bear trap? When I visited Meziadin Lake, a trap was being kept at the park, although the BC Parks attendant informed me that it had not been used for a while. Meziadin Lake Provincial Park is in the Nass Basin and rewards the visitor with excellent views of the Coast Mountains. As you travel north from Highway 16, this is the first of three provincial park campgrounds on Highway 37. It is just south of Meziadin Junction, the turnoff for Stewart, which has a shop, cafe, gas station, and tourist information. The park also has a small convenience store, but the widest range of services is found in Stewart, 50 kilometres to the west.

> Facilities

This 335-hectare park has 66 open gravel campsites that can accommodate every size of vehicle but offer little privacy. However, a few are situated on the lakeshore and offer breathtaking views of the lake. There is no sani-station, and because of the prevalence of bears in the area, garbage has to be stored in a concrete structure on the site and all items used for cooking, eating, and drinking must be kept in a vehicle day and night. The pit toilets are wheelchair accessible, and a recent upgrade has brought Wi-Fi to the park. Eighteen sites have electrical hook-ups and long stays (up to four weeks) are permitted. Reservations are accepted at 25 sites.

> Recreational activities

Recreational pursuits offered by the lake include swimming, boating, and fishing for rainbow trout and Dolly Varden. There is a boat launch, a small dock, and the nearby Meziadin River has a salmon-counting fence. The road to Stewart provides a breathtaking view of more than twenty glaciers, including Bear Glacier, which comes right down to the road. Stewart and Hyder (in Alaska) are early gold- and silver-mining communities located about 65 kilometres from the campground, and Stewart has a number of pleasant cafes and restaurants.

> Additional information

This campground seems to be the busiest on Highway 37 and is a popular place for those interested in fishing. Bears are particularly active during the salmon-spawning season, so visiting Hyder at this time of year provides the best chance of seeing both black and grizzly bears. We spent an unforgettable three hours in Hyder watching grizzly bears fish salmon out of the stream, rip them apart, and devour them. It is an image I will never forget. When we got back to our tent at 8:00 PM, it was dark and raining heavily. A couple in a neighbouring RV took pity on us and invited us in for the remains of their chicken stew and alcohol. We retired to our tent two very happy campers. We stayed in August 2004, swam in the lake with a beaver, enjoyed brilliant weather, and saw grizzly and black bears, then repeated the experience a few years later as Meziadin delivered the goods yet again. A truly wonderful location.

MOBERLY LAKE

> Location

This campground is well maintained and a real delight to stay in, but at certain times of the year, you'll have to watch out for black bears, which feed on the abundant berries growing in the area. Positioned in the valley of the Moberly River on the south shore of the lake, between the foothills of the Rocky Mountains and the northern Great Plains, Moberly Lake Provincial Park is reached by turning off Highway 29, 25 kilometres northeast of Chetwynd, and taking a good gravel road 3 kilometres. All services are available at Chetwynd, 25 kilometres away, and more limited ones are at the Moberly Lake townsite, 11 kilometres from the campground.

> Facilities

One hundred and nine large, private camping spots set in a forest of mature white spruce and aspen make this a desirable destination. Streams flow through the campground and a few sites overlook the lake. Grassy sites are available, and there is ample space for the longest RV. There is a sani-station and only pit toilets. Some facilities are wheelchair accessible, and reservations are accepted at 67 sites.

> Recreational activities

A number of activities can be undertaken both within the 98-hectare park and in the surrounding area. The park has a boat launch, and it is possible to fish for Dolly Varden, northern pike, bull trout, lake trout, whitefish, and char. A developed beach and changing facilities make swimming a delight. There are also a number of walks and trails, and a children's play area has been built near the lake. A wealth of birdlife can be observed in the area, including bald eagles, American kestrels, belted kingfishers, and common loons. About an hour's drive away, the W.A.C. Bennett Dam, one of the largest earth-filled dams in the world, houses a visitor centre with interpretive programs and a restaurant, and the nearby Peace Canyon Dam is also well worth a visit. There are also opportunities to go golfing in the area.

> Additional information

Sixty-five million years ago Moberly Lake formed part of a great inland sea and the adjacent land was inhabited by dinosaurs. Moberly Lake was named after Henry Moberly, a Hudson's Bay Company trader and trapper, who settled on the shores of the lake in the mid-1800s. It has special significance to the Dane-Zaa First Nations, who knew it as "the lake that you could depend on" because it was a consistent food source. They also believed it had a hole in its bottom (or no bottom at all) and that an ancient creature lives in the lake—so be careful when you go swimming ...

MONKMAN

> Location

Monkman Provincial Park is a wonderland of waterfalls and scenic lakes surrounded by the Hart Range of the central Rocky Mountains. The park was established in 1981; 22,000 hectares were added in 1999 to take in the Upper Fontiniko Creek Valley and Limestone Lakes areas, which contain old-growth spruce forests and unique geological forms. Accessing this massive park requires travelling 60 kilometres south from Tumbler Ridge on a gravel road, a trip that may deter some visitors. Services are located at Tumbler Ridge.

> Facilities

Twenty-two camping spots are found here, a number of them less than 50 metres from the Murray River. All accommodate every type of recreational vehicle, and some have specific areas for tents. Backcountry campsites are also available. Campers will find fire pits, picnic tables, hand-pumped drinking water, and pit toilets at this location. There is no firewood, however, and campers are asked to take garbage with them when they leave the park.

> Recreational activities

Among the biggest attractions here are the hiking trails. A short trail leads to the spectacular 60-metre-high Kinuseo Falls, where a viewing platform ensures excellent photography opportunities. A 7-kilometre (one-way) trail leads to the Murray River, where a suspension bridge can be crossed, taking hikers along the much longer Monkman Pass Memorial Trail into the park's backcountry. The latter route follows the original one of the Monkman Pass Highway (see below). Powerboats can be launched on the Pine and Murray rivers, and the Murray River can be canoed below the falls. Fishing in the lakes and rivers yields trout, char, grayling, and whitefish. The campground also has a playground and horseshoe pit, and the area is very rich in wildlife, including grizzly and black bears, mountain goats, moose, and caribou. Caving is also a popular pastime in this locale.

> Additional information

In 1922, Alex Monkman, a fur trader, farmer, and visionary, dreamed of creating a route to link the farms of the Peace River to Hansard, northeast of Prince George. In 1936, he formed the Monkman Pass Highway Association, and a year later work started. Unfortunately, the project was plagued by a lack of funds, and all work ceased in 1939 with the outbreak of the Second World War. Today, the Monkman Pass Memorial Trail follows much of the original highway, while the pass bears the name of the pioneer whose dream was never realized.

MUNCHO LAKE

> Location

Muncho Lake is an area of parkland covering over 88,000 hectares in the Terminal and Muskwa ranges of the Rocky Mountains, an area noted not only for its wildlife but also for its classic Rocky Mountain features, such as folded and vaulted rock and alluvial fans. Like many provincial parks along the Alaska Highway, it owes its existence to the rout and is situated at kilometre 681, about 250 kilometres west of Fort Nelson. A gas station, restaurants, and small shops are located, quite unusually, in the park itself. When travelling to or from Muncho Lake, stop near kilometre 650 of the Alaska Highway and look for stone sheep licking the mineral rocks. The best time for viewing is at dawn or dusk in the late spring and early fall.

> Facilities

Thirty campsites are positioned in two campgrounds on the shores of Muncho Lake, a vast expanse of jade-coloured water. The more northerly campground, MacDonald, has 15 spots that are quite close to the road and provide little privacy. Strawberry Flats (my preference) is the more southerly location, with 15 spots that are more private, some on the waterfront. There is no sani-station, and facilities are basic in both campgrounds (fire pits, drinking water, pit toilets, picnic tables). The campground does not accept reservations.

> Recreational activities

Muncho Lake, 12 kilometres long and over 2 kilometres wide in places, is typical Canadian Rocky Mountain scenery and offers endless photo opportunities. The 90-kilometre drive through the park on the Alaska Highway is often described as the most scenic stretch of that route. While staying here, campers can follow hiking trails, go boating (there is a boat launch at MacDonald Campground) and fish for trout, Arctic grayling, Dolly Varden, and whitefish. The lake tends to be cold in the summer, so it is not a popular swimming location. The park is also noted for its wildlife, including black bears, stone sheep, mountain goats, caribou, deer, and wolves.

> Additional information

Muncho Lake takes its name from the Kaska language: "muncho" means "big lake." The lake's jade colour comes from the copper oxides leached in from the surrounding bedrock, coupled with the refraction of sunlight on sediments brought into the lake by glacial meltwater. The scenery here is spectacular, but the weather can be quite cool and windy. In the summer months, you can take a boat tour of the lake—a perfect opportunity to spend more time in this breathtaking location that few are lucky enough to experience.

NAIKOON

> Location

Naikoon Provincial Park is a photographer's paradise: the atmospheric conditions and the variety of plants and wildlife yield fantastic photography opportunities. The only provincial park with camping facilities on Haida Gwaii, Naikoon is found on Graham Island, the most northerly island of the archipelago, which is served by scheduled ferries from Prince Rupert. The park has two campgrounds: Misty Meadows is located near Tlell, 42 kilometres north of Skidegate on Highway 16, while Agate Beach is 26 kilometres northeast of Masset on a secondary road. Services are available in Port Clements, Tlell, Masset, and Queen Charlotte.

> Facilities

The 43 sites at Agate Beach are close to the ocean and somewhat exposed; in contrast, the 30 vehicle and 6 tent sites at Misty Meadows are situated under pine trees. Misty Meadows is my preference, as it is less exposed. When I was here, each campsite had a hanging basket full of flowers at its entrance—a wonderful touch. Neither site has a sani-station or flush toilets. There is limited wheelchair access at Agate Beach. Wilderness camping is also permitted throughout the park, and three wilderness shelters are located along East Beach near the mouth of MaaGan Gandlaay (Cape Ball River) and at Sk'aw Gandalaa (Cape Fife).

> Recreational activities

Numerous recreational activities can be enjoyed in this 69,071-hectare park, and visitors frequently spend a week or more here. The visitor centre is located on Highway 16, 2 kilometres south of Tlell, and is open from June 15 to September 15 and interpretive programs are offered. Hiking trail details are posted on the information board at the entrance to each campground, and the park has 100 kilometres of beach to explore. It is possible to dig for clams and to swim in the Tlell River, and coho salmon and steelhead can also be caught. Opportunities to see wildlife abound: the Tow Hill, Drizzle Lake, and Rose Spit Ecological Reserve have been established in the park to protect the flora and fauna. It is illegal to camp, fish, hunt, or use motorized vehicles in these ecological reserves.

> Additional information

The islands of Haida Gwaii, renowned for overcast skies and frequent fogs, are often referred to as the "Misty Islands." Campers should come well prepared for cold, damp conditions, even if you're planning to visit in July and stay in a vehicle. If you wear the correct gear, you can enjoy walking along deserted windswept beaches, and there are excellent opportunities to see an assortment of sea mammals and birds—Haida Gwaii boasts the second-highest eagle population in the world. According to the BC Parks website, "Naikoon" is a corruption of the Haida name for Rose Spit, Nai-kun, which means "house point."

NISGA'A MEMORIAL LAVA BED (ANHLUUT'UKWSIM LAXMIHL ANGWINGA'ASANSKWHL NISGA'A)

> Location

North of Terrace, you can camp adjacent to Canada's most recent volcanic eruption, which experts believe took place in the mid-1700s. The Nisga'a Memorial Lava Bed is the first provincial park to be managed jointly by a First Nation and BC Parks. Also known as Anhluut'ukwsim Laxmihl Angwinga'asanskwhl Nisga'a, this 17,717-hectare park is reached by turning off Highway 16 at Terrace and travelling 100 kilometres north on the Nisga'a Highway, which turns to gravel after the first 70 kilometres. There is a visitor centre and information kiosk at the entrance to the park. Full services can be found at Terrace; grocery stores, restaurants, and gas stations are in the five local Nisga'a communities of Gitlakdamix (New Aiyansh), Gitwinksihlkw (Canyon City), Lakalzap (Greenville), Kincolith, and Nass Camp. Watch for logging trucks, especially if you're driving the road on a weekday.

> Facilities

The campground here was established beside Vetter Creek in 2000 and has 16 shaded vehicle/tent spaces within a deciduous forest. Facilities include flush and pit toilets, firewood, and picnic tables. One campsite and one pit toilet are wheelchair accessible.

> Recreational activities

This park is the first in the province to combine an interpretation of natural features and Indigenous culture. The Nisga'a Tribal Council has established a visitor centre (open from mid-June to Labour Day) to illustrate its traditional culture, display aspects of the Nisga'a lifestyle, and arrange tours of the Tseax Cone volcano. In the summer, 3-kilometre-long guided walks are offered (see nisgaanation.ca/lava-bed-park for more information). In addition to touring spectacular lava beds, there are other hiking options, and Lava Lake offers opportunities for swimming, boating, and fishing for salmon and trout. The lake has one gravel boat launch and there's another one at Nass River.

> Additional information

It is believed the Tseax Cone erupted in 1775, destroying two Nisga'a villages and killing as many as 2,000 people. The lava flow rerouted the Nass River and dammed other waterways. Visitors now see a sparsely vegetated lava plain that stretches over 10 kilometres. Be forewarned: walking on the lava beds, although fascinating, is hard on the feet, so be sure you have appropriate footwear. This is another fascinating and unique area of BC to visit. Besides the spectacular geography, you might also be lucky enough to view moose, bear, marmots, and goats. In 2020 and 2021, this park was completely closed due to the COVID-19 global pandemic, but reopened again in 2022.

ONE ISLAND LAKE

> Location

After thirty years living in BC, I still have not had the opportunity to visit this park (indeed it is one of only a handful I haven't visited), but all of the people I have spoken to who know the area stress the cleanliness of the lake's water. It is a Class C park, jointly maintained by BC Parks and the local community, so while it is called a provincial park, the services it provides may not be the same as at other provincial parks. Somewhat off the beaten track, One Island Lake does not have the advantage of being a conveniently situated roadside campground for one night's stop, but it will guarantee a quiet night's rest. The 61-hectare park is situated 60 kilometres southeast of Dawson Creek in the foothills of the Rockies. Turn off Highway 2 at Tupper, where services are available, and take an unpaved road 38 kilometres to the campground.

> Facilities

There are 30 campsites available on the east side of the lake, some backing onto the lake. Services are limited to the basics (drinking water, fire pits, picnic tables, pit toilets).

> Recreational activities

This park is popular with residents of Dawson Creek in summer and winter. It is possible to swim, fish, water-ski, windsurf, and go boating here. There is a boat launch, and, since the lake is stocked annually, fishing for rainbow and brook trout is reputed to be excellent (with catches reaching over 2 kilograms in size). A fish-cleaning stand is provided near the boat launch, and there's an annual Father's Day fishing derby. There are no developed hiking trails, but there is a small playground, should you have small children or the urge to stop fishing and play yourself.

> ## Additional information

One Island Lake Provincial Park is representative of the Kiskatinaw Plateau ecosystem, and moose, white-tailed and mule deer, and beaver are found here. The lake's original name was "HOP Lake," after the first letters of the last names of the three men who helped build the first access road: Len Hodgson, Bill Oakford, and Art Pearson. It was renamed "One Island Lake" by government surveyors, because of the small island in one corner of the lake. The people who established the settlement of Tupper were Sudetens (Czechoslovakians from the Czech–Poland border) who escaped Hitler by settling here in the 1930s. For those who do not like travelling on gravel roads, Swan Lake Provincial Park has a nearby alternative campground.

PAARENS BEACH

> ## Location

Watch the sun go down and the stars come out from this lovely campground on the warm southern shores of Stuart Lake. At nearly 70 kilometres in length, Stuart is one of the largest lakes in the province and located amidst the Nechako Plateau Hills. It's a little less than 2 hours northwest of Prince George on Highway 27. Approximately 15 minutes away by car is the historic town of Fort St. James, which has all services.

> ## Facilities

The 50-hectare campground contains 42 sites; 6 are close to the water's edge and 3 are walk-in sites. With a few exceptions, the sites are large, private, and partly wooded. Only the basic amenities are provided (pit toilets, drinking water, picnic tables, fire pits). Reservations are accepted at 20 sites.

> Recreational activities

This provincial park boasts an 800-metre sandy beach, including a roped-off swimming area, and BC Parks has made it ideal for families by providing a change house, picnic shelter, multiple picnic tables, horseshoe pits, a play area for children, and a large grassy area perfect for ball games. Stuart Lake is also an ideal location for sailing and windsurfing, but users must be cautious because sudden strong winds can easily develop on this large lake. Campers can also fish for rainbow trout and lake char, and there is a concrete boat launch at the south end of the park. Nearby, the reconstructed Hudson's Bay Company trading post at Fort St. James provides an account of pioneer life and is well worth a visit. Guides dressed in period costume give accounts and anecdotes of the lives of the early settlers. For the more energetic, the Mount Pope trail just north of the community takes hikers on a 2- to 4-hour hike (one way) up to the top of the mountain, which offers spectacular views of Stuart Lake below.

> Additional information

Swimmer's itch can sometimes be a problem in Stuart Lake at certain times of year. Stuart Lake is one of the largest in the province and is part of the Stuart–Takla chain of lakes, along with Trembleur Lake and Takla Lake (almost 90 kilometres long). With so much water, this area is a fishing nirvana. Paarens Beach is very close to Sowchea Bay, where there are comparable facilities, and it is easy to travel between the two to determine which provincial park provides the best camping location for your needs.

PRUDHOMME LAKE

> Location

Twenty-one kilometres east of Prince Rupert, there is a small coniferous-forested lakeside campground at Prudhomme Lake. Access from Highway 16 is immediate, and all amenities are available in Prince Rupert. By staying here, campers can enjoy the best of two provincial parks: Diana Lake Provincial Park is a stone's throw away, accessed by a 2.5-kilometre gravel road off Highway 16.

> Facilities

Prudhomme Lake offers 24 spacious campsites on the water, though large RVs may have difficulty accessing some of these spots. There is no sani-station and only basic facilities (picnic tables, pit toilets, pump water, fire pits). One campsite and one pit toilet are wheelchair accessible. Noise from passing traffic is easily audible, although the road is not that busy, especially at night. Reservations are accepted at 10 of the sites.

> Recreational activities

Although the activities at Prudhomme Lake are limited to fishing for steelhead, rainbow trout, and Dolly Varden, Diana Lake has a day-use area that's good for swimming, canoeing, and sunbathing. From Diana Lake it is possible to take a trail that meanders through the coastal rainforest to Diana Creek Falls, or to fish in the creeks that run through the park. A short drive away, Prince Rupert offers many leisure activities, including the Museum of Northern BC, Kwinitsa Railway Station Museum, a self-guided walking tour, and an eighteen-hole golf course. In the nearby community of Port Edward, you can visit one of the BC coast's oldest fishing canneries—Northern Pacific Cannery. Open from May 1 to September 30, this site is well worth a visit as it represents a unique piece of BC history (for more information, visit northpacificcannery.ca). We visited in early August and had the place to ourselves.

> Additional information

In August and September, it is possible to see salmon spawning in Diana Creek. Black-tailed deer also inhabit this area. From Prince Rupert, air charters to the Khutzeymateen Grizzly Bear Sanctuary, 45 kilometres north of the city, can be arranged. This area of 445 square kilometres is home to the largest-known grizzly bear population on the BC coast and one of the largest in the world. I see Prudhomme Lake primarily as a convenient overnight camping location for visiting Prince Rupert, or if you need a place to spend the night prior to catching a ferry.

PURDEN LAKE

> ## Location

Exceptional photography opportunities can be had at Purden Lake, especially in the early morning as the mist slowly clears over the calm waters of the lake. Situated in the foothills of the Rockies, less than an hour's drive from Prince George on a paved road 2 kilometres off the Yellowhead Highway, this popular campground is regularly used by both Prince George residents and visitors. Services such as gas, propane, and restaurants are conveniently located less than 5 kilometres from the campground, although its proximity to Prince George means campers are within an hour's drive of every amenity.

> ## Facilities

This 2,521-hectare park has 78 campsites set among trees. All sites are relatively private, and some sites are set aside specifically for tents. There are flush toilets and a sani-station, but no showers. Some park facilities are wheelchair accessible, and reservations are accepted at 41 sites.

> ## Recreational activities

Park amenities include an adventure playground and a horseshoe pit. There's also a sandy beach with a designated swimming area (be warned, there is a sharp drop-off) and changing rooms in the day-use area. Lakeside walking trails offer beautiful views of the surrounding area and make it possible to investigate a variety of plant life. There is a concrete boat launch, and water-skiing is permitted on the lake. Anglers can fish for rainbow trout and burbot. The city of Prince George, 64 kilometres away, provides a wealth of things to see and do, including the Exploration Place Museum and Science Centre (formerly the Fraser–Fort George Regional Museum) and the University of Northern British Columbia, which affords spectacular views of the surrounding landscape.

> Additional information

Thanks to the park's beautiful setting amidst undulating, forested mountains and its easy access to Prince George, Purden Lake is one of the region's most popular parks. Consequently, it is regularly full on weekends, so reservations are strongly advisable. The lakeshore is very picturesque and its beauty quite haunting.

RED BLUFF

> Location

Like Babine Lake Provincial Park, Red Bluff is situated on Babine Lake, the longest natural freshwater lake in BC. So-called because of the dramatic reddish cliffs under which it nestles, the park is a few kilometres south of the village of Granisle and a 45-minute drive from Highway 16 on a paved road reached by turning off at Topley. The 148-hectare park is jointly managed by the local community and BC Parks, which means services may vary from those at other provincial parks.

> Facilities

The campground has 34 large sites set in woodland; a few overlook the lake, while others are more open and closer to the day-use area. There is also an overflow camping area. Facilities are limited to the basic ones generally found in BC parks (picnic tables, fire pits, drinking water, pit toilets, firewood for purchase), so there is no sani-station, flush toilets, or wheelchair access in the pit toilets. Reservations are accepted at 27 sites.

> Recreational activities

Visitors can engage in numerous pursuits involving the lake, such as fishing (BC Parks boasts that cutthroat trout weighing up to 1 kilogram, rainbow trout of up to 6 kilograms, and char up to 13 kilograms can be caught here), boating (there is a somewhat rudimentary boat launch), and swimming. Hiking is possible. The Bluff Trail is an easy 3-kilometre loop interpretive trail, and a number of small trails provide the opportunity to see wildlife—black bears and moose are particularly abundant. One trail overlooks a marsh area, where your patience may be rewarded by a sighting of elusive birds and waterfowl. However, at certain times of the year, when the water level is high, this trail can be flooded. The Fulton River salmon spawning channel just south of the park also deserves a visit if you want to learn about salmon spawning and view salmon leaping up a series of channels.

> Additional information

Granisle was a copper-mining town until the mine closed in 1992. The surrounding area is known for its wildlife. Wild animals are regularly sighted along the quiet drive from Highway 16 to the park, and we saw black bears when we drove here. The lake can become extremely rough, as high winds are easily whipped up in the area. I spent a somewhat uneasy night at this campground listening to the winds high in the trees and wondering which tree was going to crash down on top of me. My fears were totally unfounded.

SEELEY LAKE

> Location

Seeley Lake is nestled among the Hazelton Mountains and located on Highway 16, 10 kilometres west of New Hazelton, where services are located. It's a quaint, picturesque 24-hectare park with fantastic views. Bring your binoculars to this park as you will be rewarded with sightings of bald eagles, ospreys, kingfishers, and a variety of waterfowl.

> Facilities

The campground is relatively small, containing only 20 sites. All of them are large, private, and wooded, and about half of the sites overlook the lake. There is no sani-station and only the basic amenities (pit toilets, drinking water, fire pits, picnic tables). The only downside to the location is that the campsites are quite near the road.

> Recreational activities

The fish that can be caught here include cutthroat and rainbow trout. Swimming is possible as there is a small sandy beach, and there is also potential for canoeing and kayaking. In May, ice can still be found on the lake, so be prepared for a cold dip if you're camping early in the season. A marsh-viewing platform on Seeley Lake provides opportunities to view a variety of bird and animal species that occupy the marsh and woods. A short trail starting at the day-use area leads to a wildlife-viewing platform. Seeley Lake is only a short drive from the 'Ksan Historical Village and Museum, a recreated village illustrating characteristics typical of a historic Gitxsan community. There are six longhouses with painted fronts and totem poles, a gift shop, and a carving school. In the summer, Gitxsan dancers perform in the early evenings. For those interested in exploring Indigenous culture further, Seeley Lake makes an ideal base from which to travel to see the totem poles of Kispiox, Gitwangak, and Gitanyow.

> Additional information

I stopped here early one morning as the mist was rising over the lake and the surrounding snow-topped mountains were just coming into view; the moment was magical. Seeley Lake also makes a lovely picnic spot for those who choose not to camp.

SOWCHEA BAY

> Location

This region is full of historical accounts of early European settlers and is an educational and relaxing recreational destination. Sowchea Bay is about 70 kilometres north of Vanderhoof, off the Yellowhead Highway, and just a

5-minute drive from Paarens Beach Provincial Park. The park's location and the recreational facilities it provides are similar to those of its neighbour; campers can easily travel between the two provincial parks to decide which campground to choose. The nearest community to both is Fort St. James, 17 kilometres away.

> Facilities

This is a particularly attractive campground with 30 sites. The advantage Sowchea Bay has over Paarens Beach is that all sites here are located on the water's edge. They are also quite large, relatively private, and set among trees—although very large RVs may find difficulties manoeuvring. There are no flush toilets, showers, or sani-station. Sowchea Bay accepts reservations at 12 sites.

> Recreational activities

Aside from the lack of day-use picnic facilities, Sowchea Bay's recreational opportunities are similar to those available at Paarens Beach. They include fishing for rainbow trout, lake char, burbot, and kokanee in Stuart Lake, as well as swimming, sunbathing, sailing, and boating (there is a boat launch at the site). In addition, the nearby community of Fort St. James provides historical interest, as well as a nine-hole golf course with views of Stuart Lake.

> Additional information

Although Paarens Beach seems to be the more popular site—perhaps because it has a day-use area—I prefer Sowchea Bay. With all sites on the beach, it is an ideal place to watch the sun set while taking a stroll along the shoreline.

The views are quite spectacular, and on a clear night the stargazing from this vantage point is awe-inspiring. Caution must be exercised by those who plan to windsurf or sail on Stuart Lake, as it is prone to high winds and waves. Swimmer's itch can also be a problem here.

STONE MOUNTAIN

> Location

High among the breathtaking Rocky Mountain scenery at kilometre 595 of the Alaska Highway is 25,690-hectare Stone Mountain Provincial Park. Camping here can either be bleak or beautiful, depending on the weather and your personal camping preferences. Full services are available at Fort Nelson, 140 kilometres east of the park, while gas and food can be obtained a few kilometres from the park.

> Facilities

The Stone Mountain Campground is situated at the end of Summit Lake. The 28 campsites here are very exposed and close to the road. All overlook the lake to varying degrees but have little privacy, as there are no trees or vegetation. Facilities here are basic (fire pits, picnic tables, pit toilets, drinking water).

> Recreational activities

The area is known for five hiking and backcountry exploration trails, accessed from the campground. These trails take up to a week to complete and let you appreciate the full beauty of this area of the Rocky Mountains. Summit Lake has a boat launch, and fishing can be attempted for trout and whitefish in the lake, and Arctic grayling and Dolly Varden in MacDonald Creek. The fishing is not fantastic because the waters are too cold to yield high fish populations. Mountaineering, horseback riding, photography, and wildlife observation are other popular activities possible in the park.

> Additional information

This campground, located on the highest part of the Alaska Highway (elevation 1,267 metres), is exposed to very cold winds. The scenery, characterized by steep bare mountain slopes, is quite beautiful, and the location provides easy access into the backcountry. The park features hoodoos (or erosion pillars), plus subalpine lakes and waterfalls. One of the primary attractions of the area is the abundant wildlife, but visitors have to be patient in order to see any of the hundreds of mountain caribou, stone sheep, moose, mule deers, black and grizzly bears, lynx, wolverines, beavers, and elk that live in the region. If the weather is good, this is also a fantastic picnic spot for anyone travelling the Alaska Highway. Check out the unusual washrooms built on stilts.

SWAN LAKE

> Location

Swan Lake is close to the Alberta border and has a colourful 50-year history. The park is found 35 kilometres southeast of Dawson Creek on Highway 2, just north of Tupper, which has basic services. A 2-kilometre gravel road leads from the highway to the campground. A comprehensive range of services is available at Dawson Creek.

> Facilities

Situated on the lakeside are 44 campsites catering to every type of recreational vehicle. There is no sani-station and only limited access for those in wheelchairs. Facilities are limited to the basic ones found in BC parks (fire pits, picnic tables, pit toilets, drinking water). Reservations are accepted for 16 sites.

> Recreational activities

Five-kilometre-long Swan Lake has an average depth of 2 metres and is only 3 metres at its deepest point. The lake favours water-oriented activities, including boating, swimming from an excellent beach, and fishing for northern pike, walleye, and perch. The park has a boat launch, and water-skiing and powerboats are permitted. Hikes around the lake can be taken from the campground. A large grassy area attracts daytrippers and picnic parties, and there is an adventure playground for children, as well as horseshoe pits and a baseball diamond. The vast number of waterfowl and migratory birds in the area makes this location attractive to the birding community, with species including the common loons, red-necked and western grebes, trumpeter swans, American wigeons, as well as sandpipers, coots, gulls, swallows, and hermit thrushes, to name a few.

> Additional information

This 82-hectare park was established on June 19, 1918, making it BC's third-oldest provincial park. It is the largest body of water in the Alberta Plateau. It's popular with residents of Dawson Creek and has a long history of hosting local social events. For those who are visiting the area for the first time, the town of Dawson Creek at Mile Zero of the Alaska Highway has an interesting pioneer village open during the summer months that's worth a visit (mileopark.ca/pioneer-village).

TĀ CH'ILĀ (BOYA LAKE)

> Location

A stunningly beautiful sight, carved by glacial action 20,000 years ago, awaits the camper who heads for Tā Ch'ilā (formerly known as Boya Lake Provincial Park). The lake is remarkable for its clarity and aquamarine colour, the result of light being reflected from the lake bottom, which is composed of marl, a mixture of silt and shell fragments. In this regard, Boya Lake is quite unlike the lakes found in many other BC provincial parks, and it is wonderful to photograph. Described by BC Parks as a "must-see" location, Tā Ch'ilā is situated 150 kilometres north of Dease Lake and 34 kilometres from the junction of the Stewart–Cassiar and Alaska Highways, which is where the nearest services are located. Two kilometres of gravel road (rudimentary when we visited in 2004, but much improved in 2013) east of Highway 37 lead to the campground itself, which sits adjacent to Boya Lake and affords truly spectacular views of the Cassiar Mountains.

> Facilities

There are 50 spaces of a variety of shapes and sizes. Some are close to the lake, some are just for tents, and most are private and set among black and white spruce trees. There is no sani-station and only basic facilities (picnic tables, pit toilets, drinking water, fire pits).

> Recreational activities

Because the lake is so clear, fishing here is not good for the serious angler, although my children had a ball catching small toe-biters a few years ago. Fishing for grayling can be enjoyed a short distance away, in Dease River. A short 1.5-kilometre lakeside trail introduces the multitude of songbirds and waterfowl attracted to the area by its topography, vegetation, and mild climate. Moose and beaver are found in the park, as are mountain goats and caribou. The lake is ideal for boating (as long as you observe the 10-horsepower motor restriction) and swimming (although the water's somewhat cold despite its reputation as one of the few northern lakes warm enough to swim in), and photographers will enjoy the mix of spectacular scenery and plant life. There is a great playpark close to the lake.

> Additional information

The quietest campground on Highway 37, Tā Ch'ilā also seems to have been personally cared for. For example, when I visited in 2014, a box where campers can deposit and select reading material was placed at the entrance. I love these personal touches; they make camping special. Weather forecasts are posted on the campground notice board—again, a lovely touch. The main draw of this campground, though, is still the crystal-clear lake and stunning views. Tā Ch'ilā is a gorgeous, quiet place to camp.

TUDYAH LAKE

> Location

Close to the junction of Highway 97 and Highway 39, between the Hart Range and the Nechako Plateau of the Rocky Mountains, this 56-hectare lakeside provincial park is perfect for the weary traveller. Tudyah Lake is 9 kilometres north of McLeod Lake on Highway 97 and 157 kilometres from Prince George. The nearest services are found at McLeod Lake.

> Facilities

Primarily used for overnight stays, this campground has a somewhat unusual feel to it because the 36 spaced-out sites are set in an open grassy meadow with a creek running through it, creating a pleasant pastoral atmosphere with good privacy. There is no sani-station or wheelchair access, but the park includes all the basic amenities (fire pits, drinking water, pit toilets, picnic tables). There are numerous potholes on the gravel campground roads, but all navigable.

> Recreational activities

It is possible to swim (be aware of the sharp drop-off), kayak, and canoe in Tudyah Lake. Anglers will enjoy fishing for rainbow trout, Dolly Varden, and whitefish in the lake and at the nearby Parsnip River. Tudyah Lake has a boat launch, and ice fishing is popular in the winter. There is a large group-camping facility and day-use area with horseshoe pits. The town of Mackenzie, 30 minutes away, has a nine-hole golf course and a recreation centre, and is situated on the banks of Williston Lake, a prime fishing spot.

> Additional information

The community of Mackenzie is at the south end of Williston Lake, a huge artificial reservoir that supplies water to the hydroelectric plant at Hudson's Hope. The town is named after Alexander Mackenzie, the first white person to reach Canada's Pacific coast by land. Mackenzie was built in 1965 in an area of wilderness as a centre for pulp, paper, and lumber manufacturing. It has a museum and is home to the world's largest tree crusher, seen on Mackenzie Boulevard, but it has little to recommend it architecturally. In 2008, the town's mill closed and with the loss of Mackenzie's main employer, the town's future is uncertain. I last visited on a Wednesday afternoon in August 2013. No one was here except one older woman in a car dating back to the 1960s. Judging by her camping equipment, which also looked about 50 years old, she seemed to have been there for decades. It was like going through a time warp. If you want a quiet place to camp, this is it!

TYHEE LAKE

> ## Location

Children adore Tyhee Lake for the beach, anglers love it for the fish, and bird-watchers are attracted to the abundant bird life. But for me, Tyhee Lake's biggest attraction is its friendly atmosphere. While it is the convention in BC parks to say hello and pass the time of day with other campers, when I stayed at Tyhee Lake, everyone I met was happy and communicative. Consequently, Tyhee Lake lives in my memory as being the "very friendly provincial park." This provincial park's family-oriented campground is a 15-minute drive east of Smithers on Highway 16, near the quaint settlement of Telkwa in the Buckley River Valley. All amenities are therefore available within a few kilometres of the park itself.

> ## Facilities

This large and well-maintained campground is set amidst an aspen forest on the side of Tyhee Lake. There are 71 campsites, a few with views over the lake. Nine of these are for tents only, but the rest will accommodate every kind of recreational vehicle. In addition to all the usual facilities found in provincial parks, Tyhee Lake has a sani-station, flush toilets, electrical hook-ups at 38 sites, and showers. Reservations are accepted at 20 sites.

> ## Recreational activities

A beautiful 200-metre beach provides access for swimming. Water-skiing is permitted on the lake, and there is also a boat launch. Fish found in the lake include cutthroat and stocked rainbow trout, while smaller anglers can go for minnows and sticklebacks. Horseshoes and volleyball are also available, as is a play area for children. An interpretive trail has been developed around the campground, and there is a marsh-viewing platform where you may see loons, red-necked grebes, ruffed grouse, and beavers. In addition, the communities of Smithers and Telkwa are pleasant places to visit. Smithers houses a wild-life museum that displays a variety of big game animals, and Telkwa's history dates back to the Old Cariboo Trail in the 1800s and, later, the Collins Overland Telegraph line. Both are lovely places to wander around in, and they have good restaurants if you're getting bored of camping fodder.

> Additional information

The large, well-kept day-use area and the park's proximity to the Yellowhead Highway also make it an ideal picnic spot if you do not have time to spend the night. But with the many activities available here, Tyhee Lake is a perfect place for family camping, and visitors usually spend more than one night. For me, the only downsides of Tyhee Lake were the jet skiers who dominated the lake in the early evening hours when I last stayed and the Canada goose droppings littering the grass.

WHISKERS POINT

> Location

Rich in Indigenous and pioneer history and situated on a sandspit jutting out into McLeod Lake, Whiskers Point is an extremely agreeable location. The campground is 130 kilometres north of Prince George on Highway 97 and about 12 kilometres south of McLeod Lake, where gas, food, and lodging are available.

> Facilities

Fifty-nine large, secluded sites set in a mature forest of spruce and pine are available. A number of them overlook the lake or are near Whiskers Creek, which runs through the campground. There is a sani-station and flush and pit toilets, and some facilities are wheelchair accessible. Reservations are not accepted at 24 locations.

> Recreational activities

McLeod Lake provides a wealth of opportunity for the water enthusiast. There is a good beach and excellent swimming, a concrete boat launch has been built, and windsurfing, canoeing, kayaking, and fishing for Dolly Varden and rainbow trout are all possible. (A note of caution: the lake is subject to suddenly changing conditions, and strong winds can easily transform the calm water.) For younger campers, there's a children's play area, horseshoe pits, and a volleyball net. The area is rich in bird and animal life, and there's also a 20-minute-long nature trail near the beach.

> Additional information

I have visited Whiskers Point but have not stayed in the campground. All the literature on this area stresses the beauty of the sunsets visible from the park, which have been described as "spectacular," "magnificent," and "breathtaking." The community of McLeod Lake, 12 kilometres north of the campground, was first established in 1805 by Simon Fraser. Known first as Trout Lake Fort and later as Fort McLeod, it was the first trading post and first European settlement west of the Rocky Mountains at the time. Although the Hart Highway (Highway 97) was developed in the twentieth century, the Tse'khene People had a system of trails developed in this region long before the Europeans came. You will not be disappointed in your decision to stay here.

THE YUKON

A N EXCURSION TO the Yukon involves considerable planning, a lot of time, and often quite a bit of money. But, oh, how it is worth it! The scenery is breathtaking, and the immense size and empty spaces make the trip worthwhile. Okay, so it is costly in gas, the drives between the small communities are long, and if you are addicted to cell phone service, Starbucks, fast food restaurants, or maintaining a clean car, this long haul is not advisable. But these issues dwarf into little inconveniences when you start to consider the benefits. Where else can you experience over 4,480 square kilometres of fresh water, see Canada's second-longest river (the Yukon), climb the country's highest mountain (Mount Logan), or drive amidst the largest protected area in the world (Kluane National Park)? When I moved from England to Canada in 1991 and started to camp in the provincial parks of BC, I was immediately frustrated by the lack of information available on these fantastic places. Now, in addition to this book, there are a plethora of websites, travel books, personal blogs, and government pamphlets detailing every aspect of all the campgrounds in BC. This is not the case for the campgrounds of the Yukon. While I have personally visited the vast majority of the forty sites included in this chapter, for the remainder I have had to rely on speaking to government officials, accessing literature (very sparse), and trawling through the various search engines and blogs for small anecdotes from the few people who have visited and documented their experiences. The Yukon Government produces a brochure listing all campgrounds, which also has information on how crowded they can become in the summer months. The same information can also be found on the Government of Yukon website at yukon.ca/en/find-campground-or-recreation-site. Visitors are also encouraged to refer to the Yukon Government's camping guide, which includes rules and safety guidelines, and can be downloaded at yukon.ca/en/guide-camping-yukon.

When I first camped in these Yukon campgrounds, over fifteen years ago, I found them to be a little primitive. During my last visit, all the washrooms were freshly painted, the picnic tables were large, highway signposts were clear, firewood was dry and plentiful, and garbage non-existent. Although mosquitoes can be a nuisance, especially at the beginning of the season and in areas with large bodies of stagnant water, by August and September these pests can be avoided for the most part.

The following Yukon government campgrounds (and one national park campground) have been organized into four areas, reflecting the territory's three major highways: the Alaska Highway, the Klondike Highway, and the Robert Campbell Highway. There is also a section for campgrounds not on these routes. Facilities in Yukon government campgrounds are similar to those in the more remote BC provincial parks. While there are no paved roads, showers, flushing toilets, sani-stations, or park employees within the campgrounds themselves, they are, for the most part, large, well-kept sites in stunning locations. Services include picnic tables, fire pits, free firewood, water (pump, tap, or from a river or lake, and often with a boil advisory), and pit toilets. A few campgrounds are wheelchair accessible. Large picnic shelters are frequently found in parks of the Yukon, which is fantastic when you are tenting and in need of a dry place to cook. Starting in 2023, a camping fee of $20.00 per night is requested if paying with cash on site. No reservations are accepted, so camping spots are on a first come, first served basis. Yukon residents can buy an annual pass for $200.00, and those over the age of 65 can get a 50 percent discount on this. Everyone camping must self-register. After finding a spot and parking, look for the self-registration sign and follow the instructions. Prepaid daily permits are also available

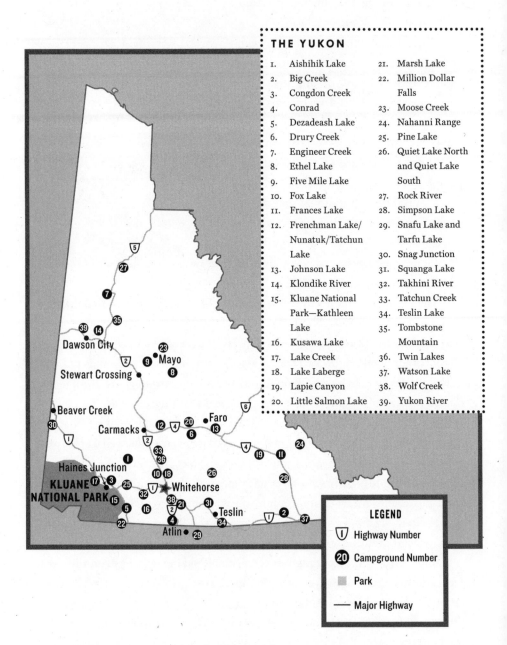

THE YUKON

1.	Aishihik Lake	21.	Marsh Lake
2.	Big Creek	22.	Million Dollar
3.	Congdon Creek		Falls
4.	Conrad	23.	Moose Creek
5.	Dezadeash Lake	24.	Nahanni Range
6.	Drury Creek	25.	Pine Lake
7.	Engineer Creek	26.	Quiet Lake North
8.	Ethel Lake		and Quiet Lake
9.	Five Mile Lake		South
10.	Fox Lake	27.	Rock River
11.	Frances Lake	28.	Simpson Lake
12.	Frenchman Lake/	29.	Snafu Lake and
	Nunatuk/Tatchun		Tarfu Lake
	Lake	30.	Snag Junction
13.	Johnson Lake	31.	Squanga Lake
14.	Klondike River	32.	Takhini River
15.	Kluane National	33.	Tatchun Creek
	Park—Kathleen	34.	Teslin Lake
	Lake	35.	Tombstone
16.	Kusawa Lake		Mountain
17.	Lake Creek	36.	Twin Lakes
18.	Lake Laberge	37.	Watson Lake
19.	Lapie Canyon	38.	Wolf Creek
20.	Little Salmon Lake	39.	Yukon River

LEGEND

[I] Highway Number

(20) Campground Number

Park

— Major Highway

for $18.00 from a number of outlets in the Yukon (gas stations, retail stores, and from Department of Environment offices; see yukon.ca/en/where-buy-yukon-angling-hunting-and-camping-permits-or-licences). It is advisable to keep cash handy for payment, though I have seen campers pay by cheque. Yukon government campgrounds are administered by the Yukon Department of Environment, which supplies information on their website. Current road conditions can be found at 511yukon.ca. Campgrounds close October 1.

CAMPGROUNDS ON ALASKA HIGHWAY

The famous Alaska Highway was built in 1942, shortly after Alaska became part of the United States, as a military access road—part of a supply route connecting the coast of Alaska to the main body of the United States through Canada. Thirty thousand US army personnel were involved in the construction of this 2,288-kilometre highway. It cuts through forests, traverses mountain ranges, and crosses numerous rivers, and stretches from Dawson Creek in BC to Delta Junction in Alaska.

The section through the Yukon, from Watson Lake to Beaver Creek, is 882 kilometres. Most of the road is paved, and signs are posted to warn drivers of the short rough sections. This is one of the best northern highways in the world, but do not expect numerous locations to stop for coffee or gas. The distances between communities can be far, and the settlements, once reached, are often small, consisting of little more than a few houses and a gas station. What the route lacks in twenty-first-century services (there is rarely cell phone coverage and in certain places, signposts inform the traveller of the absence of 911 service) it makes up in the stunning scenery and wonderful wildlife-viewing opportunities. Personally, I find the most enjoyable part the lack of vehicles. Even in the height of summer, the traffic is minimal, and it is possible to travel for over 20 minutes in mid-afternoon in August and not see another soul.

The thirteen Yukon campgrounds included in this section have been listed from south to north, from Watson Lake, adjacent to the BC border, to Beaver Creek.

WATSON LAKE

Located about 4 kilometres from central Watson Lake, where all services can be found, and near kilometre 984 of the Alaska Highway, this campground is accessed by a 2-kilometre gravel road and is a nice, quiet spot to stop for the night. Although none of the 40 campsites are on the lake (8 are pull-through), the campground is a good one, set in an area of large trees and natural vegetation. Trails with interpretive panels lead from the campground to the lake, where it is possible to swim. The 8 large pull-through sites can easily accommodate RVs of up to 45 feet. The campground is equipped with a picnic shelter and tables, water, wood, fire pits, pit toilets, and a playground. It is wheelchair accessible. The town of Watson Lake is famous for its "signpost forest," displaying over 80,000 signs and adding about 2,000 more each year. The lovely visitor centre adjacent to this forest has information and photographs about the construction of the Alaska Highway. This visitor centre also provides information on road conditions.

BIG CREEK

Situated on kilometre 1,042 of the Alaska Highway, about 61 kilometres west of Watson Lake (which has the nearest services), this campground consists of 15 sites spread out around a loop. Seven are pull-through. These sites accommodate even the largest RV (site 3 has the best view). All the sites have picnic tables, fire pits, water from a pump, free firewood, pit toilets, and a cooking shelter. Some sites have tent pads, and the campground is wheelchair accessible. When we visited, my only disappointment was that the creek was not easily accessible. One online reviewer refers to Big Creek as "Big Rig Friendly." This campground is very popular during the summer months.

TESLIN LAKE

I have fond memories of Teslin Lake as it was the first Yukon campground I stayed in, way back in 1998. When we visited again in 2013, I was surprised at how little had changed; it was still just as quaint as I remembered. Found at kilometre 1,258 of the Alaska Highway, this campground is directly accessible from the main road, but set back enough so noise from traffic is not an issue. Twenty-seven well-spaced spots are set in a lightly mixed forested area of aspen, some which overlook the lake. There are 6 pull-through sites. Services include water, picnic tables, wood, pit toilets, and fire pits. There is also a picnic shelter. A small trail takes campers to the beach, and in addition to offering swimming, the lake can be fished for lake trout, northern pike, and grayling. This is a great area to see songbirds and waterfowl during the fall migration. The nearby community of Teslin provides all services, including a very well-stocked gas station store offering coffee by donation and an excellent selection of food and camping supplies.

SQUANGA LAKE

Near kilometre 1,316 of the Alaska Highway, Squanga is named after a variety of whitefish that inhabit the lake. It has 16 vehicle sites that can accommodate all but the very largest of recreational vehicles, including 4 pull-through sites set in a pine-forested area. It offers the basic services (fire pit, pit toilet, water, wood, picnic table) as well as a picnic shelter. Despite the campground's name, only 3 sites are actually on the lake, which is just as well because it is quite shallow and muddy and does not have a beach. There are two floating docks, and the lake can be fished for pike, grayling, burbot, whitefish, and rainbow trout. When we visited, it was early and the loons were out in force, making their distinctive cries. A nice, tranquil location. Limited services are available at Johnson Crossing, about 20 kilometres east.

MARSH LAKE

This is a lovely Yukon government campground and one of the larger ones, offering 59 sites (9 pull-through) suitable for even the largest recreational vehicle in an area of spruce forest. Found at kilometre 1,379, two gravel loop roads offer spacious, quiet locations for the night. Many are adjacent to the lake and 4 have tent pads. Services provided include water, pit toilets, picnic tables, fire pits, and wood. Bear-proof lockers are provided, and there is also a picnic shelter and a beach. The park is wheelchair accessible, and there is a playpark, making this park ideal for those with young children or as a rest stop. The location is also a stopping place for thousands of trumpeter swans and other waterfowl during spring migration. When I last visited, there were bat boxes mounted high on poles and information boards about wildlife in the area. Original trapper and mining cabins around the lake date back to the 1898 gold rush. Be prepared, this campground is often full.

WOLF CREEK

Not far (16 kilometres south) from Whitehorse, the capital of the Yukon, where all sorts of services can be found (even Starbucks!), this 46-site campground is at kilometre 1,408 of the Alaska Highway. Eleven of the sites are pull-throughs. With Wolf Creek running through the middle of the campground, the campsites follow a circular drive among delightful spruce trees. The 3-kilometre Tàgáyä hiking trail located in the park follows the creek and leads to great views of the Yukon River. Some of the best sites are creekside. Services include water, pit toilets, picnic tables, fire pits, and wood. It is possible to fish in the creek for grayling. The campground is wheelchair accessible and includes a playground. The proximity to Whitehorse makes this an ideal location and, at $20.00 a night for accommodation, it is a real bargain. It is therefore very popular and often full. Access is easy to many of Whitehorse's attractions (the capital is home to 60 percent of the Yukon's population). According to Yukon government information, Chinook salmon spawn in the creek in the autumn, and there is a fish ladder located under the Alaska Highway to assist movement of the fish.

TAKHINI RIVER

Access to this small, 12-site campground is found at kilometre 1,489 of the Alaska Highway via Kusawa Lake Road, a gravel road that leads 15 kilometres into the campground. The sites overlook the river. Services are the basic ones of wood, picnic tables, pit toilets, fire pits, and water, which has to be taken from the river, accessed by quite a steep bank. If you want a get-away-from-it-all experience, this is the place for you. The site is noted for its angling opportunities, and there have been reports of 9-kilogram lake trout here, as well as grayling and pike. Takhini River is also a good place for kayakers and canoeists. While the campground is suitable for RVs under 25 feet, it is more ideal for truck campers. Those in larger vehicles would be advised to travel another 10 kilometres to Kusawa Lake (see below).

KUSAWA LAKE

This huge body of water, whose name means "narrow lake" in Tlingit, leads over 72 kilometres toward the BC border and averages 3.2 kilometres in width. It is reputed to have over thirty sandy beaches, but without a boat they are inaccessible. Others call this Raft Lake, and it has also been known as Arkell Lake, so clearly it has somewhat of an identity crisis. Access to Kusawa Lake is located at kilometre 1,489 of the Alaska Highway and is reached by travelling 23 kilometres along Kusawa Lake Road. It is a trek, and sometimes the road can be rough, but anglers say it's worth it! This road was originally constructed in 1945 by the US Army to harvest wood for the bridges of the Alaska Highway. The campground has 53 spots, including 8 pull-throughs, among spruce forest with wild rose bushes. Services include a picnic shelter, water, picnic tables, firewood, pit toilets, and fire pits. The campground is wheelchair accessible and there is a playground. From the small rocky beach there are stunning views of the surrounding mountains. As with all Yukon campgrounds set on lakes, the water is cold! This campground often gets full between June and August.

AISHIHIK LAKE

The turnoff for this campground is located at kilometre 1,546 of the Alaska Highway, and the campground is found by travelling 40 kilometres farther along Aishihik Road. The name Aishihik comes from the word "Äshèyi," which in the Southern Tutchone language means "at the head of the lake, base of the mountains, where the ranges meet." There is space for 16 camping parties, including 5 pull-through sites. Services are basic (water, pit toilets, fire pits, wood, and picnic tables), and there is a boat launch. The campground is near the Otter Falls Cutoff, which has a much larger commercial campground and services (gas station, grocery store) and access to Otter Falls, almost 29 kilometres along the Aishihik Lake Road (not suitable for large RVs). Aishihik Lake Campground is at the south end of the lake, which sometimes remains frozen until mid-June. It is possible to fish in the lake for lake trout and grayling. There is a herd of bison in the area, so take care when driving.

PINE LAKE

This is a delightful family-oriented campground set among mature spruce trees with views of the Kluane Mountains, St. Elias Mountains, and (to the north) the distinctive Paint Mountain (first named by the Southern Tutchone People, who collected red ochre from it for dyes and paints). Pine Lake is conveniently located 7 kilometres from Haines Junction at kilometre 1,572 of the Alaska Highway. There are 42 well-spaced camp-sites (including 6 pull-throughs), with some located on the lake. Services include a boat launch, playground, picnic tables, wood, water, fire pits, and pit toilets. There is a nice sandy beach with easy access to the lake, which even in August we found to be very cold. Trails ribbon through the park. Trout, grayling, and northern pike can be fished in the lake. This camp-ground seems to be popular with both locals and tourists, so it its often full in the peak summer months. On the downside, there may be mosqui-toes as the campground has areas of stagnant water. Anyone who comes here must visit the fantastic new visitor centre at Haines Junction, which has full details about the region as well as Kluane National Park. There is also a good bakery, open from the end of April until mid-September (villagebakeryyukon.com).

CONGDON CREEK

When we visited Congdon Creek in August 2013, it was closed to tent campers because of the prevalence of bears. I have since read a number of reviews of the campground, and it appears bears are always a potential problem. In 2016, the Yukon govern-ment removed a number of soapberry bushes to address this issue—bears love soapberry—and more recently, an electric fence has been installed around 20 sites; tent camping is only allowed behind this fence. Congdon Creek is located near kilometre 1,666 of the Alaska Highway, on the shores of Kluane Lake. Although the 62 camping spaces are quite open among spare vegetation of spruce and alder, they are well spaced and suitable for every type and size of vehicle. All facilities are available (fire pits, water, wood, pit toilets, picnic tables), and the location also has a boat launch and a playground. My family swam in the freezing cold waters of this huge lake. In thirty years of Canadian camping, I have never swum in such a cold lake. But the fantastic views made the experience worthwhile. Not surprisingly, we had the lake—which is the largest in the Yukon, covering approximately 400 square kilometres—to ourselves. There is a short, 500-metre interpretive trail along the shoreline for those who prefer not to access the water and the reportedly superb trout fishing. This is one of the best campgrounds in the Yukon.

LAKE CREEK

In the foothills of the Kluane Mountain Range and found at kilometre 1,791 (23 kilometres south of Koidern), this small 27-site campground has accommodation for 13 larger RVs. Services are basic (wood, creek water, picnic tables, fire pits, and pit toilets). Although the sites are large and well spaced in a lightly forested area, this roadside camping spot is basically just for overnight stays. The sites are wooded and 3 are lakeside. Noise from traffic can be heard, but it is not excessive and declines tremendously at night. Bears can be a problem from mid-July to late September. For those interested in gold panning, Edith Creek Bridge (kilometre 1,782) is only 9 kilometres away and is reputed to be the place to strike it rich!

SNAG JUNCTION

Just 60 kilometres north of Lake Creek Campground is Snag Junction, a small, 15-space facility found at kilometre 1,850 of the Alaska Highway. Snag Junction is the last (or first, depending on which way you are travelling) Yukon government–operated campground on this stretch of road. The services consist of wood, fire pits, pit toilets, picnic tables, and water. Although some sites are near the lake, they are not only tight but also quite open, and some are a little uneven, so settling in with a large RV can be challenging. If you are travelling in a large RV, consider this spot for a picnic rather than an overnight stay. The village of Snag is famous for recording the lowest temperature in Canadian history: −63°C, on February 3, 1947. Moose are often seen in this area. Nearby Beaver Creek (just a 15-minute drive away) is Canada's most western community, with a number of services, including a visitor centre.

CAMPGROUNDS ON
THE KLONDIKE HIGHWAY

Stretching from Whitehorse to Dawson City, this 332-kilometre route can be easily completed in a day, but it has many fantastic campgrounds ideal for picnics or overnight stays. Winding through some breathtaking scenery, lakes, and areas devastated by immense forest fires, this historic route, first used by gold prospectors, leads north to what was once the largest community west of Chicago. Ten campgrounds are included along this route, listed south to north.

CONRAD

This is the Yukon's newest campground, opened in 2016, and located 16 kilometres south from Carcross on Tagish Lake's Windy Arm, covering 45 hectares. Services are available at Carcross. A total of 35 sites (2 pull-through) are available, some with views over the lake. Picnic shelters, water, and bear-proof garbage and food storage are available. A playground has recently been completed. Hikes can be taken from the campground, which is adjacent to the Conrad Historic Townsite, a small silver mining community established in 1905. This newer campground has become a hit with locals and tourists, so it is often full.

LAKE LABERGE

Made famous in Robert Service's poem "The Cremation of Sam Magee," the spectacular 64-kilometre-long lake is one of many at the headwaters of the Yukon River. The campground is located at kilometre 225 of the gorgeous Klondike Highway and is reached via Deep Creek Road. Travel along for about 3 kilometres (the first kilometre is paved). There are 16 campsites, set in a lightly forested environment, with 12 pull-throughs. However, the size of the sites may make those with the larger RVs think twice about staying, as manoeuvring is tight. Services include picnic tables, water, firewood, fire pits, kitchen shelters, and pit toilets. There is a boat launch, and a few sites have direct access to the water. Fishing opportunities include lake trout, grayling, and northern pike. The lake is prone to quickly developing storms, so be vigilant if you venture out in a small canoe. The Yukon government boasts this is the only place in the territory to see double-crested cormorants.

FOX LAKE

This quaint campground is suitable for anyone, from those camping in tents to those rolling in with the largest RVs. Found at kilometre 248 of the Klondike Highway, this campground has 43 sites (9 pull-through) set around a circular drive. Facilities include fire pits, pit toilets, water, wood, picnic tables, and a picnic shelter. There is also a boat ramp and a small playground. Fishing for lake trout and burbot is possible from the shores of the campground, and there are even better opportunities for grayling fishing year round. For the bird-watcher there are ample opportunities to see waterfowl. Fox Lake was named by a US airman forced to make a landing here in 1943. Connected to Lake Laberge by Fox Creek, this is a great spot to stop for a picnic, as it allows the chance to see the lake the highway skirts around in more detail and at a slower pace. I understand this is one of the Yukon's more popular camping locations, so it is often full.

TWIN LAKES

These two tranquil, vibrantly coloured lakes, positioned on either side of the Klondike Highway, are not that large. The campground is found at kilometre 308 of the highway and has 31 spaces, divided into two areas. The first has back-in sites, suitable for all but the very largest RV and privately located among aspen trees and light vegetation. The second area has 10 spaces in a large gravel parking lot with views of the western lake. Some of the spaces are directly on the lake, making for a great get-away-from-it-all camping experience. All sites have individual picnic tables and fire pits, and the campground has water, firewood, and pit toilets. There is a boat launch and a small dock.

Campers can swim (but like all Yukon campground lakes, the water is cold and may have thawed only a few days before your arrival) and fish for trout, grayling, and pike. The best opportunity to see the elk that inhabit the area is in spring.

TATCHUN CREEK

This is one of my favourite Yukon campgrounds. We did not overnight here but spent a very enjoyable couple of hours over lunch. My two sons spent the time in the river, letting the fast-flowing waters propel their bodies down the small rapids: whitewater body rafting. We had the place to ourselves in mid-August, so they also did a bit of skinny-dipping, which was all fine until three young women from the Canadian government's Department of Fisheries and Oceans quietly arrived to take samples of the water! The campground is found at kilometre 382 and only has space for 12 sites (including 4 pull-throughs), all well spaced in a lightly forested area with easy access for even the largest RV. Some spaces are on the actual banks of the creek. Facilities include water, wood, fire pits, pit toilets, and picnic tables. Anglers can fish for grayling (June to September) and salmon (July to August), but note that fishing is not permitted from August 1 to September 30 to protect spawning chinook salmon. The campground is located just 2 kilometres north of Five Finger Rapids, a location of the Yukon River where early explorers had to navigate through five channels. A steep staircase consisting of 217 or 239 steps (I did not count them, but the tourist literature varies on the exact number) leads to a good lookout and photographic opportunities. Although the campground is near the road and traffic is audible, the road is not very busy, especially at night, and it is an ideal picnic spot as it is almost midway between Whitehorse and Dawson City.

ETHEL LAKE

Confession time: I have not personally visited this location (over 200 kilometres from Dawson City). It is reached by travelling 24 kilometres on Ethel Lake Road after turning off the Klondike Highway at kilometre 524. This gravel access road is narrow and twisting and therefore not recommended for the largest RVs or anyone who has concerns about their vehicle. There are 10 camping spots on a narrow strip of elevated land, a boat launch, and fishing possibilities for lake trout, northern pike, and grayling. It is also a good place to spot moose. The facilities are the usual ones found in Yukon government campgrounds (water, pit toilets, wood, picnic tables, fire pits). Although this campground does not seem to be on anyone's "must visit" list, photographs of the lake do look wonderful. As there are not many spaces it is frequently full in the summer.

FIVE MILE LAKE

Although not technically on the Klondike Highway, this campground can be reached by turning west at Stewart Crossing (kilometre 534) and driving 58 kilometres on the road to Mayo. This route is known as the Silver Trail and leads to the community of Keno City, one of the richest silver mining areas in Canada. Located 8 kilometres from the town of Mayo, there are 26 camping spots here, shaded by spruce and willow trees. Most require you to back in, but there are 3 pull-throughs. Services include water, pit toilets, picnic tables, fire pits, and wood. There is also a picnic shelter and playpark. A small hiking trail winding around the lake provides access to adjacent wetlands, where it is possible to see mule deer. Swimming is possible in the lake. The village of Mayo, developed during the gold rush, has services for visitors and companies undertaking mineral exploration in the region. Mayo also boasts being both the coldest and warmest spot in the Yukon, but I understand other areas also challenge Mayo for this honour.

MOOSE CREEK

This is a great camping spot—as long as the mosquitoes are elsewhere. We visited in late August when there was no evidence of bugs, but I was told they can be an issue earlier in the season. Located at kilometre 559, this campground has 6 tent sites and 4 pull-throughs in addition to 26 others designed around two loops, in a forest of aspen and low vegetation near the Moose Creek and Stewart River. A 2.5-kilometre trail leads around the campground through a boreal forest to the Stewart River. Apparently, birds such as the northern waterthrush, Wilson's warbler, and common yellowthroat frequent the area to feed on the mosquitoes, and it is possible to fish in the creek and river. Facilities for camping are wheelchair-accessible and include picnic tables, fire pits, water, pit toilets, and wood. There is also a playground.

KLONDIKE RIVER

If you intend to camp and visit Dawson City, there are two Yukon government-run options: Klondike River and Yukon River. My preference is Yukon River (see below), but perhaps this is because my first impression of Klondike River was that it was a little gloomy (to be fair, I visited it on a grey evening when there were few campers around). Klondike River is located at kilometre 697 of the Klondike Highway, 20 kilometres from Dawson City. The 35 well-spaced sites, set in a forested region of natural vegetation, can accommodate every size of recreational vehicle and are positioned on a loop road for easy access. Facilities include pit toilets, water, fire pits, wood, and picnic tables. There are a couple of picnic shelters, a playground, and a 2-kilometre trail and boardwalk among giant white spruce and willows leading to the river. The campground is not near the road, so traffic noise is not an issue.

YUKON RIVER

Technically this campground is not on the Klondike Highway. It is located just north of Dawson City on the Top of the World Highway and accessed by driving through Dawson City and taking the George Black Ferry, a great little (free) ferry service that provides passage across the Yukon River. The Yukon River Campground is basically the first spot you reach after disembarking from the boat. A wonderful location awaits on the banks of the Yukon River with convenient access to Dawson City. The ferry operates from 5:00 AM until midnight and runs from mid-May to mid-October, depending on the ice build-up. This is the largest Yukon government campground, with 102 spaces (20 pull-through) arranged in a large loop and able to accommodate every size of vehicle. This includes a number of sites on the river, some designed specifically for tents. Sites are well spaced in a lightly forested area set away from the road, so there is no issue with the noise from traffic. Facilities include picnic tables, wood, pump water, fire pits, and pit toilets. There are picnic shelters and a playpark, and the park is wheelchair accessible. As the campground has bears, tent campers should store food high up and out of reach. The campground has a viewing platform that looks toward the cliffs, where families of the rare peregrine falcon reside. This is a great, convenient place to camp, easily walkable to Dawson City, and very busy during the Dawson City Music Festival in July and at other times.

CAMPGROUNDS ON THE ROBERT CAMPBELL HIGHWAY

Named after Robert Campbell, a Hudson's Bay Company fur trader and the first European to enter what is now known as the Yukon, this road stretches 583 kilometres north from Watson Lake to Carmacks and was completed in 1968. The highway traces the route that Campbell took west. Those who choose to travel this route will be treated to a quiet drive, with few services but amazing landscapes, although the view is often obscured by trees. Ten lovely campgrounds punctuate the road, encouraging the traveller to stop and appreciate the scenery. Ross River and Faro are the main communities on this stretch.

SIMPSON LAKE

This small campground only has 10 spaces, but what it lacks in size it makes up in quality—all the sites are quite large and can accommodate all but the biggest RVs. Most are positioned on the lake, and 1 is pull-through. Located at kilometre 81 of the highway, the sites are situated on a loop road on a gorgeous lake. Facilities include picnic tables, wood, water from a pump, pit toilets, fire pits, and a floating dock. There is a picnic shelter, playpark, and access to the lake for swimming, but no beach. The lake also provides opportunities for fishing for lake trout, Arctic grayling, whitefish, burbot, and northern pike, and the campground is noted as a good base for hunting in the fall. One camper reports staying here in mid-September and being the only one in the campground until the early evening, when he was joined by a pack of wolves, who moved on once the bear arrived . . .

NAHANNI RANGE

To reach this campground it is necessary to turn off the Robert Campbell Highway (kilometre 108) and take the Nahanni Range Road, a route not recommended for tourist traffic as it is rough and frequently washed out. The information centre at Watson Lake can provide details of the road conditions, which vary considerably from year to year. The road leads to Tungsten, 198 kilometres away in the Northwest Territories, and the campground is located at kilometre 84 of this rough road. There are only 11 spaces

(3 pull-through), and services are minimal. Water is obtained from the creek via a steep bank. A large forest fire in 2002 swept through the campground, which is still recovering, but poplar and willow trees offer some privacy. Tungsten is home to a tungsten concentrate mine, which was opened in the early 1960s, then closed and reopened again several times between the 1980s and early 2000s. This remote location is not on many campers' must-see lists. According to the Yukon government, the site receives minimal maintenance each year because of its remote location, and it is primarily utilized in the autumn by hunters. Pack out garbage.

FRANCES LAKE

This is a truly great place to camp. Although the vast lake can experience windy conditions, making boating a challenge, the views are fantastic and the wind keeps the mosquitoes away. Situated at kilometre 171 of the Robert Campbell Highway and accessed by taking a 1.6-kilometre gravel road, the campground has 24 sites that must be reversed into. All are large and many are close to the lake itself (making it a more desirable location than Simpson Lake). Services include water, wood, picnic tables, fire pits, and pit toilets. There is a picnic shelter, boat launch, and a nice sheltered beach. Fishing is good for lake trout, grayling, and northern pike. The location is popular with fishermen, hunters, and, at certain times of the year (when the wind abates), mosquitoes. If the lake water is high, this campground gets flooded at the beginning of the season.

LAPIE CANYON

Located at kilometre 364, just to the west of Lapie River Bridge, this campground boasts 20 camping spaces, including 5 pull-throughs. Although the spaces can accommodate large RVs, the narrow road leading to the campground and the tight manoeuvring room make this a better destination for camping vehicles under 35 feet. Services include pit toilets, water, firewood, picnic tables, a picnic shelter, and fire pits. The canyon is small, and a brief trail leads from the campground for adjacent exploration of the river and canyon. The trail was closed in 2022 until further notice. It is possible to fish for lake trout and grayling, and to kayak and canoe in the rapids.

JOHNSON LAKE

If you are looking for a campground adjacent to services, Johnson Lake is for you. Situated about 8 kilometres from Faro on a gravel access road, the turning is situated at kilometre 415. The delightful 15 spots are positioned along Johnson Lake, and 7 are pull-throughs. Services include pit toilets, wood, water from a pump, picnic tables, fire pits, and a picnic shelter. Swimming is possible, but the lake is reedy and there is no beach. Float planes also use the lake. With a population of almost four hundred, Faro has a visitor centre, a post office, a recreational centre, a liquor store, and even a nine-hole golf course. It is possible to rent canoes here, and there are a number of trails. Try the delightful and easy Van Gorder Falls Trail, which crosses Van Gorder Creek and leads to a deck overlooking the falls.

DRURY CREEK

There is a lovely beach at this campground, which is referred to in the literature as both Drury Lake and Drury Creek but is actually on Little Salmon Lake. From here it is possible to brave the freezing water and swim, or sit on the shore and watch the various waterfowl. Situated on kilometre 468 and accessed by a short road, this campground only has 10 sites, including 5 pull-throughs (numbers 8 and 10 are the best ones). Services include a boat launch, picnic tables, wood, water, fire pits, and pit toilets. There is good fishing for northern pike, grayling, whitefish, and lake trout, and there is a fish filleting table for those who are successful in this pursuit. At this location, the highway follows the northern side of Little Salmon Lake. The campground is on the eastern end of the lake.

LITTLE SALMON LAKE

Found at kilometre 501 of the highway, by all accounts there is little to do here except fish. With 22 camping sites, including 7 pull-throughs, the spots can serve RVs up to 45 feet. Some of the camping spots are directly on the water. Almost a fjord, this good-sized lake is reputed to be a fine place for pulling northern pike, grayling, whitefish, and lake trout from the cool waters. There is a nice sandy beach, but the access to the lake is reedy. The campground has a boat launch and standard services (water, wood, pit toilets, fire pits, and picnic tables) and, I understand, can get quite windy.

FRENCHMAN LAKE, NUNATUK, AND TATCHUN LAKE

Frenchman Lake is one of three campgrounds found off the highway at kilometre 543 on the narrow gravel Frenchman Lake Road (the others are Nunatuk and Tatchun Lake). Frenchman Lake is located by travelling 7 kilometres down the road. It has 10 spaces, including 2 pull-throughs arranged in a gravel lot and accommodating every size of vehicle. Seven kilometres farther is the second campground, Nunatuk, which has 15 spots (4 pull-throughs), and 26 kilometres farther is Tatchun Lake, with 20 smaller spaces, about half of which are on the lake itself. All the campgrounds are situated on the beautiful clear waters of Frenchman Lake; they have boat launches and are equipped with the standard services of picnic tables, water (either from a pump or the lake), wood, fire pits, and pit toilets. There is fishing potential for trout, pike, and grayling, and canoeing or kayaking excursions are easily available. If you are travelling along this route, be prepared for some rocky roads. Although the driving distance of the loop is only 46 kilometres, the gravel can be rough in places, especially between Nunatuk and Tatchun Lake.

OTHER YUKON GOVERNMENT CAMPGROUNDS

The campgrounds in this section are found along four routes: the Haines Highway, which leads south from Haines Junction to Haines, Alaska; the Dempster Highway, which leads north from the Klondike Highway and crosses the Arctic Circle to Inuvik, Northwest Territories; Canol Road, which stretches north from the Alaska Highway at Johnsons Crossing; and Atlin Road, which is accessed from Jakes Corner on the Alaska Highway.

HAINES HIGHWAY: KLUANE NATIONAL PARK—KATHLEEN LAKE

In 1979, Kluane National Park (21,980 square kilometres) in the Yukon and the adjacent Wrangell–St. Elias National Park and Preserve in the United States (53,602 square kilometres) were together awarded UNESCO World Heritage status. The area is not only home to abundant wildlife but also contains the largest non-polar icefield in the world and some of the most spectacular glaciers.

Just driving along the Haines Highway in the shadow of the mountains is a stunning experience; even when travelling at the peak months of July and August, it is not uncommon to drive for 30 minutes and not see another vehicle. Within the national park is Kathleen Lake Campground, the only vehicle-accessible campground in a national park in the Yukon, and as such it has a few different qualities from Yukon government campgrounds. Open from mid-May to early September and located at kilometre 220 of the Haines Highway, 27 kilometres south of Haines Junction on an amazingly good road, Kathleen Lake Campground has 38 large sites suitable for every size of recreational vehicle (all back-ins), arranged around a loop of cottonwood and spruce trees. There are pit toilets (with hand sanitizer), wood (included in the camping fee), water, picnic tables, fire pits, and bear-proof storage lockers. It is necessary to self-register and pay a camping fee. A trail leads from the campground to the lake and day-use area, which has an indoor cooking shelter complete with information boards. There is a dock and a boat launch, and it is possible to swim in the lake (be prepared for slippery stones when wading in). The first night we stayed here, Kathleen Lake had waves and was dark and inhospitable, but the next evening at 9:00 PM it was calm and (relatively) warm and wonderful. Reportedly there is good fishing for lake trout in June and July, and kokanee and grayling from June to September (a National Parks fishing permit is required). Kathleen Lake is nearly 122 metres deep in places and hosts the only established campground in the park. From this location it is possible to take a number of much longer overnight hikes into the park itself. Anyone with ambitions to do this must register with park officials (consult the Parks Canada website).

HAINES HIGHWAY: DEZADEASH LAKE

The Dezadeash Lake Campground has only 20 spaces and is not for people driving the largest RVs, or even vehicles greater than 30 feet in length. Even if you are not intending to camp, it is well worth stopping here as the views are stunning and it is nice to appreciate the lake close up and maybe fish for northern pike, grayling, and lake trout. Found at kilometre 198, the campground is on a small promontory with many camping spaces on the water's edge. The only drawback is that winds can quickly whip up. The lake is not very deep and so it is one of the Yukon's warmest. Facilities include picnic tables, fire pits, wood, water (from the lake), and pit toilets. There is a picnic shelter and a boat launch. Ten kilometres to the south is the St. Elias Lake Trailhead, part of Kluane National Park, which leads to a subalpine meadow.

HAINES HIGHWAY: MILLION DOLLAR FALLS

There are three theories about how these falls got their name: the construction camp initially located here cost $1 million to establish; there is $1 million worth of construction equipment buried here; and a plane carrying $1 million crashed here and the money has yet to be found. We were told to camp at Million Dollar Falls when booking whitewater rafting on the Tatshenshini River, as it is the nearest campground from which to start these excursions. The campground is on the site of an old construction camp established in 1944 during the building of the Haines Road. Located where the road crosses the Takhanne River, this little gem has 28 vehicle-accessible sites, all of which must be backed into, but all quite large and well separated among a natural forest situated on a loop road. There are also 6 walk-in tent sites. Services include pit toilets, fire pits, wood, water, and picnic tables, in addition to a picnic shelter and playground. A small boardwalk interpretive trail leads to a viewpoint overlooking the 60-metre falls and onto another small lake. Fishing for grayling, Dolly Varden, rainbow trout, and salmon is possible. The Takhanne River also has

salmon running in July, and while this is lovely for the angler, it is also lovely for grizzly bears; consequently the campground is known as a grizzly feeding area and is sometimes closed due to the grizzly activity. Like Dezadeash Lake, this is a great place to stop for a walk or picnic even if you do not intend to camp.

DEMPSTER HIGHWAY: TOMBSTONE MOUNTAIN

The gravel Dempster Highway is found at kilometre 675 of the Klondike Highway and leads 740 kilometres to Inuvik. It hosts three Yukon government campgrounds: Tombstone Mountain, Engineer Creek, and Rock River. An excellent guide to this route is produced by the Yukon government and can be found on the government website (yukon.ca/hike-camp-tombstone). Although it is possible to drive the highway in a day (12 to 16 hours), it is better to stop. The road is part of the Trans Canada Trail (tctrail.ca) and is named after North-West Mounted Police corporal William John Duncan Dempster. It crosses the Arctic Circle and straddles the continental divide on three separate occasions. Tombstone Mountain Campground is located in Tombstone Territorial Park next to the meeting of Blake Shale Creek and the North Klondike River at kilometre 72 of the Dempster Highway. Found 1,034 metres above sea level, the campground has 39 sites for RVs in addition to 12 tent sites. Located off a loop drive and suitable for every size of vehicle, it has water, picnic tables, pit toilets, wood, a cooking pit, and a picnic shelter. There is an interpretive centre (open May to September) at the campground providing information about the park, displays, and talks. Trails lead from this location, and the information centre provides current reports about wildlife viewings, weather forecasts, and even hot tea. The campground is wheelchair accessible and regularly fills up. In addition to this roadside facility for vehicle camping, there are also backcountry camping opportunities at Grizzly, Divide, and Talus lakes.

DEMPSTER HIGHWAY: ENGINEER CREEK

Located at kilometre 193, Engineer Creek Campground has 11 spaces located below Sapper Hill. Sapper is the nickname given to an army engineer, and it was used in 1971 to refer to the Third Royal Canadian Army Engineers who built the bridge over the Ogilvie River. The Ogilvie River and Mountains were named after William Ogilvie, a land surveyor, explorer, and the Yukon's fourth commissioner. All camping spots are back-ins, but they are quite large, with a few positioned along the creek itself. There are picnic tables, water (from the creek), pit toilets, wood, and a cooking shelter. The water from the creek contains iron, which colours the rocks red. There are opportunities to fish for grayling, and it is also possible to sight peregrine falcons and golden eagles here.

DEMPSTER HIGHWAY: ROCK RIVER

Make sure the bug repellent is at hand when you visit this riverside campground, which is notorious for black flies. Located at kilometre 446 of the Dempster Highway in an isolated spot on the west side of the Richardson Mountains, this campground's sites are situated among white spruce trees adjacent to the river and protected from the wind. The 17 camping spots (including 3 pull-throughs) are positioned around a loop and suitable for vehicles of all sizes. Facilities include pit toilets, water, wood, fire pits, picnic tables, and a picnic shelter. The Arctic Circle is 40 kilometres south and from this point, for six weeks following mid-June, the sun does not sink below the horizon. This area is the traditional caribou-hunting ground of the Gwich'in Peoples.

CANOL ROAD: QUIET LAKE
NORTH AND QUIET LAKE SOUTH

The 825-kilometre Canol Road was constructed between 1942 and 1944 to provide access to the oil fields adjacent to Norman Wells. Rebuilt in the 1950s, this gravel road is not recommended for RVs or trailers. The two Yukon campgrounds found on this route reflect these limited access issues. The road is reached from Johnsons Crossing (kilometre 930) on the Alaska Highway. There are two campgrounds: Quiet Lake North and Quiet Lake South. Quiet Lake South is at kilometre 76 of Canol Road and has 12 sites, including 1 pull-through. Services include pit toilets, water, picnic tables, fire pits, and wood. Quiet Lake North (at kilometre 99) is smaller, with only 10 sites, but it has all the same services, plus a boat launch. The main activity at these campgrounds is fishing for lake trout, northern pike, and Arctic grayling. A Yukon government signpost at the campground explains that Quiet Lake was named by John McCormick, one of four prospectors who panned for gold in the region in 1887. Although gold was found, the area is now recognized more for fishing than for prospecting. The lake is 27 kilometres in length and set among stunning scenery. Travelling on the gravel roads adjacent to the campground reveals rusty trucks and historical vehicles abandoned following the construction of the road.

ATLIN ROAD: SNAFU LAKE AND TARFU LAKE

While on holiday in the Yukon in 2013, I spoke to a young woman who had travelled extensively in the region and she explained the best road in the territory was the one to Atlin (technically British Columbia's northernmost town, but so far north that many Yukoners consider it part of their territory). When we headed in that direction, I saw what she meant. You reach the community of Atlin by turning off the Alaska Highway at Jakes Corner and driving 95 kilometres south. Atlin gets its name from the Tlingit word "Áa Tlein," meaning "Big Lake," and was famed for one of the richest gold strikes in 1897–98 during the Klondike Gold Rush. The first campground reached when travelling toward Atlin is Snafu Lake, located at kilometre 26 on the Atlin Road. Snafu is a military acronym for "Situation Normal—All Fouled Up." There are 9 relatively small sites with picnic tables, fire pits, water, firewood, and pit toilets. Although the sites can accommodate RVs up to 30 feet, larger vehicles will have difficulty. There is a boat launch and fishing possibilities for grayling and trout. Canoeing is also possible. A little farther along is Tarfu Lake (kilometre 32), located on a hillside of pine and aspen trees. Tarfu is another military acronym, this one for "Things Are Really Fouled Up." Like the previous campground, the sites here are better for RVs under 30 feet. Services for the 11 campsites at Tarfu Lake are the same as at Snafu Lake. Tarfu Lake is reported to be a great place for fishing and canoeing. The small community of Atlin is well worth a visit; it has a small museum, a gallery, and all manner of services.

MULTI-DAY CAMPING TOURS

DESIGNED FOR INDIVIDUALS travelling in a vehicle, this chapter provides suggestions for one-, two-, and three-week camping excursions starting in the Lower Mainland of British Columbia. However, these itineraries can easily be amended to accommodate personal preferences or alternative starting points. While I offer brief synopses of the roads to take for each of the recommended tours, a good map is required for anyone planning to camp and travel in BC and the Rockies. One excellent resource is the *British Columbia Road & Recreational Atlas*, which provides comprehensive coverage of the province's major and minor highways, as well as data on places, area boundaries, trails, elevations, lakes, and parks. The fact that it is an 8-by-11-inch bound mapbook and not a 4-by-4-foot paper map makes it easy to consult in the car (and helps keep it in one piece). Alternately, Tourism BC's official Road Map and Parks Guide lists all provincial parks. Both publications are readily available at tourist information offices, and the *British Columbia Road & Recreational Atlas* is carried by most bookstores in BC (and from hgdistribution. com). The BC Government also provides a digital road atlas, free of charge, that can be downloaded ahead of time and used on a tablet or laptop (see gov. bc.ca/gov/content/data/geographic-data-services/topographic-data/roads). Travellers should also check road conditions and potential closures by calling the Drive BC automated phone service at 1-800-550-4997, or by consulting their website (drivebc.ca) or Twitter (@DriveBC) for up-to-date information. For those campers uncomfortable travelling without a reservation, each of the one-, two- and three-week tours has a "fully reserved" option, where it is possible to book all camping spots in advance. Anyone planning to vacation in the peak months of July and August without reserving ahead should be prepared to encounter some full campgrounds and plan alternative options.

7-DAY TOURS

> Trip 1: A Little Taste of the Province

Although this route may appear to involve a lot of driving, for those who like this pastime it provides a good introduction to the province and to some lovely provincial parks, as well as a taste of some of the best scenery. It is a circular tour: you start by travelling north to Highway 97, east on the Yellowhead Highway, south on Highway 93, then west on Highway 3.

DAY 1 Lac La Hache	DAY 4 Kootenay	DAY 6 Kettle River
DAY 2 Mount Robson	National	Recreation Area
DAY 3 Mount Robson	DAY 5 Moyie Lake	DAY 7 E.C. Manning

> Trip 2: Popular Provincial Parks (Fully Reserved)

This itinerary gives campers the security of knowing they have accommodation in some of the most popular campgrounds in the province. It includes campgrounds on BC's mainland, Vancouver Island, and the Gulf Islands, making for wonderful ferry trips and minimal driving. After staying at Alice Lake, travel south on the Sea-to-Sky Highway to Horseshoe Bay and take the ferry to Vancouver Island. From there, it is just a short drive north on Highway 19 to Rathtrevor. After Rathtrevor, head south on Highway 19 to Goldstream. To reach Montague Harbour, take a ferry from Swartz Bay to Galiano Island.

DAY 1 Alice Lake	DAY 4 Rathtrevor	DAY 6 Montague
DAY 2 Alice Lake	Beach	Harbour Marine
DAY 3 Rathtrevor Beach	DAY 5 Goldstream	DAY 7 Montague

> Trip 3: Vancouver Island and Gulf Island Hopping

Like Trip 2, this route has some fantastic ferry rides through breathtaking scenery. From the Lower Mainland, Montague Harbour on Galiano Island is reached by ferry at Tsawwassen. Ruckle Provincial Park is on Salt Spring Island, and ferries regularly leave from Galiano for Salt Spring. From Salt Spring, take a ferry to Swartz Bay; from here, the Island Highway leads to Goldstream and Bamberton. French Beach is located south of Victoria on Highway 14.

DAY 1 Montague Harbour Marine	DAY 3 Ruckle	DAY 6 Bamberton
	DAY 4 Ruckle	DAY 7 French Beach
DAY 2 Montague Harbour Marine	DAY 5 Goldstream	

> Trip 4: Circle Tour

This easy-to-complete circular excursion takes campers to some of the less popular camping spots that are still easily accessible from Vancouver. It involves driving north on the lovely Sea-to-Sky Highway (Highway 99), turning briefly off it to access Birkenhead, and continuing along this scenic road until it joins Highway 97 just north of Cache Creek. At Cache Creek, you take Highway 97C south to Kentucky–Alleyne. From this campground, travel south on Highway 5A to Highway 3, which leads through E.C. Manning Provincial Park and back to Vancouver.

Kentucky–Alleyne Provincial Park is within easy reach of Vancouver.

DAY 1 Nairn Falls	DAY 4 Kentucky–Alleyne	DAY 6 E.C. Manning
DAY 2 Birkenhead Lake		DAY 7 Emory Creek
DAY 3 Birkenhead Lake	DAY 5 E.C. Manning	

> Trip 5: The Hiker's Dream

This trip is designed for driving one day and hiking the next. To reach Wells Gray, take the Coquihalla (Highway 5) to Kamloops and then head north on Highway 5. After Wells Gray, continue north on Highway 5 until it joins the Yellowhead Highway (Highway 16). After Mount Robson, take the fantastic Glacier Highway (Highway 93) south until it meets Highway 1. (Pray for good weather, as the views along this road are some of the best in the province.) Travelling west on Highway 1 leads to Yoho. From Yoho it is possible to drive back to Vancouver in a day. For those who want a less hurried route, take

The spectacular beauty of Mount Robson Provincial Park draws outdoor enthusiasts from all over the world.

Highway 1 as far as Kamloops, then Highway 97 until it reaches Highway 99, which you can follow to Vancouver.

DAY 1 Wells Gray	DAY 4 Mount Robson	DAY 6 Yoho
DAY 2 Wells Gray	DAY 5 Yoho	DAY 7 Marble Canyon
DAY 3 Mount Robson		

14-DAY TOURS

Wells Gray is one of the best provincial parks in BC.

> Trip 1: A Bigger Taste of the Province

Two weeks is a good length of time for touring the province. On the first day of this itinerary, there is little driving involved, as campers head out of Vancouver on Highway 7 to nearby Golden Ears. After camping here, continue on Highway 7 to the junction with Highway 3 and then take Highway 3 through E.C. Manning. After E.C. Manning, travel north to Kamloops. A number of routes are available, but my advice to those who have time is to take 5A. From

Kamloops, take Highway 5 north until it joins the Yellowhead Highway. Travel east on the Yellowhead until you get to Highway 93, which can be taken all the way south to Kootenay National Park and beyond, where it meets Highway 95. From Jimsmith Lake, follow Highway 3, then 3A to Crawford Bay and the longest free ferry ride in the world over Kootenay Lake, where Highway 31 leads to Kootenay Lake Provincial Park. Travel south from Kootenay Lake on Highway 3A and take a slow drive along Highway 3 back to Vancouver, with a stop at sẁiẁs (Haynes Point) in Osoyoos.

DAY 1 Golden Ears	DAY 7 Mount Robson	DAY 11 Jimsmith Lake
DAY 2 E.C. Manning	DAY 8 Mount Robson	DAY 12 Kootenay Lake
DAY 3 E.C. Manning	DAY 9 Kootenay	DAY 13 Kootenay Lake
DAY 4 Paul Lake	National	DAY 14 sẁiẁs
DAY 5 Wells Gray	DAY 10 Kootenay	(Haynes Point)
DAY 6 Wells Gray	National	

> Trip 2: Stress-Free BC (Fully Reserved)

This itinerary only includes campgrounds that accept reservations. Travel along Highway 7 to Highway 3 and continue east on this road until it meets Highway 97. At this juncture, you will adopt a northward direction as the road leads toward Highway 1, dividing into Highways 97, 97A, and 97B. All these roads lead in the direction of Shuswap Lake. After staying at Shuswap Lake, drive west on Highway 1 to Kamloops, then take Highway 5 north to the Yellowhead Highway and the stunningly beautiful Mount Robson Park. Retrace your steps to Kamloops and follow Highway 5A south to Princeton and the nearby Otter Lake Provincial Park. The return journey to Vancouver leads you back on Highway 3.

DAY 1 Golden Ears	DAY 6 Okanagan Lake	DAY 11 Mount Robson
DAY 2 Golden Ears	DAY 7 Okanagan Lake	DAY 12 Mount Robson
DAY 3 E.C. Manning	DAY 8 Shuswap Lake	DAY 13 Mount Robson
DAY 4 E.C. Manning	DAY 9 Shuswap Lake	DAY 14 Otter Lake
DAY 5 Okanagan Lake	DAY 10 Shuswap Lake	

> Trip 3: Vancouver Island and Gulf Island Hopping

On this lovely, relaxed excursion you will be able to explore the camping highlights of Vancouver Island and the Gulf Islands. From the Lower Mainland, Montague Harbour on Galiano Island is reached by ferry at Tsawwassen. Ruckle Provincial Park is on Salt Spring Island, and ferries regularly leave from Galiano for Salt Spring. From Salt Spring, a ferry is needed to reach South Pender Island, the last Gulf Island on the tour. Travel from South Pender Island to Vancouver Island's Swartz Bay by ferry. At Swartz Bay, the Island Highway (Highway 1) leads south to Victoria. Take Highway 14 from Victoria to French Beach. Backtrack a bit for the return journey north, stopping at Goldstream and then taking the Island Highway as far as Parksville. At Parksville, head west on Highway 4, which meanders across Vancouver Island to Pacific Rim National Park (the road from Port Alberni to the coast is particularly lovely). Return along this road to the Island Highway and continue north until reaching Campbell River. Highway 28 just north of this town leads into Strathcona Park. Return to the Lower Mainland by ferry from Nanaimo.

DAY 1 Montague Harbour Marine	DAY 5 Prior Centennial	DAY 10 Pacific Rim
	DAY 6 French Beach	DAY 11 Miracle Beach
DAY 2 Montague Harbour Marine	DAY 7 Goldstream	DAY 12 Strathcona
	DAY 8 Bamberton	DAY 13 Strathcona
DAY 3 Ruckle	DAY 9 Pacific Rim	DAY 14 Strathcona
DAY 4 Ruckle		

The small town of Coalmont, near Otter Lake Provincial Park, sprang to life during the gold rush.

> Trip 4: Fruit and Freedom—The Okanagan and the Kootenays

This tour offers the best of both worlds, as the somewhat more populated Okanagan is visited in conjunction with the calm, quiet Kootenays. The quickest way to reach Bear Creek, the first provincial park campground on the itinerary, is to take Highway 1 out of Vancouver, then the Coquihalla Highway to Merritt. Turn east on Highway 97C toward Kelowna. Alternatively, instead of the Coquihalla, take Highway 3 through E.C. Manning Park to Princeton, then Highway 5A north to Highway 97. From Bear Creek, drive north to Vernon, and then take Highway 6 east to

Beautiful Manning Provincial Park is a hiker's paradise.

reach Mabel Lake. After staying here, continue on Highway 6 until the turnoff for Highway 31A; this leads to Highway 31 and, by travelling north, to Kootenay Lake Provincial Park. From Kootenay Lake, travel south on Highway 31 and take Highway 3A to find Kokanee Creek. A short drive south on this road leads to Champion Lakes. Continue the journey back to Vancouver on Highway 3, stopping at Otter Lake and E.C. Manning or any other campgrounds that look appealing.

DAY 1 Bear Creek	DAY 6 Kootenay Lake	DAY 11 Otter Lake
DAY 2 Bear Creek	DAY 7 Kootenay Lake	DAY 12 Otter Lake
DAY 3 Mabel Lake	DAY 8 Kootenay Lake	DAY 13 E.C. Manning
DAY 4 Mabel Lake	DAY 9 Kokanee Creek	DAY 14 E.C. Manning
DAY 5 Rosebery	DAY 10 Champion Lakes	

> Trip 5: Rocky Mountains and the National Parks

It is easily possible to visit all the "big" parks in a two-week period, but a few long days in the car are required. This tour has been designed to compensate for these long travelling times with two- or three-night stays in some of the largest and most spectacular parks in the province. To take this excursion, leave Vancouver on Highway 1, and then take the Coquihalla north to Kamloops. Just north of Kamloops is Paul Lake Provincial Park. The following day, take Highway 1 east to Glacier, and a few days later proceed the few kilometres to Yoho. From Yoho, Highway 1 East leads to Lake Louise. From here, head south on Highway 93 to Kootenay National Park. Continue on Highway 93, which eventually becomes Highway 95 and joins Highway 3. Highway 3 travels across the bottom of the province and leads back to Vancouver.

DAY 1 Paul Lake	DAY 6 Yoho	DAY 11 Moyie Lake
DAY 2 Glacier	DAY 7 Yoho	DAY 12 Kettle River
DAY 3 Glacier	DAY 8 Kootenay	Recreational Area
DAY 4 Glacier	DAY 9 Kootenay	DAY 13 E.C. Manning
DAY 5 Yoho	DAY 10 Kootenay	DAY 14 E.C. Manning

21-DAY TOURS

> Trip 1: A Huge Taste of the Province

If travelling hundreds of kilometres a day across remote regions of the province is a pleasurable notion for you, then this trip will be a dream. I undertook it in 19 days, which required a lot of driving—over 6,500 kilometres. It is not an itinerary for those who suffer from motion sickness. Leave Vancouver on the Sea-to-Sky Highway and travel north on what I believe to be one of the best roads in the world. When the road joins Highway 97, head north. This is the Gold Rush Trail. After stopping at Lac La Hache and turning east

Magnificent falls in Wells Gray Provincial Park.

just north of Quesnel on Highway 26 to visit Barkerville, return to Highway 97 and proceed north to Prince George. From here, turn west on the Yellowhead Highway (Highway 16). At Terrace, take Highway 97 south to Lakelse, after which you should be prepared to travel north on this highway as far as the Alaska Highway. (Be warned that sections of Highway 37 between Dease Lake and Meziadin Junction are unpaved.) Upon reaching the Alaska Highway, head south as far as Dawson Creek, then drive Highway 97 south to Prince George. At Prince George, travel east on the Yellowhead Highway to Mount Robson, and then head south on Highway 5 to Kamloops. At Kamloops you can choose between returning to Vancouver via the fast Coquihalla or on Highway 1 through the Fraser Canyon.

DAY 1 Lac La Hache	DAY 9 Meziadin Lake	DAY 14 Gwillim Lake
DAY 2 Ten Mile Lake	DAY 10 Tā Ch'ilā	DAY 15 Bear Lake
DAY 3 Ten Mile Lake	DAY 11 Liard River	DAY 16 Bear Lake
DAY 4 Sowchea Bay	Hot Springs	DAY 17 Mount Robson
DAY 5 Sowchea Bay	DAY 12 Liard River	DAY 18 Mount Robson
DAY 6 Tyhee Lake	Hot Springs	DAY 19 Wells Gray
DAY 7 Lakelse Lake	DAY 13 Buckinghorse	DAY 20 Wells Gray
DAY 8 Lakelse Lake	River Wayside	DAY 21 Emory Creek

> Trip 2: Best of the Mainland (Fully Reservable)

Many of the campgrounds that are part of this itinerary are ideal for families and those who require more comfort when camping, such as flush toilets, showers, and nearby stores. To reach the first campground, leave Vancouver on Highway 1, then take Highway 3, which meanders through E.C. Manning Park. Continue east along this road until you reach Osoyoos, and then head north on Highway 97. After staying at Ellison, continue the journey north on Highway 97 until you reach the junction with Highway 1. At this stage, head west as far as Kamloops, then north on Highway 5 to the Yellowhead Highway and Mount Robson. After Mount Robson take the Yellowhead Highway west to Prince George, then travel north on Highway 97 as far as Crooked River. On the next stage of the journey, take Highway 97 south as far as the turn for Highway 99, just north of Cache Creek. You will spend the final days of your camping tour driving the wonderful Highway 99 back to Vancouver.

DAY 1 E.C. Manning	DAY 8 Ellison	DAY 15 Ten Mile Lake
DAY 2 E.C. Manning	DAY 9 Mount Robson	DAY 16 Green Lake
DAY 3 E.C. Manning	DAY 10 Mount Robson	DAY 17 Green Lake
DAY 4 Okanagan Lake	DAY 11 Mount Robson	DAY 18 Green Lake
DAY 5 Okanagan Lake	DAY 12 Crooked River	DAY 19 Alice Lake
DAY 6 Okanagan Lake	DAY 13 Crooked River	DAY 20 Alice Lake
DAY 7 Ellison	DAY 14 Ten Mile Lake	DAY 21 Porteau Cove

> Trip 3: Vancouver Island, the Gulf Islands, and the Sunshine Coast

An easy-to-complete excursion featuring beautiful drives and numerous ferry rides, this route follows the same one detailed in the 14-night Vancouver Island and Gulf Island Hopping itinerary. However, upon leaving Strathcona Provincial Park, extend the tour by taking the ferry from Courtenay to Powell River on the Sunshine Coast. Next, drive south on Highway 101. To end the journey, take the ferry back to Horseshoe Bay.

DAY 1 Montague Harbour Marine	DAY 8 Bamberton	DAY 15 Strathcona
DAY 2 Montague Harbour Marine	DAY 9 Rathtrevor Beach	DAY 16 Strathcona
DAY 3 Ruckle	DAY 10 Rathtrevor Beach	DAY 17 Strathcona
DAY 4 Ruckle	DAY 11 Pacific Rim	DAY 18 Saltery Bay
DAY 5 Prior Centennial	DAY 12 Pacific Rim	DAY 19 Saltery Bay
DAY 6 Goldstream	DAY 13 Pacific Rim	DAY 20 Porpoise Bay
DAY 7 Goldstream	DAY 14 Miracle Beach	DAY 21 Porpoise Bay

Dress warmly when strolling Naikoon's windswept beaches.

> Trip 4: Gold Rush Trail and Haida Gwaii

The drawback of this trip is that the same roads have to be travelled on the outbound and the return journeys. However, the scenery en route to Haida Gwaii more than compensates. From Vancouver, go north via Highways 99 and 97 as far as Prince George, then follow the Yellowhead Highway west to Prince Rupert, where a 6-hour ferry ride connects you to Haida Gwaii. Retrace the same route back until just north of Cache Creek, where you can continue on the Gold Rush Trail south (Highway 1) down the Fraser Canyon all the way to Hope.

DAY 1 Lac La Hache	DAY 8 Prudhomme Lake	DAY 15 Beaumont
DAY 2 Sowchea Bay	DAY 9 Naikoon	DAY 16 Beaumont
DAY 3 Sowchea Bay	DAY 10 Naikoon	DAY 17 Ten Mile Lake
DAY 4 Tyhee Lake	DAY 11 Naikoon	DAY 18 Ten Mile Lake
DAY 5 Lakelse Lake	DAY 12 Naikoon	DAY 19 Green Lake
DAY 6 Lakelse Lake	DAY 13 Naikoon	DAY 20 Green Lake
DAY 7 Lakelse Lake	DAY 14 Kleanza Creek	DAY 21 Emory Creek

Illecillewaet is just one of three campgrounds in Glacier National Park.

> Trip 5: The Rockies and the Larger Provincial and National Parks

Designed with the hiker in mind, this itinerary features some of the best parks in the province. On leaving Vancouver, take either Highway 1 or the quieter Highway 7 to the junction with Highway 3. Travel east on Highway 3 to Castlegar, then take Highway 3A to Kokanee Creek. Continue along Highway 3A until it rejoins Highway 3, which turns into Highway 95 and leads north into Kootenay National Park. Next, travel north to meet Highway 1, and then drive west through Yoho and Glacier national parks as far as Kamloops, where Highway 5 leads north to the Yellowhead Highway and Mount Robson. From Mount Robson head west on Highway 16 (the Yellowhead Highway) as far as Prince George and then south on Highway 97, back through the Fraser Canyon to Vancouver.

DAY 1 E.C. Manning	DAY 8 Kootenay	DAY 15 Wells Gray
DAY 2 E.C. Manning	DAY 9 Yoho	DAY 16 Wells Gray
DAY 3 Kokanee Creek	DAY 10 Yoho	DAY 17 Mount Robson
DAY 4 Kokanee Creek	DAY 11 Yoho	DAY 18 Mount Robson
DAY 5 Moyie Lake	DAY 12 Glacier	DAY 19 Mount Robson
DAY 6 Kootenay	DAY 13 Glacier	DAY 20 Ten Mile Lake
DAY 7 Kootenay	DAY 14 Wells Gray	DAY 21 Downing

SPECIAL INTEREST
CAMPING RECOMMENDATIONS

ALTHOUGH MANY CAMPERS are content to explore any and every provincial park they find, a number of people have special needs or interests and seek camping facilities that will accommodate them. Here are some suggestions for those folks.

HIKING

Numerous provincial and national parks offer superb hiking. Most offer easier walking, but among the best known for varied hikes are the larger provincial parks such as Wells Gray, E.C. Manning, Mount Robson, Strathcona, and Tweedsmuir (South), as well as Banff, Jasper, Waterton, Yoho, Glacier, Kootenay, Pacific Rim, and Kluane national parks. It is easy to spend a week or more at any of these locations and only begin to touch the beauty they offer.

PUBLISHER'S BOOK RECOMMENDATIONS: *Popular Day Hikes: Vancouver Island* (Theo Dombrowski; Rocky Mountain Books), *Waterfall Hikes in Southern British Columbia* (Steve Tersmette; Rocky Mountain Books), *Popular Day Hikes: Waterton* (Andrew Nugara; Rocky Mountain Books), *Destination Hikes: In and Around Southwestern British Columbia* (Stephen Hui; Greystone Books), and *105 Hikes: In and Around Southwestern British Columbia* (Stephen Hui; Greystone Books).

DIVING

A number of campgrounds in BC offer diving potential, but the most notable ones in the province are Saltery Bay on the Sunshine Coast (home to Canada's first underwater statue), Ellison in the Okanagan (the province's only freshwater dive park), and Porteau Cove (less than 1 hour's drive from Vancouver).

HOT SPRINGS

What better way to relax than in warm mineral pools? Kootenay, Banff, Jasper, Whiteswan Lake, Lakelse Lake, and Liard River Hot Springs parks all offer this idyllic environment within their boundaries. If you don't mind a short drive, Dry Gulch is close to Radium Hot Springs (in Kootenay National Park); Martha Creek is close to Canyon Hot Springs; Kootenay Lake and Kokanee Creek are close to Ainsworth Hot Springs; Arrow Lakes, McDonald Creek, and Summit Lake are all close to Nakusp Hot Springs; and McDonald Creek also has Halcyon Hot Springs nearby.

CANOEING AND KAYAKING

With an abundance of lakes, the possibilities for canoeing and kayaking are almost limitless. Those who seek serious paddling excursions should consider Champion Lakes, Wells Gray, Bowron Lake, Okeover Arm (with access to Desolation Sound), and Sasquatch. BC Parks offers canoes for rent at a number of provincial parks, including E.C. Manning and Golden Ears, and you can rent canoes at Yoho National Park's Emerald Lake.

PUBLISHER'S BOOK RECOMMENDATION: *Sea Kayaking* (David Dowd, Greystone Books).

If you don't own a canoe or kayak, some parks have rentals available.

GOLD PANNING

Although the potential to pan for gold exists in many provincial parks, Emory Creek, Kettle River, Stemwinder, and the aptly named Goldpan are good places to try.

PUBLISHER'S BOOK RECOMMENDATION: *Gold Panning in British Columbia* (Jim Lewis and Susan Company; Heritage House Publishing).

HORSEBACK RIDING

Relive that pioneer spirit by exploring BC parks on horseback. Horses can be rented from businesses adjacent to Babine Lake, Tweedsmuir (South), Golden Ears, and E.C. Manning provincial parks, as well as Yoho National Park, for riding on specifically designated trails in these parks. Other parks also allow horseback riding, including Big Bar Lake, Tunkwa, Ts'il?os, and Glacier National Park.

BIRDWATCHING

You can spot wonderful birdlife almost everywhere in BC, but the parks that are particularly notable include Vaseux Lake, E.C. Manning, Kootenay National Park, Big Bar Lake, Green Lake, Inkaneep, Kilby, Rolley Lake, Paul Lake, and Naikoon. All are excellent destinations for amateur ornithologists.

PUBLISHER'S BOOK RECOMMENDATION: *Birds of British Columbia and the Pacific Northwest* (Richard Cannings, Tom Aversa, and Hal Operman; Heritage House Publishing).

FISHING

All anglers have their own tips for the best fishing location, and BC parks provide thousands of spots to choose from (see gofishbc.com). Of particular note are Elk Falls, Stamp River, Wells Gray, Charlie Lake, Babine River Corridor, Kokanee Creek, Whiteswan Lake, Tunkwa, Jewel Lake, Summit Lake, Vaseux Lake, Beatton, Premier Lake, Cowichan River, Skagit River, Bridge Lake, and Goldpan. The many rivers and lakes in the Yukon also offer world-class fishing opportunities.

PUBLISHER'S BOOK RECOMMENDATION: *Trout School: Lessons from a Fly-Fishing Master* (Mark Hume with Mo Bradley; Greystone Books).

To catch your dinner, all you need is a fishing rod and some luck.

ISLANDS

Island campgrounds are magical, since the neighbouring communities (if any) on these quiet oases are quite distinct from those of the Mainland. Smelt Bay, Montague Harbour Marine, Sayshutsun (Newcastle Island Marine), Fillongley, Ruckle, and Sidney Spit Marine all provide fantastic camping retreats.

BEACHES

Tidal beaches are attractive to every age group, but especially to children. The following recommended sites are all on Vancouver Island: French Beach, Pacific Rim National Park, Rathtrevor Beach, Miracle Beach, and Sidney Spit Marine. There are also spectacular lakeside beaches to be enjoyed at Gordon Bay, sẃiẃs (Haynes Point), Okanagan Lake, and Birkenhead Lake on the Mainland.

PUBLISHER'S BOOK RECOMMENDATION: *Secret Beaches of Southern Vancouver Island* (Theo Dombrowski; Heritage House Publishing).

FAMILY

BC Parks has a number of family-oriented campgrounds that have activities for children, playgrounds, and numerous safe environments to explore. Alice Lake, Kokanee Creek, Rathtrevor Beach, Shuswap Lake, Tyhee Lake, Porpoise

Bay, Cultus Lake, Big Bar Lake, Golden Ears, Wasa, Miracle Beach, E.C. Manning, Sasquatch, Champion Lakes, Bear Creek, Paul Lake, Kikomun Creek, Monck, and Ten Mile Lake are but a few fantastic locations. To catch your dinner, all you need is a fishing rod and some luck.

PUBLISHER'S BOOK RECOMMENDATION: *Family Walks and Hikes in the Canadian Rockies 1* and *2* (Andrew Nugara; Rocky Mountain Books), and *Best Hikes and Nature Walks with Kids in and Around Southwestern British Columbia* (Stephen Hui; Greystone Books).

SENIORS

Campgrounds that are generally smaller and away from large centres of population make ideal places to sit, relax, read, maybe take a gentle hike, and generally unwind. Try sx̌ʷəx̌ʷnitkʷ (Okanagan Falls), Emory Creek, Fintry, Jewel Lake, Kentucky–Alleyne, Norbury Lake, Whiteswan Lake, Crooked River, Kleanza Creek, or Meziadin Lake.

USEFUL INFORMATION

MAPS

Tourism BC produces a map of the province that details all of the provincial parks and summarizes their facilities. The *British Columbia Road Map and Parks Guide* is available from most tourist offices and bookstores. Another excellent guide of the province is the *British Columbia Road & Recreational Atlas*, featuring up-to-date colour maps (1:600,000 scale). BC Parks produces visitor brochures featuring maps and other information on provincial parks in six regions: Kootenay Rockies; Vancouver, Coast, and Mountains; Thompson Okanagan; Vancouver Island; Cariboo Chilcotin Coast; and Northern BC regions. These are complimentary and available at visitor centres, tourism information offices, and provincial parks around the province. Digital brochures and maps for most individual provincial parks are also available for download on the Parks BC and Yukon Government websites.

WEBSITES

Several informative websites give details about camping in BC.

For the majority of the parks listed in this book, the BC Parks website has the most up-to-date information on all of the provincial park campgrounds and can be accessed at bcparks.ca.

For current details about the national parks included in this book, visit pc.gc.ca.

Make BC provincial park reservations through discovercamping.ca. For national parks, the equivalent is reservation.pc.gc.ca.

The following websites are also useful:

> General Information

- pc.gc.ca
- sanidumps.ca
- weather.gc.ca
- wildsafebc.ca

> Alberta

- travelalberta.com
- albertaparks.ca
- banfflakelouise.com
- banffnationalpark.com
- field.ca/yohonationalpark/
- gulfislandsnationalpark.com
- jasper.travel
- kootenayrockies.com
- mywaterton.ca
- seerevelstoke.com

> British Columbia

- travel.bc.ca
- fishing.gov.bc.ca
- bcadventure.com
- bcferries.com
- britishcolumbia.com
- campingrvbc.com
- canadianrockies.net
- drivebc.com
- gocampingbc.com
- hellobc.com
- sitesandtrailsbc.ca
- spacesfornature.org
- travel-british-columbia.com

> The Yukon

- 511yukon.com
- alaskahighwayjourney.com
- dempsterhighway.com
- northofordinary.com
- travelyukon.com
- yukon.ca/en/outdoor-recreation-and-wildlife/campingyukoninfo.com
- yukonwild.com

INDEX OF PARKS

BCP = *BC park*
NP = *National park*
YP = *Yukon park*

Aishihik Lake (YP), 269
Alice Lake (BCP), 69
Allison Lake (BCP), 98
Arrow Lakes (Shelter Bay) (BCP), 150

Babine Lake Marine (BCP), 217
Babine River Corridor (BCP), 221
Bamberton (BCP), 29
Banff (NP), 180
Bear Creek (BCP), 99
Beatton (BCP), 222
Beaumont (BCP), 223
Beaver Creek (BCP), 151
Big Bar Lake (BCP), 202
Big Creek (YP), 266
Birkenhead Lake (BCP), 70
Blanket Creek (BCP), 152
Boundary Creek (BCP), 100
Bowron Lake (BCP), 203
Boya Lake (BCP). *See* Tā Ch'ilā
    (Boya Lake) (BCP), 256
Bridge Lake (BCP), 102

Bromley Rock (BCP), 103
Buckinghorse River
    Wayside (BCP), 224
Bull Canyon (BCP), 204

Carp Lake (BCP), 225
Cedar Point (BCP), 205
Champion Lakes (BCP), 153
Charlie Lake (BCP), 227
Chilliwack Lake (BCP). *See* Sx̱ótsaqel
    / Chilliwack Lake (BCP)
Congdon Creek (YP), 270
Conkle Lake (BCP), 104
Conrad (YP), 272
Cowichan River (BCP), 30
Crooked River (BCP), 228
Cultus Lake (BCP), 71

Dezadeash Lake (YP), 281
Downing (BCP), 206
Drury Creek (YP), 279
Dry Gulch (BCP), 154

Elk Falls (BCP), 31
Ellison (BCP), 105
Emory Creek (BCP), 74

E.C. Manning (BCP), 73
Engineer Creek (YP), 283
Englishman River Falls (BCP), 33
Ethel Lake (YP), 274

Fillongley (BCP), 34
Fintry (BCP), 106
Five Mile Lake (YP), 275
Fox Lake (YP), 273
Frances Lake (YP), 278
French Beach (BCP), 35
Frenchman Lake/Nunatuk/ Tatchun
   Lake (YP), 280

Glacier (NP), 184
Gladstone (Texas Creek) (BCP),
   108
Golden Ears (BCP), 76
Goldpan (BCP), 109
Goldstream (BCP), 37
Gordon Bay (BCP), 38
Green Lake (BCP), 208
Gwillim Lake (BCP), 229

Haynes Point. See sẁiẁs
   (Haynes Point) (BCP)
Herald (BCP), 110
Horsefly Lake (BCP), 209

Inkaneep (BCP), 112
Inland Lake (BCP), 77
Jasper (NP), 185
Jewel Lake (BCP), 113
Jimsmith Lake (BCP), 156
Johnson Lake (YP), 279

Johnstone Creek (BCP), 114
Juan de Fuca (BCP), 39
Juniper Beach (BCP), 115

Kekuli Bay (BCP), 116
Kentucky–Alleyne (BCP), 118
Kettle River Recreation Area (BCP),
   119
Kikomun Creek (BCP), 157
Kilby (BCP), 78
Kin Beach (BCP), 41
Kinaskan Lake (BCP), 230
Kiskatinaw (BCP), 231
Kitty Coleman (BCP), 42
Kleanza Creek (BCP), 233
Klondike River (YP), 276
Kluane (NP)—Kathleen Lake (YP),
   280
Kokanee Creek (BCP), 158
Kootenay (NP), 188
Kootenay Lake (BCP), 160
Kusawa Lake (YP), 268

Lac La Hache (BCP), 210
Lac Le Jeune (BCP), 120
Lake Creek (YP), 271
Lake Laberge (YP), 272
Lakelse Lake (BCP), 234
Lapie Canyon (YP), 278
Liard River Hot Springs (BCP),
   235
Little Qualicum Falls (BCP), 43
Little Salmon Lake (YP), 279
Lockhart Beach (BCP), 161
Loveland Bay (BCP), 44

Mabel Lake (BCP), 121

Marble Canyon (BCP), 123

Marsh Lake (YP), 267

Martha Creek (BCP), 162

McDonald (NP). *See* SMONEĆTEN (McDonald) (NP)

McDonald Creek (BCP), 164

Meziadin Lake (BCP), 237

Million Dollar Falls (YP), 282

Miracle Beach (BCP), 46

Moberly Lake (BCP), 230

Monck (BCP), 124

Monkman (BCP), 240

Montague Harbour Marine (BCP), 47

Moose Creek (YP), 275

Morton Lake (BCP), 48

Mount Fernie (BCP), 165

Mount Revelstoke (NP), 192

Mount Robson (BCP), 125

Moyie Lake (BCP), 166

Muncho Lake (BCP), 241

Nahanni Range (YP), 277

Naikoon (BCP), 242

Nairn Falls (BCP), 80

Nancy Greene (BCP), 168

Newcastle Island Marine (BCP). *See* Sayshutsun (Newcastle Island Marine) (BCP)

Nisga'a Memorial Lava Bed (BCP), 244

Norbury Lake (BCP), 169

North Thompson River (BCP), 127

Okanagan Falls (BCP). *See* sx̌ʷəx̌ʷnitkʷ (Okanagan Falls) (BCP)

Okanagan Lake (BCP), 128

Okeover Arm (BCP), 81

One Island Lake (BCP), 245

Otter Lake (BCP), 129

Paarens Beach (BCP), 246

Pacific Rim (NP), 50

Paul Lake (BCP), 131

Pine Lake (YP), 269

Porpoise Bay (BCP), 82

Porteau Cove (BCP), 83

Premier Lake (BCP), 170

Prior Centennial (NP), 52

Prudhomme Lake (BCP), 247

Purden Lake (BCP), 249

Quiet Lake (North and South) (YP), 284

Rathtrevor Beach (BCP), 54

Red Bluff (BCP), 250

Roberts Creek (BCP), 84

Rock River (YP), 284

Rolley Lake (BCP), 86

Rosebery (BCP), 171

Ruckle (BCP), 55

Saltery Bay (BCP), 87

Sasquatch (BCP), 88

Saysutshun (Newcastle Island Marine) (BCP), 56

Seeley Lake (BCP), 251

Shuswap Lake (BCP), 132

Sidney Spit Marine (NP), 58

Silver Beach (BCP), 133

Silver Lake (BCP), 90

Simpson Lake (YP), 277

Skagit Valley (BCP), 91

Skihist (BCP), 134

Smelt Bay (BCP), 60

SMONEĆTEN
(McDonald) (NP), 61

Snafu Lake and Tarfu Lake (YP),
285

Snag Junction (YP), 271

Sowchea Bay (BCP), 252

Sproat Lake (BCP), 62

Squanga Lake (YP), 267

Stamp River (BCP), 63

Stawamus Chief (BCP), 92

Steelhead (BCP), 136

Stemwinder (BCP), 137

Stone Mountain (BCP), 254

Strathcona (BCP), 65

Summit Lake (BCP), 173

Swan Lake (BCP), 255

sẇiẇs (Haynes Point) (BCP), 138

Sx̱ótsaqel / Chilliwack Lake (BCP),
93

sx̌ʷəx̌ʷnitkʷ (Okanagan Falls) (BCP),
140

Syringa (BCP), 174

Tā Ch'ilā (Boya Lake) (BCP), 256

Takhini River (YP), 268

Tatchun Creek (YP), 274

Ten Mile Lake (BCP),
212

Teslin Lake (YP), 266

Texas Creek (BCP). *See* Gladstone
(Texas Creek) (BCP)

Tombstone Mountain (YP), 283

Ts'ilʔos (BCP), 213

Tudyah Lake (BCP), 257

Tunkwa (BCP), 141

Tweedsmuir (South) (BCP), 214

Twin Lakes (YP), 273

Tyhee Lake (BCP), 259

Vaseux Lake (BCP), 142

Wasa Lake (BCP), 175

Waterton Lakes (NP), 194

Watson Lake (YP), 266

Wells Gray (BCP), 143

Whiskers Point (BCP), 260

Whiteswan Lake (BCP), 176

Wolf Creek (YP), 268

Yahk (BCP), 178

Yoho (NP), 197

Yukon River (YP), 276

IMAGE CREDITS

Interior photographs are by Jayne Seagrave, with the following exceptions, used by permission:

BC Ferries/Scott Arkell: 29; BC Parks: 216 (*top*); Government of Yukon: 270, 273 (*right*), 282 (*both*); Parks Canada/Rob Buchanan: 146 (*both*); Parks Canada/Rick Reynolds: 296; Trevor Julier: 22, 73, 97, 99, 107, 118, 129, 147, 160, 181, 184, 186, 188, 192, 193, 194, 196, 198 (*bottom*).

Colour insert photographs are by Jayne Seagrave, unless otherwise credited.

ALSO BY JAYNE SEAGRAVE

ISBN 978-1-77151-162-9 (*paperback*)

Chicago, St. Louis, London, Vienna … bestselling author Jayne Seagrave has travelled there, and she's done it solo. Now she wants her readers to know that not only can they do it too, they should.

---

touchwoodeditions.com
hgdistribution.com

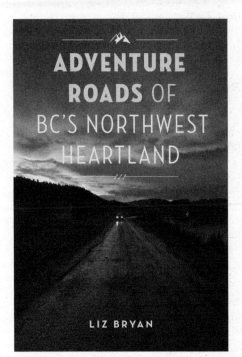

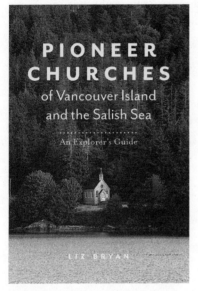

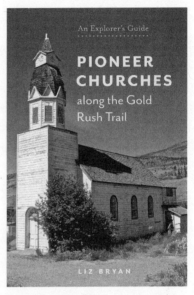

ISBN 978-1-77203-305-2 *(paperback)*   ISBN 978-1-77203-401-1 *(paperback)*

Colourful, concise travellers' guides to the historical churches of BC, dating back to the 1800s.

heritagehouse.ca
hgdistribution.com

JAYNE SEAGRAVE is a bestselling travel writer and has published an eclectic range of books over a twenty-five-year writing career. Born in England, Jayne moved to Canada more than 30 years ago. She is the author of *Camping British Columbia, the Rockies, and the Yukon* (now in its ninth edition), *Camping with Kids in the West*, and *All the World's a Stage: The Story of Vancouver's Bard on the Beach*. In 2021, she published her first work of fiction, *The Games Women Use* (Vanguard Press). She lives in Vancouver, where she is now retired. Find a full list of her writing at jayneseagrave.com.